the Dancing HAND of GOD

VOLUME I

*Unveiling the Fullness of God
through Apostolic Signs, Wonders and Miracles*

James Maloney

WESTBOW
PRESS
A DIVISION OF THOMAS NELSON

ISBN: 978-1-4497-3125-0 (e)
ISBN: 978-1-4497-3068-0 (sc)
ISBN: 978-1-4497-3067-3 (hbk)

Library of Congress Control Number: 2011960127

WestBow Press books may be ordered through booksellers or by contacting:

WestBow Press
A Division of Thomas Nelson
1663 Liberty Drive
Bloomington, IN 47403
www.westbowpress.com
1-(866) 928-1240

Printed in the United States of America

WestBow Press rev. date: 11/17/2011

Dedication

To the late Frances Metcalfe and the Golden Candlestick ministry: I pray, by the grace of God, your fifty and more years of intercession and ministry in worshiping our Lord will find the fruit of your sacrifices within these pages.

Acknowledgements

In the course of my life and ministry, there have been many wonderful men and women who have helped shape the person I am today and, therefore, this book. It would take more than space allows mentioning them all, but I could not call this book complete without gratefully acknowledging the following people:

My best friend, confidant, sounding board and "pastor" — my beautiful wife, Joy, for her unwavering support, unconditional love and unending patience; she is unquestionably the most gifted and intelligent woman I have ever met, and I am most grateful for her partnership these past thirty-plus years. My son, Andrew, a man with a spirit of excellence — I recognize the supreme importance of raising up the next generation, and he truly is a person of his mother's and my spiritual DNA. Many of the insights in expounding the teachings of this book come directly from him, and for all of his help in editing the manuscript I thank him. My lovely daughter, Alisa, who I knew would live up to her namesake, "joyful," when I held her in the palm of my hand and told the Lord, "I claim her." I love you all!

My brother-in-law, David Alsobrook, is quite possibly, I consider, the single greatest Bible teacher in modern history. I am most appreciative for his doctrinal insight that helped shape my foundation in the Word. The late Brant Baker and all who were a part of the Shekinah Fellowship team: their love and impartation, encouraging a teenager in the release of the miraculous, left more of an impression on me throughout my life than they could ever know. Drs. Chuck and Mary Ann Flynn, for all of their timely prophetic wisdom, are two of the finest people I know, and I consider myself most blessed to acknowledge them here. Also, Mario Murillo — simply one of the most dynamic and profound revivalists of our time, in my opinion — his distinct message and release of tremendous power continue to be true inspirations that influence my life to this day.

Table of Contents

Foreword

History has been shaped by people with extraordinary courage. When the courageous ones are friends of God, they impact mindsets and culture for generations. The secret place with God is where friends are made.

In the place of intimacy with God is where eternal victories are won. A true friend prefers the favor of God to the recognition of man. King David was one such individual. He fought the lion and the bear when no one was looking. But David's victory in secret qualified him to beat Goliath when two entire nations were watching. That is a common destiny for a friend of God. God will often trust them with the recognition of man because favor with God is all that matters to them. They earn God's trust, and in turn, God entrusts them with power and authority to do the works of Christ on a very large scale. What is available for everyone is realized by only a few. Dr. James Maloney is such a man: a friend of God, and a chosen vessel of the Lord.

One of the greatest privileges in life is to honor a friend of God. In honoring them, we honor God Himself. He takes it personal. In this case, it is my privilege to honor James for his service to the Lord and for his wonderful book, *The Dancing Hand of God*. I don't know of another book quite like it. It is revelatory, insightful, inspirational, and perhaps most importantly, it is timely. We need this book! Whether it's the report of miracles, the story of his call into ministry, or the insights into church life of the last days, each justifies the careful study of this book. Theories can inspire the imagination. But stories and teachings from authentic biblical experiences release the power for personal transformation. That will no doubt be a byproduct of reading this book.

The story of his call into ministry is one of the most unusual and delightfully supernatural stories I've ever heard. And I never get tired of hearing it. I am fascinated by how God pursued and called James. And while my personal call was so different from his, my understanding of God is expanded through such variety.

James' experiences in the miraculous fascinate me. My heart so longs for the authentic ministry of Jesus to be seen in the earth that each of Dr. Maloney's stories gives me an education. I for one am not satisfied with nice ideas. I must have the real, or at least be in its pursuit. Every time we're together, I get to hear more of the most unusual ways that God uses this man. My faith is strengthened, and my focus becomes more resolved. He has that effect on me.

I need men like James Maloney in my life. The wisdom I gain from them is priceless. And I need books like *The Dancing Hand of God*. There's so much mystery in the life of miracles. Yet Dr. Maloney unravels things that were never meant to remain hidden, as the realm of mystery has become our inheritance.

I pray that as you read this book your heart will burn — burn with new passion for God, burn with hunger for truth, and burn with desire for the authentic gospel that displays miracles, signs and wonders. The ingredients needed for such a fire exist on the pages of *The Dancing Hand of God*.

Bill Johnson

Senior Pastor – Bethel Church, Redding, California

Author – *When Heaven Invades Earth* and

Face to Face with God

Chapter One

Unveiling the Fullness of God

THE DANCING HAND OF GOD

I just love it when God shows off by displaying His power to the world. It is so amazing that God is not only willing, but also desirous, of revealing Himself to us. Zephaniah 3 says that God dances over His children with delight, and that He is mighty in the midst of them. That's an impressive image. The "dancing hand of God" is a concept taken from 1 Corinthians 12, which speaks of the gifts of the Spirit.

The concept was brought out by the late John Wimber. Verse 11 of 1 Corinthians 12 says that the Spirit divides gifts out to men individually as He wills. The Greek word translated "manifestations" in Verse 7 of that chapter is the Greek word *phanerosis* (Strong's #5321). It means "to shine," "to exhibit," or "to render apparent." Based on an encounter he had with God, John Wimber extrapolated one of the meanings of *phanerosis* as the finger of God pointing to specific people and unveiling an aspect of His nature to them. In other words, we can envision the finger of God singling out one person to be granted a word of wisdom, then dancing to another person, and they have a word of knowledge, etc.

Phanerosis could also convey tributaries (or fingers) of a river, flowing out to people, diversified as God sees fit. This meaning gives the image of the one river (the Spirit) with many streams going out to God's people. Again, this was a revelation that John Wimber had during an encounter with the Lord. I think it is a phenomenal revelation concerning the manifestations of the Holy Spirit; one that I attest to in my own experiences with the Lord, as this book will show.

As God's hand moves among His servants, the supernatural gifts of the Holy Spirit testify to His delight in working through those He calls His children. It is my desire that this book show more clearly the "dancing hand of God" which unveils the fullness of the Father's heart through apostolic signs, wonders, and miracles, and that it will unveil more fully—though by no means exhaustively—God's desire to lavish His favor upon us.

I want this book to speak to the apostles first. After all, this is an apostolic book. But I want this book to be uplifting to *apostolic people*, as well. I realize we are not all called into full-time five-fold ministry, but I am firmly convinced that God wants every one of His children to be apostolically motivated. It is for this reason that I have chosen to write this book in a very conversational voice.

I've endeavored not to make it sound like I'm simply dictating from a set of typed notes. I believe the information presented herein lends itself to a very practical approach. I've noticed a tendency in many charismatic books to write almost archaically, and it often comes out a tad dry for my taste. I really want to avoid that here. Be warned—I ain't always gonna write with the proper grammar. I might even use sentence fragments. Sometimes.

I've also tried to find a balance between storytelling and teaching. In other words, while this book should sound like I'm talking to you over a cup of coffee, it also presents material in a systematic way. I've included outlines at the end of each chapter that I encourage you, in whatever capacity you serve in ministry, to present to those around you. I want you to *use this material to turn the face of a hurting world toward God.*

As you read, you'll find that some chapters will be more inspirational in content, while others will be "meatier" in theology. I've done this purposely, because I've read some books that feel like homework, and I think it's nice to ease up a bit every now and again to allow a reader to recharge before plowing ahead. I'm sure you've had similar experiences where a new book—while truly amazing—makes your brain hurt if you read it too long. I hope I'm not the only one who's had that experience!

With the advent of the Apostolic Reformation, there have been well over two hundred books on apostles and their functions in the Church. (This does not include the books that are *opposed* to the manifestation of the apostolic in the body.) With so many "pro-apostle" books available on any number of topics from church government to financial release, from fathering disciples to military-like leadership skills, workplace anointing, and so on, you might be thinking *Why this book? Why now?*

That's a good question. Here's my answer: I have attempted to wait these nearly ten years of the Apostolic Reformation to allow the general concept of the apostle to manifest itself to me and the church. In short, just like you, I have been *learning* what an apostle is ... and is not. I do not claim to be an authority on all things apostolic—quite the opposite, actually. This book is by no means intended to be a complete theological study on the apostles and their functions.

Rather, I wanted to deal with the heart principles behind the motivation of the apostolic. Why? Because I feel that no matter what one's apostolic release is supposed to be (governmental, fathering, workplace, etc.) there should be a dynamic of supernatural anointing that backs up the apostolic claim. Hence, *any* person with an apostolic desire should be able to benefit greatly from this book.

Before we get into this book of supernatural encounters, I want to make something very clear: I endeavor to be a man of God's Word. I have dedicated more than thirty years of my life to studying it as best as I can. While I was saved in the Jesus Movement, I attended a Bible school that was rooted in a systematic, theological study of the written Word of God. I cut my spiritual eyeteeth on the Word of Faith movement (not that I subscribe to *everything* Word of Faith.) My point is, I give the Bible the utmost preeminence in *any* expression we see in the Church. What do I mean by that? It takes the Word and the Spirit operating together in perfect unison! (John 4:23).

If we lack an understanding of God's eternal, inerrant Word, we open ourselves up to "dead-works legalism" and religiosity (that's bad) or to excess and hyper-emotional mysticism and esoteric experientialism (that's bad too.) The only way we keep a balance is through a vibrant, personal one-on-one relationship with Jesus Christ and His Word. This book should always drive you to seek Him more.

This book is about the release of the supernatural, and in my most humble of opinions, there is a true purpose behind encounters like that. I urge you as you read this book, whether you are skeptical of supernatural experience or a full-blown "mover and shaker," to keep everything in context and subjection to the written Word of God—the only infallible source we possess.

The Purpose of Supernatural Encounters

This book is largely autobiographical. It is about my life's work and shares some of the most miraculous encounters God has graciously permitted me to participate in. However, this book is more than just an autobiography; it provides teaching based on those encounters that you as the reader can adapt to your life.

Whenever God has graced me with a visitation or a physical touch of His presence, it has not been just for my benefit alone. These encounters are also to release a fuller understanding of His heart, His desires and His power in the church as a whole. To me, that's the nature of apostolic ministry. Not that I call myself an apostle. It's not a title I really use for myself. But I believe these experiences establish an attribute of the Father in the day-to-day lives of His children.

When a supernatural act goes forth into the natural world, it confirms the Kingdom of God. The reality of the spiritual world (which the Bible says is more real than this one) crashes through the veil that covers this natural world. (Isaiah 25:7)

As I relate these experiences for the benefit of others—firstly to the apostles, secondly to apostolic people—my prayer is that God will release a *breaker anointing* among His people so that they can enter into these miraculous encounters. I am no special person. I have nothing in myself that God is not desirous to give to every Spirit-filled believer in the world. I want this book to instill within you the knowledge that these encounters are for everyone as the Holy Spirit wills and directs you in them.

By mixing what you are about to read with faith, a holy discipline, and a passion for His presence, you can enter into this anointing (Hebrews 4:1-2). This is for everyone! It's not an excuse to give over to the newest Christian fad, but rather a call to cultivate a lifestyle of sensitivity to God's supernatural presence and a deeper relationship with Jesus Christ founded on systematic, biblical study.

I believe that the encounters presented in this book are to be used to release a breaker anointing—something that apostles and apostolic people are to operate in on a regular basis. Some revelations—not every revelation out there, mind you—are keys to an apostolic release.

It hit me when I started writing this book, that many of the dreams, visions, visitations, and manifestations that I've been permitted to witness have revealed an attribute of the gift of the apostle in signs, wonders, and miracles. I want to share them with you to create a new expression of the apostolic.

In the early '90s, some initial books on the office of the apostle launched the Apostolic Reformation (as it's been titled by many theologians). God used those books as forerunners into a new anointing and fresh concepts regarding the Church. It is my sincerest hope that this book launches an expression of the apostle to the people.

I have waited ten or more years during the Apostolic Reformation to be released by God to write this book. I believe the Church is ready to embrace this type of apostolic expression now. I recognize it is not the *only* expression of the apostle, and as I wrote earlier, this book is by no means authoritative on everything apostolic. It is, however, material and experiences compiled over nearly forty years of ministry that I believe God wants to use to create a new expression through the apostolic people.

I want to point out that throughout the book I will be referring to apostles, but because an Ephesians 4:11 apostle is called to equip the saints with an apostolic spirit, one could usually replace *apostle* with *apostolic people*, excepting that which is specifically related to one who stands in the office of an apostle. I'll save the tedium of writing both out each time, but you will know that when you see *apostle*, it most often also applies to an *apostolic people*.

A friend of mine, Bill Johnson, once said, "Wherever I have found the activity of God — that activity can also become my possession." How true this is! What he's saying here is that when someone sees God move in a particular, supernatural fashion in another person or in a geographical location, that someone can have an expectation to see God move in a similar way in their own life. God does not give an expression of Himself to one person and not to another.

The startling testimonies you are about to read are put here to encourage you to expect these supernatural encounters to be reproduced in your life, if you want them. Now, let me give a word of caution about this: do *not* miss the supernatural by only looking for the spectacular! When you read these awesome encounters that God has done — and I'm the first to admit, they *are* awe-inspiring — do not be under the persuasion that I am minimizing the "smaller" supernatural things that God does. Look, any move, any manifestation of God is an incredible gift to His people. I can honestly say I am just as thrilled to see God heal someone of an ingrown toenail as opposed to lung cancer! It is all through His grace and mercy. But I believe we are quickly approaching a time of greater impartation, and God is calling His people to expect those overwhelming signs and wonders in a deeper measure.

It's not arrogance to presuppose that if God wants people healed of ingrown toenails, He also wants them healed of cancer. Of course, the Body of Christ has seen both throughout its history, but more and more, our faith to see the cancer healings will grow to be the same as the toenail healings. That's the purpose of this book: to encourage that kind of faith and expectation.

THE BREAKER ANOINTING

The Holy Spirit is separating the sheep from the sheep in the Body of Christ. What I mean by that is God is raising up people with an apostolic spirit upon them — saints who jut out a little further than the person next to them. People of an excellent spirit, people of another (or different) spirit, people who will break out. They aren't *better* people, but they *are* leaders of the pack, and the pack will always follow the leader. There is nothing wrong with followers if they align themselves with true leaders.

Daniel 5:11-12 says, "'There is a man in your kingdom in whom is the Spirit of the Holy God... Inasmuch as an excellent spirit, knowledge, understanding, interpreting dreams, solving riddles, and explaining enigmas were found in this Daniel....'"

That word *excellent* is represented by the Chaldean word *yattiyr* (Strong's #3493), meaning "to jut over, to exceed, very exceedingly excellent." Daniel was a leader, so much so even the king took note of his words.

Numbers 14:24 reveals, "'But My servant Caleb, because he has a different spirit in him and has followed Me fully, I will bring into the land where he went, and his descendants will inherit it.'" *Different* here is translated from the Hebrew word *acher* (Strong's #312), and it means "another (man), strange, to be unique and peculiar." Caleb was a leader, and if the children of Israel had followed his and Joshua's advice, it would have saved them forty years of wandering around in a wilderness.

Micah 2:13 writes, "'The one who breaks open will come up before them; they will break out, pass through the gate, and go out by it; their king will pass before them, with the Lord at their head.'" *Breaks open* is conveyed in the Hebrew word *parats* (Strong's #6555), meaning "to make a breach, to burst out, to press, scatter, urge, a breaker." God is raising up people who are on the cutting edge of His expression. These people are wedges of grace, one could say; innovators who go ahead of others and break open the way for them to follow. These breakers pave the way.

The point here is — who do you want to be? I'm convinced that God's called every believer to be a breaker, a wedge — to a certain extent — making a way for others to follow them. You are to be a person of an excellent, different spirit! Now, you may not be an apostle, *per se*, but you can align yourself with the breaker anointing represented in the apostles around you. Not everyone is an apostle, but God expects them to support the apostolic, breaker anointing — that anointing which breaks through a structure prohibiting the move of God.

All the above phrases represent the apostle and by association the apostolic person. They predicate being an icebreaker, one who is a peninsula, one who juts out a little further than the rest. They mean a forerunner, a point person, a leader. That breaker anointing I believe the Holy Spirit is incorporating into the Body. I want this book to be a catalyst for that anointing.

The Bible says that the signs of an apostle are perseverance in signs and wonders and mighty deeds. (2 Corinthians 12:12) To me, that means that anyone who is apostolic in their ministry *must* operate in the supernatural on a regular, consistent basis — be that in healing, workings of miracles, deliverance, prophecy, etc. It also bears noting that the signs of the apostle can be more than just straightforward healing or deliverance. They can also have supernatural strategies and planning or a breakthrough anointing in church government; people who have a gifting in dealing with church struggles and factions, wisdom from above, strategies of heaven to defeat the strategies here on earth. There can also be a supernatural patience in persecution. Just because something supernatural is not explosive to the eyes, ears, taste, touch or smell that doesn't make it any less supernatural. The apostolic is altering our definition of what is *supernatural*.

But if we were to be completely honest, generally, we would all agree we're not seeing the miraculous as often as we should. The tangible supernatural is something that I believe God is bringing to the apostles and then His apostolic people.

A time is fast approaching that restores the supernatural to the Body of Christ in greater measure, when His sent ones will rise up in power and authority, confirming that the Father is a God of miracles we can see. It has only been the past few years that the Lord has authorized me to share many of these experiences in my life. That tells me that a *kairos* moment is coming soon to usher in a new flood of the miraculous that will not only empower the Body of Christ but will confirm His reality and authority to the world at large. The Greek word *kairos* speaks of an appointed time within the flow of normal, calendar time (*chronos*.)

Let's face it, friends, if a man who has no arm instantly grows an arm in front of a thousand people, it confronts them with the reality of the Father's love and authority. It forces them to either accept or reject Him. It's confrontational and it's real. The disciples themselves asked, "Who is this Man that even the winds and the sea obey Him?" (Matthew 8:27) So if we are to imitate Christ in His earthly ministry, should not the winds and sea also obey us sent in His name to do His business?

The purpose of every miracle, every sign and wonder, is to release the apostolic spirit. They do warfare in the spiritual realm and tear down the demonic strongholds over this earth. Truly, we don't fight with flesh and blood, but against demonic principalities, and the weapons we use are not carnal weapons. (Ephesians 6:12) The miraculous is one such type of weapon; the miracles themselves are weapons of warfare. I know they are not the *only* weapons we have, but they are some of the most *neglected* weapons we have.

How else do we combat the New Age? Stand against the onslaught of Islam? Work against the apathy of those in the world? By operating in signs, wonders and miracles that testify of the validity and authority of the Kingdom of Jesus. It's a simple premise, but one that is not talked about much in Charismatic circles.

A Passion Being Born

There is a cry among God's people. There is a passion being born, a thirsting for the power and glory of God to permeate the earth. David sang, "So I have looked for You in the sanctuary, to see Your power and Your glory." (Psalm 63:2) This is the song of God's people today.

Paul the apostle, in Philippians 3:10, outlined quite possibly the greatest need of every believer, "...that I might know Him...." "Know" in the Greek is *ginosko* (Strong's #1097), and it implies "knowing absolutely." I believe that Paul is seeking to know Him in an *explosive, experiential way*. I mean, there is a knowing, and then there is a **knowing**. One can know something abstractly, as a concept, but it is entirely different to *know* something in experience.

A certain sense of dissatisfaction has to come in the Body of Christ, a sense of restlessness to want more of His power manifested; we need a passion to know Him more fully. Proverbs 29:18 admonishes us, "Where there is no revelation, the people cast off restraint...."

Look, I know that we are ultimately satisfied in Jesus. I realize that. Don't misconstrue my intentions. But, if I can phrase it this way, we need to be dissatisfied with our current level of satisfaction. We need Him *more*. If the power of God is truly limitless, then we should be ever pursuing manifesting a deeper level of that power. I don't think it's wrong to covet more of Him expressed in our lives. We should all be an explosive representation of His power on the face of this earth. We see in Exodus 33:18 that Moses had a wonderful relationship with God, but he wanted to see more. We should act likewise.

We must press beyond the veil and be utterly consumed with His zeal. In the Old Testament tabernacle, there was the outer court; and then there was the Holy Place and the Most Holy, separated by a veil (Exodus 26:33), which of course was torn in two when Christ was crucified. (Matthew 27:51, Mark 15:38, Luke 23:45) So in our temple today (meaning ourselves, since we are the temple of God according to 1 Corinthians 6:19), one could say the veil separating us from God's most intimate domain is comprised of *discontent, disappointment* and *deception.* Apostolic ministry rends that veil in two, creating an avenue for God's zeal to consume us totally.

Many people live without His zeal in their lives because of a wound of disillusionment. They say, "My life is too difficult, and I can't ever seem to get ahead." Or perhaps a false manifestation burned them in the past, and they felt let down by God and His ministers. But an apostolic anointing *disarms* disappointment. It restores *inspiration* in the testimonies of those caught up in God-encounters.

Apostles *dismantle* wrong concepts people may have of God, like skillful surgeons taking God's Word to cut out all hindrances. It's almost as if they make room for a miracle to occur because, see, many people are deceived; but the apostolic anointing restores proper *instruction* and increases purpose, which breaks off those deceptions and creates a space for God to move.

God is raising up an apostolic people who *discharge* wisdom and virtue, and the anointing in their lives will *impart* a sense of peace and contentment to overcome the discontent of the world.

Lastly, apostles *dissuade* the people of religious leaven that spoil the whole lot. (1 Corinthians 5:5-7; Galatians 5:9) In this day of rampant religiosity that provides no actual substance for the people, God is commissioning apostles with a mandate to *increase* the sense of freedom in worshipping Him that is obviously lacking in many religious, ultimately unfruitful churches. This freedom scares some people who are used to church services following a particular pattern. These religious spirits are working furiously to stifle any sense of expression that is not "normal"... whatever that means.

Now, I believe all things are to be done decently and in order (1 Corinthians 14:40), and I'm not ignorant of the misuse and foolish overreacting that has been prevalent in the Church during any new type of renewal expression. But we tend to forget the first part of that verse: "Let *all things* be done...." I, for one, am willing to allow God to work through a little bit of flesh in order to experience Him in deeper measure in spirit and truth. Notice, I wrote "work through," not "excuse." But remember, "... we have this treasure in earthen vessels, that the excellence of the power may be of God and not of us." (2 Corinthians 4:7) It does not excuse flesh — that is something to burn away, to crucify, so a true expression of God's Spirit can come forth. There is too much mixture of carnality and spirituality in the Body. We'll explore this topic at great length in the course of this book.

Let me be clear here, I do *not* advocate abuse of the supernatural. Those who minister behind the pulpit, I believe, are compelled to present the gospel of truth in King Jesus with a certain level of decorum and modesty. Even though Paul said, "We are fools for Christ's sake..." (1 Corinthians 4:10), I don't believe he handled himself like a maniac. Expressions in God are not excuses to act like fools, giving over to every whim of the flesh or every new fad; but on the other side of the token, we cannot be afraid of a new expression from God out of some mentality of false religiosity. When properly motivated by His Spirit, that expression may just be the new level He wants to take us into so that we might know Him in deeper, greater demonstration. Why must we continually fear something new? Be cautious, yes, but also be open. That's what the Apostolic Reformation is coming to set straight.

In short, apostles *restore, renew, release* and *reform*. They make a way for God's zeal to consume us, moving us into His holiest of holy places where we get to commune with Him in as close to a face-to-face encounter as is possible on this earthly plane. We have to catch fire, so to speak, and become ablaze for an intense, burning desire to *know* Him.

As Jesus said in John 6:53, "Most assuredly, I say to you, unless you eat the flesh of the Son of Man and drink His blood, you have no life in you." I have heard it taught — and I think it's a neat idea — that the phrase *eat the flesh* should convey a concept of devouring in a noisy, crunching manner. You know, licking the plate clean, and then licking your fingers. I mean, *eating*. Further, the phrase *drink His blood* means in a gulping, slurping, sloshing manner. Letting it dribble down your chin — really *drinking*.

We need to seek ravenously after the revelation of God, otherwise we're not really eating or drinking, you know? We need to come up higher. We need to have a deeper, all-consuming revelation of God the Father. God's apostolic people are some of the tools He has given the Church to reach this goal.

THE EYES OF OUR UNDERSTANDING BEING ENLIGHTENED

Ephesians 1:17 says, "...That the eyes of your understanding being enlightened...." I picture that word *enlightened* as meaning a "photo flash." A flash of His person, His purpose, burned upon the negative of your life, like the negative of a photo. It means that we know, that we know, that we know, that we know.... The Father of Glory will imprint the Spirit of wisdom and revelation in the knowledge of Him upon you. (Ephesians 1:15-23) Our cry should be that we might know Him. Knowing Him will defeat the challenges of the enemy. Our faith in Him is what combats the snares of the enemy. We know that Romans 10:17 says, "So then faith comes by hearing, and hearing by the word of God." He anoints us to hear this word so that the eyes of our understanding may be enlightened.

The Lord may have graciously bestowed a ministry upon me spanning almost four decades, but I'm convinced the best is yet to come for all of us in the Church. Upon reading some of the supernatural encounters contained here, I know one of the main questions people will have right after *Is he telling the truth?* will be *How come I've never heard of this guy before? If these encounters are all real, why isn't he more world-renowned?*

Those are both valid questions. The first I will highlight in a moment because the answer to the second is simpler. Now, I might be somewhat known in certain circles, and I feel God blessed with an international ministry, but He has not permitted me to promote heavily what I do. Early on, He purposely told me not to resort to unnecessary advertisements and gimmicks. He said there would be a measure to which I would remain hidden, and therefore He would entrust to me certain encounters with Him. Prayerfully I would convey a revelation of God in greater fullness — so that it would affect the next generation with deeper faith and confidence to see Him move mightily by their hands. So the majority of my life's work has remained hidden, in that sense. And that's fine with me... because I just want to see miracles! We've seen literally thousands of miracles that no one has ever heard about, except for the people who received them, their families and the folks immediately around them. I don't lose any sleep if no one else knows about them.

Now don't get all offended here. This isn't some false humility; I trust you recognize that. I don't believe it's wrong to publicize a ministry as God wills. Let's be honest, we'll promote this book to a certain extent. But I do believe we have too much self-advertising in the Body of Christ. There have been "well-known" ministers who advertise a great anointing that they don't really have, and people end up getting hurt or disappointed. I'd rather let these encounters speak for themselves without undue promotion on my end, and I'll leave the book sales to God! It's only been the last couple of years He's even permitted me to write these encounters down at all, but I am sure God wants to use this book to promote a greater expression of Him to humanity. That's the most important thing.

Now in partial response to the first question above: I want this book to be a blessing, but I recognize one of the difficulties in writing a book about signs, wonders and miracles is that it opens one up to possible scrutiny and criticism. Now, I know that I'll stand before God and give an account to its accuracy, and I dare not leave a legacy of "fluff." In nearly forty years of full-time ministry, I have endeavored not to embellish or exaggerate any miracle I've witnessed. In my early ministry, I had received incorrect information on a couple of incidents related to me by pastors from the churches I was preaching in. And after further research, I found out the experiences were not as accurate as I first believed. I feel confident in commenting that that has probably happened to every minister to a certain degree. It's not an excuse, but my point here is to convey just how honest I am trying to be in sharing these encounters with you. I do not want to puff an experience up into something more than it was intended to be.

I can't stop people from nay saying, and there will be a certain amount of backlash to a book of this nature. I'm prepared to accept that because I believe in a miraculous God who wants to be miraculous for everyone, if they'll just let Him.

Anyone who knows my ministry, I trust, also knows my heart. The stream from which I write is one of compassion and love, dedication to a deeper relationship with Jesus. I am as human as the next minister —

maybe even more so! I have nothing in myself to offer you, as you will see from my testimony. I hope this book conveys the humility that I strive to show as the cornerstone of my ministry.

I believe any supernatural experience is to convey the love of God to humanity, and because God loves us so much, we ought not to make excuses for the operation — or lack thereof — of God in ministry. For this reason, I highly esteem daily prayer, speaking in tongues and the tangible, physical presence of the Lord, the prophetic move of God among His people, the deliverance ministry of Jesus in today's world, the healing of the sick and the teaching of the infallibility of the Word of God in a concise realistic, homiletic fashion.

Many of the miracles I'm sharing here have written documentation and/or multiple eyewitness testimonies to validate the experiences. Some of the encounters happened to me in my private times with the Lord, but I believe the Holy Spirit will bear witness to you the intent of my heart. I need to say that I have no desire to open myself — or these precious people the Lord healed — up to a barrage of scoffers demanding proof of these experiences. For one thing, most of these people do not desire any sort of recognition — positively or negatively — and have asked we reference them anonymously. In communicating with them, they've conveyed to me how they and their families rejoice at the miraculous touch of God in their lives, but they leave it up to the direction of the Holy Spirit to give witness and testimony to these occurrences as He sees fit.

Ultimately, one will believe me or not as one chooses. However, I trust in the Father that He will convince you of my desire to present the truth of His love and power. Those who know me know I endeavor to be a person of integrity, and I encourage those who don't know me to search the face of God for a revelation of my intentions. With every miracle I encounter, I am staggered into a humbled, broken stance. The fact that God is willing to use any of us to work His power is simply astonishing. Yet, He does. And I believe He is commissioning me to share with you these encounters to lift you up, to encourage you to seek His breaker anointing, and I'll leave it to Him to convince you of my honesty.

When I was attending Christ for the Nations Institute in Dallas, Texas, as a teenager, someone handed me a book by Smith Wigglesworth that shared the amazing things he saw. The book inspired my faith, and the Holy Spirit spoke to my heart that these miracles truly happened. I bore witness to Wigglesworth's truthfulness, and that book changed my life. I pray the same thing will happen with this book. Please know that I have a reverential fear of the Lord and will never lead His people astray by compromising the truth He has revealed to His servants.

Most of the cardinal truths we have today come from supernatural experiences in the past. If you are not Jewish, the reason you are saved today is because Peter had a vision out of heaven that salvation was also for the Gentiles (Acts 11.) The reason you are filled with the Holy Spirit today is because a rushing, mighty Wind filled those in the Upper Room (Acts 2.) If the Bible is truly the authoritative Word of God, and God cannot change (Malachi 3:6), then He operates just as supernaturally today as He did in times past (Hebrews 13:8.) And the experiences He has permitted me to witness are not only for *my* edification, but for the edification of the entire Church as well. (1 Corinthians 14:26)

I give all praise and honor to the Lord for working through His earthen vessels, and I want to see more of Him revealed. But God does not give supernatural encounters just for the sake of having a supernatural encounter. Miraculous interventions are to testify of the dominion of King Jesus over this natural world, not just simply to feel "warm and gooey" in your body. The sole purpose for any sign and wonder is to reveal His divine nature. Any miracle, visitation or prophetic word is to create a permanent link between the Kingdom of Heaven and the kingdom of earth, for it is indeed an adulterous generation that seeks after a sign just to be impressed by the sign itself (Matthew 16:4.) Every part of this book points to the love of the Father, the authority of His Son and the power of His Holy Spirit to unveil more of Their delight in moving among the Church.

We know the scriptures provide the final revelation of all things, and again, I am a stickler to the written Word of God. But I am also convinced that further supernatural experiences — subject to the Word — happen today to *confirm* that Word to His people. (Hebrews 2:4) That is why I have written this book. I'm going to share with you some of the most significant, miraculous encounters that God was gracious enough to share with me for your benefit. I pray they uplift you; I trust that they will encourage your faith, bolster your confidence in the sure Word. But more than that, I hope they ignite within you a passion to see the fullness of Him revealed through apostolic anointing. This book should admonish you in love to step out in faith and *expect* to see God move in your life. That's the only way to convince the world our God is the one, true God and all others are false, mute idols. Permit me humbly to attempt unveiling the love of the Father as best as I can.

"Unveiling the Fullness of God"

THE DANCING HAND OF GOD

- 1 Corinthians 12:7 – "manifestation" – *phanerosis* (Greek)
- God's fingers dance among His people, dealing out many gifts of the Spirit as He wills, like tributaries of a river
- Coined by the late John Wimber

THE PURPOSE OF SUPERNATURAL ENCOUNTERS

- The purpose of supernatural encounters is to unveil the fullness of God
- They release an apostolic *breaker anointing* (see below)
- To have supernatural encounters and be apostolically motivated is everyone's calling. Do *not* miss the supernatural by looking only for the spectacular
- "Wherever I have found the activity of God, that can become my possession." – Bill Johnson

THE BREAKER ANOINTING

- Daniel 5:11-12 – "excellent spirit" – *yattiyr* (Chaldean)
- "to jut over, to exceed, very exceedingly excellent"
- Numbers 14:24 – "different spirit" – *acher* (Hebrew)
- "another (man), strange, to be unique and peculiar"
- Micah 2:13 – "breaks open" – *parats* (Hebrew)

- "to make a breach, to burst out, to press, scatter, urge, a breaker"
- The Holy Spirit is separating out people within His Church, those who jut out a little further than the rest, people of another spirit who break open, as a wedge, going before the people as a forerunner and a leader, unveiling the fullness of God through apostolic anointing
- 2 Corinthians 12:12 — the signs of an apostle, through perseverance, in signs, wonders and mighty deeds
- An apostolic person operates in the supernatural on a consistent basis — healings, workings of miracles, deliverance, prophecy, words of knowledge, words of wisdom in strategies and planning for church government, supernatural patience through persecution

A Passion Being Born

- Apostolic anointing *disarms* disappointment and restores *inspiration*
- Apostles *dismantle* wrong concepts of God and restore proper *instruction*
- Apostolic people *discharge* wisdom and virtue, and the anointing *imparts* peace and contentment
- Apostles *dissuade* the people of religious leaven that spoil the freedom of the rest and are commissioned with a mandate to *increase* the sense of freedom in worshipping God
- Apostles *restore, renew, release* and *reform*

Chapter Two
Unveiling the Fatherhood of God

BEATEN AND BRUISED

I was born in the mid-Fifties in the slums of Kansas City, Missouri. According to my adoptive mother, based on what she felt were reliable sources, my birth mother was a German immigrant, who was married to a man incarcerated for one reason or another. During his time in jail, my mother sought solace from a minister. During one of their counseling sessions, my mother had an affair with the preacher, and I was conceived illegitimately — the result of their adultery.

My mother was just a teenager herself. She would venture out into the city in search of food, but days at a time would pass in which there was nothing to eat. Milk stolen from the neighbor's porch was all she ever had to give me. More often than not, tap water filled my bottle, and a dresser drawer served as my crib. She had no diapers for me; I wore a wool blanket rarely rinsed out. It caused unimaginable, fiery welts.

With all of that, Mom's greatest fear was the dreaded day when her husband would return home from prison. She'd never found the courage to warn him of the shock he would encounter upon his homecoming — a child born of another man. Apparently, he had tried to kill someone with his bare hands, so they placed him in solitary confinement, thus she had never seen him since becoming pregnant.

The day of his parole came, and the man returned home only to find a toddler that he knew couldn't possibly be his sitting on the one-room apartment floor. A spirit of rage filled him to jealous frenzy, and he stormed across the room and smashed his heavy boot in my face, breaking my nose, disfiguring my features. He picked me up by the ankles and slammed me into the wall like a battering ram. The protection of the Lord was the only thing that spared my life.

Many months of brutality followed. My mother was often a victim as well, and it finally forced her to face reality. She knew she couldn't keep me any longer. After more than two years of malnutrition, I was surely doomed to die at the hands of her insane husband. To make matters worse, she had just given birth to a girl, but she was hoping her husband would be appeased with this new baby — a child he had fathered — if I was removed and forgotten. She tried to sell me to some friends of hers. Meanwhile, the physical abuse was continuing to get worse and worse.

Being so young, thankfully I don't really remember the beatings. But I do remember being locked in a closet, sometimes for up to two days at a time, with nothing more than a bottle of water. I remember being in the dark, afraid and alone, crying out, but no one would answer my wails.

After learning of my horrible condition, her friends stepped in and got the government involved. They sued for protective custody and won, and they adopted me into their new family. Eventually we moved to Southern California.

I received much-needed medical attention that slowly nourished back to health. All of my baby teeth were decayed, each one needing to be capped with silver. Smooth skin finally replaced the welts and puffy sores from my woolen diapers. I remember feeling that each meal would surely be my last, so I ate adult-sized portions at each setting. (After the first year, I finally realized that there was no need to gorge — food would be plenteous every day.) I no longer slept in a dresser drawer. I had my own brand new bed, and although I wasn't yet toilet-trained, I never wet that bed one time. I was so proud of it.

My new parents treated my inward afflictions as well, but my emotions were so damaged that I was unable to reach out and trust. In fact, I didn't start talking until four years of age. The abuse and neglect suffered at the hands of my mother and her husband left permanent impressions upon my character.

I slept downstairs, and whenever I heard the steps of my adoptive parents upstairs, I would wake up in a panic, fully expecting that big, heavy boot to come crashing down on my face once again. As I grew older, I no longer remembered the beatings and the hunger, but nothing could erase that part of my early childhood. I remembered being left alone and abandoned in that closet — that sickening feeling in the pit of your stomach that you are unwanted. The outward bruises had long since healed, but the inward bruise of rejection responded to no natural cures. Shuddering with an empty, lonely feeling, I knew it would badger me my whole life. That feeling would always inwardly cripple me.

Adoption in itself did not prove to be the ultimate solution for my search of acceptance. Within a few years, I simply filled the role of one of America's many forgotten teenagers. Not behaving badly enough to demand constant correction, nor on the other hand acting exceptionally outstanding, I developed a middle-of-the-road personality easily ignored. There was the typical generation gap that developed in the 60s and 70s between parent/child relationships.

So since I was no longer that mistreated, little boy with sad eyes salvaged from the slums by my adopted parents' pity, they had done their part to the best of their abilities in instructing me to become independent, to learn to take care of myself. Like in so many American families, the mark of maturity was having no need to rely on others.

The Wounded Cry

I became suicidal at fourteen. There were many times while walking the twisty roads of my mountain hometown that a passing car seemed like a perfect opportunity to take my life. I could feel this heavy hand pushing me toward the vehicle, and this voice inside my head would say, "Go ahead. Just end it all." At just the last moment, I would push against the invisible hand and continue home, feeling miserable, embarrassed and all alone.

Finally, I'd had enough. It was New Year's Eve, 1970. After another futile attempt to make those yearly resolutions for self-improvement, I concluded that all such man-made penances were useless. I suffered from such a lack of self-esteem and purpose. Those feelings of being unwanted still lingered on. I sensed no reason to live at all. I knew that I'd reached the end of my rope, and I was just going to kill myself and escape this world. I was so confused. I thought about trying to pray, but I didn't know how. In an act of desperation, I cried out from my bed, "God, if You're really real, You're going to have to reveal Yourself to me, because I can't take this anymore." It wasn't like I was threatening God; it was just a statement of fact. I had nothing left within myself to keep going. I was crying out for reality. If God was concerned with my life at all, He was going to have to fill this vacuum within me. I cried myself to sleep that night, and if you've ever done that, you know what a miserable experience it is. I was ashamed of my tears, for they were surely marks of weakness.

On New Year's Day, 1971, in the early morning hours while it was still dark, I was fitfully sleeping when a small light appeared on the floor at the foot of my bed, and it woke me up. I sat up in bed, rubbing my reddened eyes, staring at this light as it grew brighter and brighter, bigger and bigger, filling my room with this wonderfully warm and holy Presence. This feeling of peace like I'd never known enveloped me, and

I was sure there was Someone in this light. I had no idea who this Light was, but instinctively I got out of bed and fell to my knees. For some reason, I knew the Person in this light was Someone I should honor and revere, Someone of royalty deserving of my praise and worship.

Now, folks, let me tell you: if Buddha had been in that light, I would have worshipped Buddha. If it had been Mohammed, I would've worshipped Mohammed. But it wasn't Buddha, and it wasn't Mohammed. It was the Lord Jesus Christ!

Jesus opened my eyes that day. I felt that I should stick my hands up into the light, and as I did, I saw two outstretched hands reaching out for mine. I just somehow knew the Person in the light was Jesus Christ. My hands and forearms, up to my elbows, disappeared into that Light. I was shaking all over, and then I heard the most beautiful voice say to me, "I have heard your cry for acceptance. I have heard your cry for reality, and I love you just the way that you are."

You cannot possibly know how long I had waited to hear those words. Tears of joy bathed my lifted face. Suddenly I had meaning in my life.

All of my natural surroundings were blurred, and sometime later, I found myself hiking down the snowy mountain where I lived, winding down toward the village with this unique Presence guiding me all the while. Passing by many familiar souvenir shops (we lived in a mountain resort community), I felt particularly drawn to this little dress shop at the end of the row that I had never much noticed before that day.

"Can I help you?" The shopkeeper's voice shook me into awareness.

"I need a Bible," I replied with no premeditation. Suddenly I was confiding all my secret feelings to a total stranger. To my surprise, the kindly woman listened with an attentive ear; and when I'd finished, she not only presented me with a Bible but also another book.

"You'll enjoy this," she said simply. The other book was entitled *I Believe in Miracles* by Kathryn Kuhlman.

Little did I know at the time that God had directed me to someone who had the Answer to my searching. A couple of weeks later, she sent me to a friend of hers (one of my junior high school teachers) who shared with me the plan of salvation. The moment I heard that God would forgive my sins through the shed blood of His Son Jesus — the Person in the light — I immediately asked to receive the gift of eternal life this person was talking about. It was by faith that I knew He had cleansed me. I was saved by grace. Nothing I could do by good works, no religion, could save me. I'd been raised Reformed Catholic in name only, but we hardly ever darkened the door at Mass. But that day, I discovered a true Christian is one who knows Christ in a personal relationship, that he or she is a brand new creation. I was born again from Heaven above. That may sound so simple to you, but to me — an American heathen, Southern California-style — it was the most profound thing I'd ever heard!

THE TOUCH OF FAVOR

Many years later, here I was an evangelist on this nasty train in India. I mean, if you've never experienced mass transportation in India, you have no idea how horrible traveling truly can be. There was this little boy crawling up and down the narrow, filthy aisle. I just stared in disbelief. He was probably five or six, creeping along on his hands and knees. His only clothing — if you can really call it that — was a tattered shred of burlap wrapped about his loins. Each rib protruded violently above his bloated stomach. Matted black hair that had never been washed shadowed hollow eyes filled with shame. He acted like a whipped puppy, tail tucked between the legs. He would not dare look up into my face.

To some people in India, if you're as desolate as this little boy, it must be because in a previous life, you were some horrible person, and the multitude of Hindu gods was punishing you for being such a wretched mortal. In some of the other, more-strict Hindu sects, cultural caste systems prohibit others from intervening on your behalf. However, the conductor of this particular train ignored the karmic consequences, being touched with pity, and allowed this little orphan to live in the bathroom of the coach. When the train began to move, that was the boy's cue to venture out into the aisle and beg for his daily bread. He literally lived off the morsels that people dropped into his palm.

He'd learned two words in English, which he used appropriately: "Ma" for the women, "Pa" for the men. He was so afraid to lift his eyes from the floor. Instead, he raised one grimy hand toward me and beseeched.

"Pa, pa."

I was dumbfounded.

"Pa, pa," he ventured again, meekly.

I gave him something to eat. But what I wanted to do, more than anything in the world, was gather that sickly boy in my arms and love on him, hug him just once, tell him that he was not a worthless human being, and that people still cared. Of course, he wouldn't have permitted me to do so. The social mores of his culture would've made that impossible. It was his plight in life, and he was resolved to it.

Later, I made my way back to the bathroom where he slept. The floor stood in an inch of stagnant, fetid toilet water. There he was, in the corner by the urinal, curled up in a fetal position, sucking his thumb, stroking his grubby hair with his free hand. I could only watch as he rocked himself back and forth on the wet floor, mothering himself to sleep.

I wish this story had some happy ending. But in reality, how lonely the unloved of this world truly feel! I know because I once felt like they did.

Perhaps the loneliest were the lepers in Jesus' day when He walked this earth, going about and doing good. Take a moment to picture the leper in Mark 1:40 — an outcast forbidden to enter society because of his flesh-eating disease. Imagine this lonely leper on the brow of a hill, looking down upon the multitude being touched and healed by the Master. His imposed restrictions prevented him from approaching Jesus. What rejection, despair, hopelessness must have weighed upon that sad man! He kept hearing shouts of victory resound across the valley; he saw people rejoicing in the distance. He knew he could have none of that.

Then a thought struggles from the back of his mind. Perhaps he said to himself, "You know, it just doesn't matter anymore. I don't care what people say — I'm just going to rush down into the midst of that crowd and reach out to Jesus." And with that singular step of faith, he broke forth from the chains of darkness and desolation that had been snaring him for so many years.

This man ran to Jesus, perhaps despite the repulsed reaction from the crowds that were most likely crying out, "Unclean! Unclean!" He threw himself at Jesus' feet and could only say one thing. He'd heard the reports that this Man could heal.

"I know You can make me whole ... if You will. You can make me clean."

Look, he knew that Jesus *could* do it, but the truth he wanted to hear was if Jesus *would* do it. He was asking, "Are You willing? Are You willing to touch an unclean leper? Am I as important as the other sick people You have touched and healed today?"

To which Jesus replied, "I am willing," forever and always answering the question: "Are you willing?" Yes! He is willing!

Jesus touched the leper. "Be made whole."

This man needed much more than just physical restoration, my friends – he needed an inner work of healing power for his mind and emotions. He needed the entire complex of his very being touched and transformed. He needed the confidence of God Himself poured into his character. He needed wholeness for his entire self: spirit, soul and body.

The apostolic breaker anointing answers this need. God has commissioned the apostles and apostolic people to meet the needs of the unloved, the unwashed and the unappreciated. The supernatural encounters of God – like the case of the leper getting healed – show the world at large that there *is* a God in heaven who is concerned for your welfare, emotionally, physically and ultimately spiritually.

In the seventeenth chapter of Luke, we find a different story with an account of ten lepers who came to Jesus. The record states that Jesus simply spoke a word of instruction to these ten men to go show themselves to the priests. As they obeyed His direction, He cleansed them of their plague as they went their way. These lepers didn't require the actual touch of Jesus. The power carried in just His words was enough to heal them as they responded in obedience.

Why then did Jesus consider it necessary to touch the lonely leper found in Mark 1? Perhaps He discerned that this leper needed more than just a word. In the case of the ten lepers, it's apparent they came in a group, meaning they took care of each other. If one could not feed or clothe himself, the others could help. If one stumbled and fell, others could assist him. These lepers had each other's company.

As far as we know, the leper in Mark's account came to Jesus by himself. Due to the lack of human fellowship, it's possible this person needed more than just the spoken word. He needed that divine-human touch found only in one Person, Jesus Christ, the God-man. He longed for that Dancing Hand of God to extend toward his tormented body and mind. In slavery to a disease of fiery torture, his leprosy burned from his flesh clear down into his very soul! This man needed the touch of favor.

Scripture says that Jesus was moved with compassion, full of eager yearning, and He put forth His hand and touched the leper. Jesus was unveiling the Fatherhood of God, for He came as an extension of the Father's Dancing Hand. He came to demonstrate a Father's love. Jesus said, "He that has seen Me has seen the Father," (John 14:9) because the Son only performed that which He saw His Father do. Jesus sounded forth a trumpet, announcing the year of Jubilee — the year of deliverance.

"'The Spirit of the Lord is now upon Me, because He has anointed Me to preach good tidings to the poor. He has sent Me to proclaim release to the captives, and recovering of sight to the blind, to set at liberty them that are bruised and proclaim the acceptable year of the Lord." (Luke 4:18-19)

Indeed, the leper was healed that day, and the bruise in his heart was cured.

THE OPPRESSION OF HUMANITY

Please bear with me for a few pages; I'm outlining a problem that vexes millions of people worldwide. If you'll trust me a little, you'll see that the solution to this problem lies in an apostolic anointing that unveils the Fatherhood of God. I am not one of those preachers who present sad situations without offering an answer, but first we need to recognize one of the key traps Satan has laid out.

One of the greatest plagues today around the world is the fear of rejection. Unwanted children are thrown into garbage bins or simply aborted and discarded as unwelcome tissue. Others live only to face the rejections caused by broken homes. These young people suffer guilt and condemnation, forced to decide which parent they will live with. Divorce can make them choose whether to love Mom or Dad most. No wonder so many women and men dread marriage! They've lost the security and self-identity only found in a stable home. Now please don't misunderstand me, I know these poor people are simply innocent victims. Many times the Moms and Dads themselves are victims, and the circumstances surrounding the divorce seem beyond their control. But the fact remains that we have a lot of bruised, hurting walking wounded in this world.

Adopted children suffer a fear of rejection to some extent. I know because I was one. They often wonder why it happened to them, and why they were not good enough to be kept. Even if a parent gives up a child in an act of unselfishness, the young person may misunderstand the motives.

Many children are raised in an environment that produces a failure complex within them. They are never spoken to kindly; they are never heard — just seen. Parents continually speak negatively to their children, and these words begin to serve as a curse. This in turn causes the child to be conformed to the words spoken. In frustration, many children turn to alcohol or drugs to cope with their feelings of inadequacy. Many withdraw into a fantasy world to escape the harsh surroundings in their households. Yes, rejection is a prime tool of Satan to bruise a once-tender heart. It takes a special miracle, an apostolic unveiling of God's supreme love and authority to break that rejection. This goes beyond the level of inner healing that has been operating in the Church, as important as that noble process is. This even goes beyond deliverance, something as equally necessary. The work of God, through His apostolic people, truly binds the wounds of the rejected, the disenfranchised and the unwanted.

Again, don't misunderstand; many inner-healing and deliverance ministers *do* operate in a breaker anointing. My point here is to show that we need more of an apostolic unction operating in these ministers' lives than what we've presently had. I believe many inner-healing and deliverance ministers are apostolic in function, and the Lord is going to ramp up a greater anointing to produce a quicker, deeper work. As the Spirit begins to move apostolically among these fine people, we are going to see that it doesn't take years and years of therapy to overcome this wound of rejection. Don't forget, the leper was completely restored all at once. Remember, the human soul is finite – there is only so much of it God has to deal with, and He is doing a quicker work in these end times.

In these times, too many young people have lost their self-identity. A girl receives her self-esteem primarily from her father. If he does not build a relationship of love, acceptance and appreciation, her opinion of herself as a woman will undoubtedly be low. In turn, a mother who shows little support of her son's capabilities can produce a lack of self-respect. Often without a proper father image, the boy loses any sense of identity and turns to homosexuality. If the father commits abuse against the daughter, she also will often turn to homosexuality or promiscuity.

Parents who mistreat their children are often victims themselves of childhood abuse. A broken down relationship with their parents creates an emotional vacuum. Since they don't love themselves, it becomes impossible to love others. A vicious cycle continues throughout the generations, producing a multitude of lonely victims.

Most well adjusted people cannot understand how a person becomes lonely. They know that by showing themselves friendly, they win friends. But a lonely person cannot reach out. Due to the inward bruises, they decide to "never be hurt again," so they thrust up a wall of protection, isolating themselves in a hardened exterior.

Proverbs 18:8 says that the words of a talebearer are wounds that enter down into the innermost parts of the belly. Truly, that foolish childhood rhyme – "Sticks and stones may break my bones, but names will never hurt me" – is simply untrue. Proverbs goes on to state that a strong spirit sustains a person through physical infirmity, but a wounded spirit, who can bear? A merry heart does good like a medicine, and a healthy spirit can take a person through their problems, but inward wounds inhibit an afflicted person from reaching out. Instead, they give up the battle when faced with a crisis.

Jeremiah the prophet identifies with the children of Israel in chapter 8, verse 21. He laments he is wounded and bruised as he sees the hurt of the daughter of his people. In verse 22, he asks, "Is there no balm in Gilead?" As you may or may not know, Gilead means "the place of worship for God's people." Is there no healing ointment there? Is there no Physician there? "Why then is not the health of the daughter of my people recovered?" he queries.

To be an apostolic people, we must answer Jeremiah's question. Isaiah 53:4 tells us that Jesus Christ took to the cross our grief; He carried our sorrows. Jesus hanged on a cross in nakedness, bearing our shame. What this means is Jesus carried our poverty so we wouldn't have to. Jesus was never poor until they stripped Him at Golgotha and divided His clothes amongst the soldiers. (Matthew 27:35, Mark 15:24, Luke 23:34, John 19:24) His needs were always met, and He encouraged His disciples to operate in the same level of faith. So many people struggling with rejection also struggle with a poverty mentality. It's like they operate on a substandard level of existence because they feel they can't climb out of the indigence of their surroundings. I am convinced there is a poverty spirit influencing millions of peoples' lives, Christian or otherwise. A poverty mentality does not necessarily mean a lack of money only. Millionaires can be impoverished emotionally, mentally, spiritually.

(Also, I'm not here to argue semantics about whether or not a Christian can have a demon. But it's obvious in many of the churches I minister in that some of the people are either *oppressed* or *suppressed* or *possessed* by a spirit that tells them they can't achieve above their current level of existence. Whatever your theology on demonic oppression, hey, let's just get rid of the thing, all right?)

God has not created us to be poor. This isn't some blatant prosperity message. I can just imagine some readers out there rolling their eyes, going, "Oh boy, here's yet another preacher harping on and on about money!" I am firmly convinced Jesus' crucifixion provided a substitute for our poverty, our lack of blessing — finances being just one part of blessing. I'm not saying everyone needs a Mercedes (although there's nothing wrong with having one.) But we have to deal with this poverty spirit in order to negate completely the wound of rejection operating in peoples' lives.

Rejection and poverty, in any form, go hand in hand. It takes a special unction on the behalf of God's people to undo those cruel philosophies. The apostolic anointing breaks the power of this poverty spirit; it shows rejected people that they don't have to struggle in a mundane, destitute existence just because their parents were poor or their grandparents lived through the Depression. A keystone mark of the apostolic person is an ability to reverse the curse of poverty in all its forms.

Jesus' body, covered in His precious blood, carried our sin. In his writings, my brother-in-law, David Alsobrook, shows how Jesus paid the price that we might have the mind of Christ. (1 Corinthians 2:16) On His way to the cross, a crown of thorns plunged deep upon His head, His hair and beard matted with blood, providing the substitution for our thought life. Our minds are free from guilt and fear because of the provision of Jesus. We only have to show people how very real this is. How do we do it?

Jesus was the "Man of Sorrows, acquainted with grief" (Isaiah 53:3) because He chose to go to the cross in our place. It's interesting to note that nowhere in the Gospels does it mention the physical pain Jesus must have felt from the scourging or crucifixion. Obviously, He did feel all the actual pain because the soldiers offered myrrh, a painkiller, to Him as He was on the cross. But Jesus refused to drink it. He was telling the whole world He wanted to bear our pain.

Even so, the writers of the Gospels make no comment of His physical pain. His emotional anguish far outweighed the bodily torture. Now, as born-again people, we know that His sacrifice on the cross was sufficient for *all* our grief and sorrow. We know that God revealed Himself to Abram by the Hebraic covenant name of *El-Shaddai*, "the Almighty God." (Genesis 17:1-2) I take that to mean the God of "more than enough" — infinitely powerful. According to many biblical scholars, *El-Shaddai* brings out the connotation of a nursing mother who provides ample milk for all her young. (*Shad* is always translated "breast" in the Hebrew.) What an amazing revelation!

But can we not be frank here and recognize that many Christians, let alone the people out there in the world, seem to be suffering from a bruising that prevents them from seeing *El-Shaddai* manifested in their day-to-day lives? How do we present this reality to them?

Jeremiah 8:11 pricks my heart when I see God's beloved repeatedly beaten down by the wound of rejection. "For they have healed the hurt of the daughter of my people slightly, saying, 'Peace, peace!' when there is no peace."

THE POWER OF A FATHER'S TEARS

So the question is: how do we undo the works of rejection in this world? I believe the answer is two-fold in apostolic function. One, the apostolic people must reveal God as the Father in love, and secondly they must reveal God as the Father in supreme authority. The rest of this chapter will deal with the first revelation.

In Mark 9:14-29, we see a powerful portion of scripture wherein a father, whose son is a demoniac, goes to the disciples for his child's deliverance. The disciples are unable to cast out the evil spirit, so the father goes to Jesus with a weakened faith and lamely says, "...If You can do anything, have compassion on us and help us."

It's interesting to note that Jesus doesn't excuse his lack of faith. The father's miserable plight does not move Him so much that He makes allowances for a lack of belief in Him. He replies, "If you can believe, all things are possible to him who believes."

Verse 24 shows the amazing response of the father. "Immediately the father of the child cried out and said with tears, 'Lord, I believe; help my unbelief.'" The father makes a proclamation of his faith, then "help my unbelief." His tears show that he is asking for enlightenment, a revelation of Jesus made known to him. The purpose of his enlightenment is three-fold in revelation; it is to understand the Father's *hope*, the Father's *heart*, and the Father's *household*. In the father's desire for his son's healing, we find each of these three motivations. It was his desire that Jesus was looking for – not his perfected faith. The tears of purpose moved the Dancing Hand of God, for of course, Jesus delivered the man's son. Tears of purpose are like prophetic intercession; they are an involvement with a particular cause, a blending of one's desires with the desires of the Father.

The Father's *hope*, when revealed, overrides any empty or dwindling hope we might be suffering under. "Hope deferred makes the heart sick." (Proverbs 13:12) We must hear from the Father and know the hope He has for His children. We must understand that He has high hopes for us. When we catch this knowledge, it reconstructs our identities, our very lives, in Him. The apostolic anointing unveils the hope the Father has for our lives.

Have you seen that movie *Roots* from the '70s? Many consider it the most powerful miniseries ever aired. The saga follows an African (eventually African-American) family throughout the slave era, the Revolutionary and Civil Wars, and then into emancipation. My point in mentioning this film is near the end when the freed slave lifts his son up to the sky, he gives a heart-stirring swell of hope to everyone who is watching this amazing masterpiece. It is similar to that scene when the Father raises His children up to the sky, and we know *He* has an overwhelming sense of hope for *our* futures. I thought the movie, for those who have watched it, would really emblazon this concept in your minds. For those who have not seen the movie, it is really worth your time.

Ephesians 2:10 proclaims, "For we are His workmanship, created in Christ Jesus for good works, which God prepared beforehand that we should walk in them." The Father's *heart*, when revealed, shows us the creative intent of God's purpose. We are His workmanship – the Greek word *poiema* (Strong's #4161), His poem with rhyme and measure. We are His work of art, being symmetrically balanced and ordered. A revelation of His heart restores identity. By understanding who He is, we see His purpose in creating us; that we are masterpieces of His artistic genius. We find our identity in knowing we are the fruit of His good labor. The apostolic anointing brings a fresh revelation of just who we are in Christ Jesus.

The second chapter of Ephesians goes on to state, in verse 19, "Now, therefore, you are no longer strangers and foreigners, but fellow citizens with the saints and members of the household of God." Before that in verses 14-18, we see that Jesus Christ has brought us into His household by breaking down walls of division. My mentor and friend, Dr. Chuck Flynn, calls this the "Householder's Anointing." The Father's *household*, when revealed, shows a divine order in His dwelling place where we meet spiritual authority. The Father's authority restores character in our lives, where we can actually live with Him, not as outcasts or aliens, but as members of His house. He is building His house with us! Take a moment to study 1 Corinthians 3:6-11.

This expression of the Householder's Anointing simply represents us as Christians coming together, each with our own unique gifts, motivations and various descriptions of the essence of Christ through our own distinct personalities. In other words, because the Father has made you different from everyone else, there is something only *you* can express as a member of His household. So then, there is one aspect of Christ's life that I can express to people; there's another aspect of Christ's life that only you can express to other people. It shows the brilliance of the Father's mastermind in bringing a full revelation of Himself through the works of His people. The apostolic anointing unveils the household of God to the children — they find their place and function in His home as sons and daughters.

No one person can represent the full manifestation of Christ on this earth. It takes the entirety of the Body — the whole Household. So that tells me something. I'm in need of you, and you're in need of me. And when we look upon the needs of humanity, as members of this household, compassion should flow forth to meet those needs. This is the essence of body ministry, as it were.

The analogy I would like to give would be, say, an example of an afflicted or sick person you might know. Chances are we all know someone sick or afflicted. Now, as a member of the household of God, you are willing to go to the hospital and sit next to their bedside, to wait upon them, speak into their lives, to make warm and glad their heart until a cure is affected in their life. That is what it means to be a member of the household of God! That's apostolic in function and essence, even if it doesn't sound very grandiose.

By bringing us into His household, He is fashioning a diverse Body to express the reality of His authority and love to others. He then gives us a mandate to cultivate these varied expressions in the next generation, continuing on His household even after we are gone. We are called to get people spiritually employed, activated to be placed on the cutting edge of humanity's needs.

RESTORING THE FAVOR OF GOD

To answer the needs of humanity requires that we have the favor of God operating in His house. If diminished, we must ask ourselves how we restore that favor to its fullest level. How do we get His face turned toward us; how do we have the Father's influence and impact resting on our lives? Here are three keys the apostles bring: *repentance*, *romance* and *reality*.

We need to have a call to repentance, just as the father in Mark 9 cried out, "Help my unbelief." We must have a Great Fathering Revival, to use a term I've heard before. Malachi 4:6, "And he [speaking of Elijah the prophet, meaning John the Baptist] will turn the hearts of the fathers to the children, and the hearts of the children to the fathers, lest I come and strike the earth with a curse." We must have the apostolic fathers' hearts turned back to their spiritual children.

Turning, in this instance, means "returning to something that was lost; to make whole, complete, alive; to restore to an original state; to restore to usefulness, acceptance, performance." It speaks of *restoration*. Further, *usefulness* here means "true purpose." *Acceptance* means "true identity" while *performance* means "true fruitfulness."

See why I like homiletic teachings?

The spiritual apostolic fathers (and of course, *mothers* as well; it is a designation of character and anointing, not gender) must lead lives that are about giving, about pouring their lives into others. "Turning the hearts" speaks of the very center, or the crux, of man's will, man's emotional makeup, man's desire and passion. Man's heart. It's possible to turn this "heart" in a positive or a negative way. The transgressions of the fathers can possibly pass iniquity on to the children — read Exodus 20:3-6. If we build up a wall of protection in the name of self-preservation, it can be passed on to the children.

As apostolic fathers, we have to realize that our lives live beyond our years in the lives of the children we bring up. We must pour into them good things. We are inspired to turn their hearts back to an understanding of just who God is, represented in our lives. The benefit of an apostolic, breaker anointing is to show people the true nature of God, and therefore, *turn their hearts* back to Him.

A call to romance speaks of rediscovering our spiritual passion. When the disciples in Mark 9 wondered why they could not cast out the demon in the boy, Jesus told them that kind of spirit would only come out with prayer and fasting. See, we need to restore an intimacy with Him in our hearts. The original King James translation of Song of Solomon 1:4 says, "Draw me, we will run after thee: the king hath brought me into his chambers: we will be glad and rejoice in thee, we will remember thy love more than wine: the upright love thee."

O Lord, draw us! Bring us into Your chambers! This is my cry, and I trust yours as well. A restoration of intimacy and romance with our God is more vital than our daily needs (as in eating and drinking.) But more than restoring intimacy, it is also restoring a confession of need within our hearts. We are powerless without His power. We need His supernatural touch!

Renewal expressions are a type of romance restoration. For those who don't know what I mean by *renewal expression*, I'm simply talking about the moves of the Spirit upon His people that create an environment for His renewing power to regenerate us, to kick start us, if you will. Renewal expressions are an intimate touch of God among His people. In a corporate setting, this might be an exuberant outbreak of unreasonable, radical joy, shouting, leaping, twirling, laughing — Charismatics call it being "drunk in the Holy Ghost." (Acts 2:5-15)

Perhaps a renewal expression will manifest in an encounter with God's peace or holiness, where the people find themselves weeping, wailing uncontrollably, or just sitting in complete, utter silence without any apparent reason. (Psalm 46:10)

As noted before, these are not excuses to cater to a catharsis of the flesh — although there can be an element of cathartic release — but rather, renewal expressions are to be genuine responses to encountering the greatness of God. If you truly met with the One who was the reason for *everything*, your response would be ecstatic or crushingly humbled, too.

These renewal expressions are the Father enticing us, courting us, if you will, with His touch, His gifts and His words. This is why the apostolic fathers must have a supernatural, breaker anointing operating in their ministries. They have to bring these enticing, renewing expressions into the household of God.

The family of God will respond to the fathers and mothers when the fathers and mothers restore a desire to display the physical power of God with all their hearts; to display not only a human desire to turn people's hearts (and that's vitally important, my friends); but also a supernatural, spiritual unction to see the people changed. It takes the breaker anointing, a dynamic release of virtue, that the apostles themselves experience personally and then translate the experience over to the people!

As they administer the Father's heart, as they release His gifts and share the words He wants them to speak, the apostles restore and renew an understanding of God's character to the people.

The family of God will respond to *strength*, *stability*, *spirituality*, and most importantly to *sensitivity*. We must learn to put down our armor, as it were, and be sensitive to the frustration and the emotional needs of the children. And most importantly, we must be sensitive to the activities of the enemy. Again, this takes a manifestation of the anointing. It takes supernatural discernment.

A call to reality is a call to sanctification. The sanctification of Jesus delivered the son in Mark 9; for He said, "'...This kind [of demon] can come out by nothing but prayer and fasting.'" Jesus sanctified Himself unto God the Father, who rewarded Him for His holiness. Hebrews 1:9 said of Jesus, "You have loved righteousness and hated lawlessness; therefore, God, Your God, has anointed You with the oil of gladness more than Your companions." Because Jesus hated iniquity, the Father gave Him an anointing higher than others, but since we are sons and daughters born of Him, our sanctification in turn grants us that higher anointing. The spiritual fathers are calling the children to a new level of sanctification that might have been lacking in times past.

A minister friend of mine, Gary Greenwald, called this turning of the hearts of the fathers to the children the "Great Fathering Revival." I like that title. It is a sign of the soon return of Jesus. So we must prepare the way of the Lord by sanctifying ourselves to His purposes. It is for this reason that the apostolic fathers in their callings, with a breaker anointing, help restore romance, repentance and subsequently restoration in the reality of God's true nature. An understanding of the nature of God leads the people into fulfilling the purposes of God. And that, dear friends, is why we're all here: to fulfill the purposes of God.

THE PURPOSES OF GOD

We need to recognize that God has a purpose for everything He wants to happen. We need to understand these purposes. We need to discover what He wants to happen before we make our own plans. Purpose is always doing the *right thing* rather than a *good thing*. Having purpose defines success. Your decisions don't move God; He is moved by His will. And His will is the only thing He desires to see fulfilled. Proverbs 19:20-21, "Listen to counsel and receive instruction, that you may be wise in your latter days. There are many plans in a man's heart, nevertheless the Lord's counsel — that will stand."

Isaiah 46:10 reads, "Declaring the end from the beginning, and from ancient times things that are not yet done, saying, 'My counsel shall stand, and I will do all My pleasure.'"

I heard one of my favorite teachers, Myles Munroe, preach about the following. It's not a direct quote, and I have mixed some of my own thoughts into this revelation, but I believe his insight into the matter was stunning, and I want to recount a portion of it here for you. We must realize that *God has already finished our purpose.*

Dr. Munroe conveyed this principle like so: God establishes the end first ... then He begins. He sets the end from the beginning ... then He starts. His setting of the destination starts the process of time. It's as if He is saying, "I never begin before I end. When I started, it was a sign that I was finished." This seems like faulty logic to an un-renewed human mind, but one must recall that God created the dimension of time, and yet is not limited by it. Remember, God is omnipresent. He simply *is.* God lives in the present, past and future simultaneously; it is all the same to Him.

Ephesians 1:4, "...Just as He chose us in Him before the foundation of the world, that we should be holy and without blame before Him in love...." Romans 8:29 says, "For whom He foreknew, He also predestined to be conformed to the image of His Son, that He might be the firstborn among many brethren." The fact that you were even born is evidence that God finished something for you to start!

In the Book of Job, chapter 36, verse 5, we find, "'Behold, God is mighty, but despises no one; He is mighty in strength of understanding.'" His mightiness shows He is sovereign in power. Ephesians 1:11, "In Him also we have obtained an inheritance, being predestined according to the purpose of Him who works all things according to the counsel of His will...." God is firm in His purpose. Malachi 3:16, "'For I am the Lord, I do not change....'" He does not despise, or that is to say *ignore*, man.

He subjects Himself, in His own counsel, to His purpose. Even though He has the sovereignty to change your purpose – *He will not.* As an illustration, let's look at Moses. (Exodus 4:13) God had a purpose for him to deliver the children of Israel. But Moses tried to rationalize his ineffectiveness to God, saying, "Send someone else. I cannot speak." Note how God actually became *angry* at Moses. We would be wise not to attack the wisdom of God, for He is firm in His decisions. Your upbringing, your fears, your timidity, your hurts, your youth — none of these sway God. God will not substitute you because He has purposed that there is something only you can do!

This revelation pushed me to a new level of thinking regarding God's will for our lives. It really hammered God's view of destiny home for me, and it has positively set the course for my life and ministry. It should for you, too!

See, purpose feeds motivation. Hebrews 11:20 states, "By faith Isaac blessed Jacob and Esau concerning things to come." When Isaac blessed his sons, he prophesied destiny over their lives, the things God commissioned them to do. His blessings quick-started the spiritual paths they were supposed to follow. Isaac spoke to them of milestones in their lives that would come to pass at later dates. He was motivating them to achieve all that God had called them to achieve.

Remember, the unveiling of the Father's heart restores identity. It unfolds destiny. This is one of the callings and functions of apostles, to reveal the destinies and purposes of others. The apostolic anointing manifests purpose; it motivates the people to achieve what God has called them to do. They *feel* God moving within them and in turn want to externalize what they're feeling to others.

In restoring intimacy, in showing the love of God, in revealing purpose, I believe the anointing of the apostles unveil Him as the Father of love. By operating in a fathering anointing that progresses through the generations, apostles can undo the works of the enemy through the trap of rejection. What an exciting and worthwhile venture to pursue!

With that said, I believe there is yet an even *deeper* understanding of the Father that apostles have a mandate to reveal. The next chapter will outline this key truth in detail: the unveiling of God as the Father of authority.

Chapter Two Outline

"Unveiling the Fatherhood of God"

THE WOUNDED CRY AND THE TOUCH OF FAVOR

- Rejection is one of the primary tools the enemy uses to warp people's view of God. He slanders God's character to them and their own character to themselves

- Mark 1:40 — the leper needed more than physical healing; he needed restoration of his emotions

- Jesus was willing not only to heal his leprosy but to touch him also, showing His ministry (and the ministry of the apostle) is not simply to deal with outside symptoms but internal roots as well

- One of the byproducts of rejection is a mentality of poverty

- The apostolic anointing breaks this spirit, showing people that God never intended for them to be poor in any facet of their lives

- Jesus' crucifixion provided the answers for everything we are lacking in our lives, for our spirits, our physical bodies and our mind, will and emotional well-being

- Not only does the apostolic anointing restore a sense of confidence in the rejected person, but it creates a drive for the mind to be restored as well

THE POWER OF A FATHER'S TEARS

- Mark 9:14-29 — it was the tears of the father of the demoniac boy that moved Jesus to compassion, not his great faith. Jesus did not excuse the lack of faith but was willing to work with the father, after hearing his call for enlightenment and an increase in faith
- As a caring Father, He responds to our tears — not just our prayers — and will work with our incomplete faith
- Apostolic people reveal God as the Father of love
- The apostolic anointing reveals the Fatherhood of God in His *hope*, His *heart* and His *household*
- The Father's *hope* overrides any empty or dwindling hope we might be suffering under. The apostolic anointing shows the people what high hopes He has for them
- Ephesians 2:10 — "workmanship" — *poiema* (Greek) — humanity is the Father's work of art. We are His masterpiece
- The Father's *heart* shows us the creative intent of God's purpose in creating us. We were made for a reason
- Ephesians 2:19 — we are the household of God, not strangers just visiting, but belonging to it, with all the rights and benefits of one who belongs
- The Father's *household* shows a divine order in His dwelling place where we meet spiritual authority. The Father's authority restores character in our lives, where we can actually live with Him as members of His house. This is the "Householder's Anointing" (Dr. Chuck Flynn)

RESTORING THE FAVOR OF GOD

- Three keys: *repentance, romance, reality*
- Repentance speaks of *turning*, "going back to an original state before something was lost — a return to the way things used to be
- Malachi 4:6 — the father's hearts must be turned back to the children and vice versa
- There is a need for a Great Fathering Revival (Gary Greenwald), a repentance from the elder generations for allowing a warped view of the Father's love to endure
- Romance speaks of a return to intimacy with the Father; our first passion is always to know more of Him
- Song of Solomon 1:4 — the Lord is drawing us into His chambers, enticing or romancing us with expressions of His love
- Renewal expressions are a type of romance restoration that are to lead to a permanent turning to intimacy with the Father
- Reality speaks of sanctification, a return to holiness as God is holy
- Hebrews 1:9 — we are to hate lawlessness and love righteousness just as Jesus did
- Apostolic anointing sets people apart for God, keeping themselves holy just for His sake because they love Him and honor His authority in their lives

THE PURPOSES OF GOD

- God never creates something without a purpose behind it; therefore, we have a purpose that God intended for us to fulfill
- Before the foundations of the world, God completed your purpose — working the end out before the beginning (Myles Munroe)
- God does not ignore man — He has a purpose that He wants us all to accomplish, and nothing on our behalves or His will dissuade Him from desiring us to complete our function
- Apostolic anointing restores a clear sense of the Father's purpose in the lives of people

Chapter Three

Unveiling the Otherness of God

THE REPUTATION OF GOD

I don't claim to have all of the answers to this problem of rejection, but I've been one of those walking wounded, someone rejected and unimportant. I know that when Jesus revealed Himself to me in that light, an attribute of the Father above was unveiled to me. And since no supernatural encounter of that nature is for one person alone, I want to share with you another apostolic attribute for confronting this disease of rejection — a revelation of God not simply as a Father, but as One who is high and lifted up. That penetrating revelation of not only the love of God as our Source, but of His majesty, His glory, His supernatural holiness.

As simple as it sounds, apostolic fathering unveils the fullness of God as *the* Father. It goes beyond the revelation that He is a giver of wonderful gifts (James 1:17) — that's vitally important. But we also have to understand that God is the Father of all life; He is the creator of all things. He is truly high and lifted up. We need to have an unveiling not only of God's love, but of God's authority.

I can remember when I was teaching at Christ for the Nations in Dallas, Texas, we had a friend of mine as a guest speaker. His name is John Kelly, and among other things, he is currently working alongside C. Peter Wagner and Chuck Pierce as the ambassadorial apostle for the International Coalition of Apostles.

I mention this by way of illustration. John has an amazing fathering anointing that goes beyond revealing God as just the loving Father. Those dear students at CFNI would flock to him at the end of each teaching session, and one could feel that dynamic anointing imparted to them. They would sit at John's feet, and he would love on them, yes. But while they were there, a deeper revelation of God's holiness, His might, His glory, His authority rested upon them. They left those teaching sessions with a deeper understanding of God as a Father, the Lover of our souls and the Holy One seated on the throne with absolute authority. It was an amazing revelation to experience!

See, God is establishing a people who will bear a great witness to the resurrection life of Jesus Christ. God wants you to experience His life in all its fullness. In the Book of Acts, we see that God gave the apostles, with power and grace, a terrific witness of the life of the Lord. (Acts 4:33) It is our responsibility, as we yield to the dealings of God, to allow the Spirit to remove any hindrance or barrier that would inhibit the flow of that *zoe* life. This expression of life, the God-kind of life, comes from a deeper revelation of how God enlarges us as His people. We not only have *acceptance* in Him, but we also have *access* to His kind of life, that expression of power in our lives. See Ephesians 1:6 and 2:18.

"Life, and life more abundantly" (John 10:10) can also be stated as power that not only meets our needs, but also the needs of those we come in contact with. That is the ministry of the believer — to show the life of God apostolically through prophetic, evangelistic pastoral teaching to the world at large. That's the purpose of five-fold ministry. God is restoring more saltiness to His people, those who have a cutting-edge influence in the world. We're being changed from glory to glory (2 Corinthians 3:18) for more of an effective witness of His life in its fullness to the world. "This society will have a rude awakening that

64 | James Maloney

there is a God in heaven!" as Mario Murillo has exclaimed. They will meet not only the love of God, but the authority of God. Amen.

As noted back in Chapter One, Moses wanted more of God revealed to him. His greatest heart's cry was, "I want Your presence, I want to know Your ways, but I beseech You now, show me Your glory." (Exodus 33:18) Ephesians 1:12 says that we should be devoted to extolling the glorious perfection of God. In John 14:8, Philip asks of Jesus, "Lord, show us the Father...." To which He replies, "...He who has seen Me has seen the Father...." In Jesus' earthly ministry, everywhere He went, He manifested the reputation of God into reality.

We can define *reputation* as "an opinion of a person's worth." If I say someone is a person of great integrity, I am giving an opinion of that person's worth. Everywhere Jesus went He perfectly and completely manifested the very Person, or character, of God — in other words, Jesus manifested the Father's reputation into reality. As in Jesus' case, God wants to place His honor upon us. We are the glory of the Lord that covers the earth as the waters cover the sea. (Habakkuk 2:14) We are the ark of His presence, bearing the glory of the Lord.

The question I want to pose to you is: **will you allow God's reputation to be seen in you?**

First Peter 2:19 says we are a "peculiar people." Now, God's definition of a peculiar people and ours is not the same. The Lord showed me once in a vision what it means to be "peculiar": to be shut up with God, enclosed with Him in a chamber-like experience, where we learn that He is our only source. As peculiar people, we are face-to-face, heart-to-heart, life-to-life with Him; and with Whomever you have that type of intimacy — that level of exchange — when you become that involved with Someone, you will become like Him, emotionally and spiritually. And when we come out of that inner chamber experience, we are so radically changed, so enriched, that the people we come in contact with cannot help but have a good opinion of who God really is, because of what they see in and through us.

God wants to cause His reputation to rest upon us — His worth, the representation of who He is. He wants His glory, His character, to be unveiled in us. The Hebrew word for "glory" is *kabod*. (Strong's #3519) It literally means "the weightiness of God." The Hebrews used it imply that the Father would bear down His weight upon them; He would cause His worth and magnificence to be felt tangibly, visibly, audibly. Today, we call this the manifest presence of God. Chapter Six will deal more heavily with the glory, but for the purposes of this chapter, we need to discuss the distinctions, or types, of glory.

Isaiah sees "the Lord sitting on a throne, high and lifted up, and the train of His robe filled the temple." (Isaiah 6:1) "The train of His robe" speaks of the Lord Jesus Christ's kingly authority and glory; "the splendor of His glory," as one translation says, filled the temple. It is the train of glory that follows after the Lord wherever He is. Remember when Moses asked to see God, and He took him to the cleft of the rock? God said He couldn't show Moses the fullness of His body because he would die, but God did permit him to see the back portion of His form. (Exodus 33:23) That is the train of glory, if you will, that follows God. That is the heaviness of His limitless power. We have to have a revelation of this attribute of God in order to undo the works of rejection and worthlessness that people labor under.

I think "[And His glory] filled the temple" conveys a continuation of habitation. From "glory to glory" (2 Corinthians 3:18), a continuance, an increase, from one level of glory to another. I envision that He came and *stayed*. His glory came and kept coming... and kept coming, and on and on. This is the household of God I mentioned earlier. See, dear readers, He has come to His house, and He keeps coming in greater degrees; He is continually coming, bringing greater unveilings, greater revelations. The fullness of life is coming in greater and greater measure based on our intimacy with Him. Hallelujah!

Teachers of the Word tell us that there are basically two levels, or degrees, of glory that God unveils, or unfolds, to us; and we are to be deepened in both. My brother-in-law, David Alsobrook, is a wonderfully gifted Bible teacher — quite possibly the best I've ever heard. You can find his teachings available at www.surewordministries.com. He was the first person I heard talk about these two levels of glory. The first level is *communicative glory*, that which He shares with His people. This is where we get the word *imminence* or "closeness, nearness" of God. People are wounded, rejected, limping because they've never had a "close encounter" with God. They've never had that loving embrace from the Father. Their love needs go unmet. As talked about in the previous chapter, part of the fathering anointing of apostles is to convey the imminence of God.

See, this is what the gifts of the Spirit are all about! As you probably know, the Greeks called it *charisma* (Strong's #5486), "the manifestation of God's grace freely given." The gifts are simply extensions of who He *is*, not just what He can *do*. God is not simply capable of healing, He *is* Healing. It is His very nature, His core person, to heal. This is why it is all right to covet spiritual gifts, with the right motivation, because all you're doing is coveting more of Him. Wounded, rejected people do not understand this. It is our mandate apostolically to unveil the reputation of God's worth to them. To see that His grace is freely given.

Every miracle, every healing, restores intimacy with an aspect of God's person, His attributes, His power. Every revelation, every deliverance, restores intimacy with His holiness. Every word of prophecy restores intimacy with the voice of God. That is communicative glory, what He shares with us.

THE OTHERNESS OF GOD

Here is the crux of unveiling the fatherhood of God to rescind the enemy's trap of rejection: there is a deeper level of God's glory and further revelation as He keeps coming and coming to His house. There is another side to God that is not shared with all. Some teachers call this the "otherness" of God.

The second level, or degree, of glory is that which David Alsobrook terms *non-communicative glory*. This speaks of the *transcendence* of God, meaning, "that which is above all." He is the Most High God, *El-Elyon*. (Genesis 14:18-20; Psalm 78:35) Isaiah 42:8: "I am the Lord, that is My name; and My glory I will not give to another, nor My praise to carved images."

Even in His desire to come near unto us, let us never forget that He is still God. So therefore, if He is God, then we are not. We can explain the otherness of God as such: here is all of His creation... and then here is God. There is no one beside Him. Wounded, rejected people need to have an unveiling of this transcendence of God, just as importantly as the imminence of Him. It's not just what He does for us, because He loves us; we worship Him because of simply who He is. What else do you do with a God but worship Him?

Any true apostle, prophet, evangelist, pastor or teacher — any person who is out there in the world doing exploits for God, moving in His grace and power — at some point in time in their lives should open their hearts to greater transcendent experiences. My life of transcendent experiences began when Christ appeared in my room — I not only knew Him as the God of love, but also that He was indeed *God*, a supreme Being capable of appearing miraculously to His creation. The only way we can truly be an apostolic, prophetic mountain-removing people, drawing the wounded into God's knowledge with lasting, magnificent results, is if we have a revelation of God's superlative transcendence above all else and before all others. This is the key to the thrust of this entire book.

I recognize that some people who have not yet had a transcendent experience can still be used powerfully, but, friends, we've come to a point in history where ministers need to expect to experience God in His transcendence. For most people, these experiences usually, but not always, occur early in their ministry.

Look at the book of Acts, chapter 9, verses 1-6. Saul is on the road to Damascus, breathing threats and murder against the disciples of the Lord. Suddenly a laser beam shoots out of heaven and knocks him to the ground.

(I know I'm being somewhat facetious here, but the effect is the same. I believe the Holy Spirit is a Gentleman — imminence. I also believe He'll knock you to the ground — transcendence. Just ask Saul of Tarsus. I don't think God appeared as some heavenly, cosmic butler in this instance: "Saul, would you kindly step over here a moment and sit on this rock, so that I might have a word with you?")

Well, anyway, let's take note of Saul's first response. He doesn't look around, wondering aloud, "I say, what is this that I'm experiencing?" No, I picture him down on the ground, gulping, breathing heavily. It says he was trembling and astonished. What was his revelation? "Who are You? *Lord?*" Bear with my paraphrasing here for a moment — I think the point I'm making is in context with the scripture. It's as if Saul was saying, "God? *You're* the One I've been persecuting?!?" He had a sudden, jolting revelation of the otherness of God. So much so, that he was blinded until Ananias laid his hands on him. That's a pretty powerful transcendent experience, wouldn't you agree?

Romans 8:15 points out that we can cry, "*Abba*, Father!" Many people believe — and it's quite right to have this notion — that God is their spiritual Daddy, a kind and loving Father. Someone you'd like to sit on His knees, let Him bounce you around, feel Him smile down upon you. Yes, that's *Abba*. What a wonderful revelation. But notice the double reference here. "*Abba*, Father!" It means something else as well.

This is how I explain it to my students. Cup your hands together in front of you. Lift them above your head; raise your eyes to the heavens, and say, "*Abba*." That's the imminence of God. It's as if you're saying, "Lord, I want that nearness. I'm in need. I'm Your son, I'm Your daughter. You're my Father. Give into me, pour into me."

Now throw your palms outward, away from you, toward Him, and say "*Father!*" See the difference? That's the transcendence, or otherness, of Him. It's as if you're saying, "If You don't do one thing for me, I love You for just who You are! Because You are the Father, I give You praise and worship."

We all need that revelation. We all need our burning bush experiences! (Exodus 3) We need a Damascus Road interruption! "Who is like unto You, oh Lord, among the heavens? Majestic in holiness, fearful in praise, doing wonders." (Exodus 15:11) If you were to do a full study of signs and wonders throughout the scriptures, you will find that there are wonders that God does in the heavens, apart from His people. There are certain things that God does that are reserved only for the heavenly places. The job of the apostles (and apostolic people), so to speak, is to relate so powerful a revelation of God's otherness that His miracles usually reserved for Himself alone in heavenly places are entrusted to us to be manifested here in the earthly plane. *Selah!*

I am firmly persuaded that God is showing off His preeminence more and more to the people of the world through the acts of the apostles. A time is fast approaching where the people of God know Him in such a depth that the very acts of Him in heaven will be manifested here on earth. That is how we overcome the bruising of rejection — by manifesting the reality of God's otherness.

THE SUPREMACY OF GOD

Gentle readers, God is immutably sovereign. God is just that: God. To me, that means God can do what He wants, when He wants, how He wants, and who He wants to use to do it through. This is a vital revelation often missed in the Body of Christ, and for those out in the world, they have no understanding of His majestic personage. We need both — a revelation of His imminence and otherness.

A revelation of God's love gives to us an understanding of the Father's heart. It is Him in *expression*. But a revelation of God's person, His holiness, yields an understanding of God's *essence*. It reveals to us His absolute authority. The Father's heart brings identity. The Father's authority brings character. "Moses, take your shoes off! The ground you are standing on is holy!" (Exodus 3) What an amazing display of authority — to cause a common bush to burn and not be consumed! The angels cry out "Holy, Holy, Holy!" (Revelation 4:8) Let's take a lesson from the humbleness of Moses and the angels. Apostles are to reveal insights into both the expression and essence of the Most High.

We will only have holiness when we recognize the holiness of God. I am not minimizing the importance of God coming to our houses in love, and let Him keep coming. We need those love encounters with Him! "Hug therapy" is wonderful. It's important. One of the words used to describe Jesus' earthly ministry is *therapeuo* (Matthew 8:7, 12:22: "heal," "healed," Strong's #2323), where we get the English words "therapy" and "therapeutic" aptly enough. Jesus is the great Therapist, don't misunderstand my intent. He embraced people; He was moved with compassion for their sakes. That is a level of revelation of the Person of God. But we have to know that there is a deeper revelation of Him; it goes above and beyond what He does for us. We worship Him just for who He is!

And here's the problem with some Christians: "If He doesn't do this for me, I'm going to leave. I'm going to quit." How arrogant! I'm embarrassed to say, during the first few years of my walk with the Lord, I was guilty of that nonsense. I'd periodically go into my prayer closet, throw the Bible down, and have the audacity and ignorance to threaten God. "God! If You don't do this for me, You're going to lose me!" How foolish! How immature!

Oh, now come on; don't act like I'm the only one who's ever been that way! I've heard Christians say, "Well, if You don't heal me, then I guess You don't love me!" Thankfully, I grew up. I had a revelation of God as the Holy One. We all need to have an unveiling. I say this lovingly, but without compromise, we have a profane mentality in the Body of Christ. How many know your body is the temple of the Holy Spirit? (1 Corinthians 6:19) We better recognize and call holy that which God calls holy. We need to meet His authority. That's what restores character.

Did you know you can have an anointing for a particular task and not have the glory of the Holy Spirit resting upon you? The gifts and callings of God are without repentance. (Romans 11:29) Ladies and gentlemen, that has to stop! Meeting God's authority creates a duty to worship, but above that, it also creates a desire to be more godly and holy in our daily lives. Just as Isaiah encountered the Lord's glory, the prophet cried out how unholy his lips were. (Isaiah 6:5) Oh, Lord, just as the angel placed the coal on Your prophet's lips, touch my lips! Create within us a life of holiness, as You are holy. Next, meeting with the glory of the Lord should also invoke a desire for evangelism. "Who can We send?" O Lord, send us!

All of us, in one degree or another, have had a transcendent experience when we worship and praise Him. Have you ever had a moment when you were intensely worshipping the Holy One, and it's like you suddenly "came out of yourself" and seemed to be lifted up? That is a transcendent experience. We need to have a further unveiling of that experience where we come out of ourselves in worship and are confronted with the love and authority of Him seated on the throne. When we meet His authority, we will worship, and we will evangelize.

It Takes More Than Miracles

How many know the event on the Mount of Transfiguration (Matthew 17) was more than just an experience for Jesus? It was an experience for His disciples as well. What God the Father was doing, when Jesus was transfigured before them, was showing the disciples the *otherness* of Christ. Elijah — the power of God — testified of His otherness, and Moses — the word of God — did likewise.

"Who do men say that I am?"

"Lord, You are the Christ, the Son of the Living God!" (Mark 8:27)

Dr. Chuck Flynn puts it this way: He is the Christ [the Anointed One], the Son [the Disciplined One] of the Living God [the Creative One]. Oh, how we need to have an understanding of this truth! The *anointing* comes upon you, so that you will *discipline* yourself, so that you can *speak creatively* to set the captives free. That is glory! That is the witness of the resurrected Life! That is freedom from the iniquity of the walking wounded!

Of course, the disciples had been seeing Him in His imminence — they'd seen Him healing, delivering and preaching. John 2:11 says they saw His glory in the manifestation of the miracles He was working. But just because people have seen miracles, they haven't necessarily been changed! Miracles simply aren't enough — the same people He was working miracles among still had Him crucified!

I believe in the coming years that the Lord is going to roll back the heavens, and we will have an unveiling of His authority, His fatherhood. We have to be ready for it. I always hear the saints in churches crying out, "Oh, Lord, show us Your glory in all its fullness!" To be honest, dear readers, I think if God were to show His glory in that magnitude, there would be a major exodus in the church. We have to be prepared for that kind of glory — it can either bless you, or it can kill you! (1 Chronicles 13:9-11) Always remember that God is not a God of mixture.

Oh, Lord, un-mix us! Make us ready for Your reputation to rest upon us!

There is a level of glory that, of course, He shares with His people. But we have to know that there is a deeper revelation of His glory that He will share with no other. (Isaiah 48:11) It is for Him and Him alone, for He is holy. That is the revelation that the seraphim have when they stand by His throne and cry out, "Holy, Holy, Holy!" Every time they go around His throne, a whole new level of the transcendence of God is revealed to them. It will take eternity to grasp His holiness.

It Takes Obedience

So how do you know you've had a transcendent encounter with His glory? Afterwards, you want to obey Him. As Mario Murillo says, "What else do you do with a God but obey Him?" Obedience is meeting authority, not just love. I've been asked by unsaved people why I don't have a desire to go and do what the world does, to roll around in the muck and mire.

I always answer them, "People who live that life have zero self esteem. If they had any esteem in Christ, they wouldn't *want* to do those things." That may sound harsh to someone who is wounded and hurt, living in self-rejection. But we can love and still not compromise, friends. For wounded people, overcoming self-hatred and a lack of self-worth requires the apostolic person to go beyond just sharing the *love* of Christ with them — it takes an encounter with His *authority*, and then they are forced to choose whether to obey Him or not.

If people would have continuing experiences with the greatness of God in all of His splendor, when they are tempted with the sins of the world, their spirits would rise up and remind them of His transcendence, His awesomeness, His purity and holiness. The ministry of those who are apostolic comes from their personal, ever-increasing experiences of a transcendent love encounter with the Father. They give *such pursuit* for the presence of His glory, and their breaker anointing shows the weightiness of God, which translates through their teaching and ministry expression. The people to whom they minister will rise up in holiness, saying "No!" to the world's devices. (Now, come on, you have to admit that's an awesome thought! Praise the Lord!)

Look, I know that no one is above temptation, and it's only by the grace of God that *any* of us are overcoming. But, see, I have no desire to do those things, not because I can't, but because I don't *want* to. I have met with divine authority and submitted. I have a reverential fear of Him. I don't want to lose that favor of God by doing something worthless. I love Him too much. My whole quest in life is to see His face turned towards me. "This is My son; I'm well-pleased." What greater compliment could be paid? Of course, I have failed Him at times, but it doesn't change the fact that my whole purpose in life is to do what is right in His sight.

In Ezekiel 1:1-3, the prophet is called into the priesthood and taken captive by the River Chebar — that is the "River of Captivity" — to Babylon — that is the "Land of Confusion." Then Ezekiel says that he came to "visions and revelations." Babylon, the most unlikely place to see the glory of God, and here's Ezekiel having visions and revelations. We, too, will have these transcendent experiences, not just in the tabernacle or in some holy place, but when we feel we are captive or in the land of confusion. And these experiences will carry us into a deeper revelation of His fullness of life. Just as in Ezekiel's case, these experiences will sustain us through difficult times.

I've been criticized by theologians for having this view. I've been called an experientialist. That all I want is to experience God!

Well... yeah.

Mea maxima culpa! "That I might know Him!" It goes beyond healing, prophesying, words of knowledge. It's simply just to know Him! That He is God, up there, high and lifted up; and He wants to touch us down here. If we have that revelation of Him, I would virtually guarantee a passion to be a sent one by Him, to have our lips touched with the burning coal, will be birthed automatically. Because we'll share His burden, how He sees humanity from His perspective.

I have heard the teachings on re-digging the spiritual wells of healing and salvation in a particular geographical area — say the nation of England or the United States. Yes, I agree with that. I've taught on that. There's a unique revelation in that mentality that I think is important. But I sometimes wonder: why are we always looking backwards? I agree with the importance of retrieving the mantles of those that have gone before us. That's vital. But why must we always focus on yesterday's experience, when there is so much that God wants to reveal in this present day? Let's experience God in a fresh way today. There are some miraculous encounters that God reserves just for Himself in these end times to unveil His otherness. The greater miracles, the greater revelations, the greater awakenings are not simply found in the re-digging or retrieving. If that were so, we would already have the greater works that Jesus spoke about. (John 14:12) We've had almost two thousand years of returning to the early Church. But those greater miracles are found in the otherness of God, in His supremacy in the world of today. *Now* is the day of salvation, *now* is the time of acceptance. (2 Corinthians 6:2) The greater miracles will come when the apostles and apostolic people have an unveiling of the otherness of God. Every apostolically motivated person needs to press in and ask with great fervency and passion for the return of the early Church and beyond, so that the latter house will be greater than the former! (Haggai 2:9)

Revelation 2:2 speaks about false apostles. It says, "I have tried their works and have found out they are liars." All true apostles, prophets, evangelists, pastors and teachers who are mightily used by God have had a revelation of the otherness of God, a transcendent experience where they know Him in His love and His authority. As I stated earlier, according to examples in scripture, this often occurs early in their ministries, but again not always.

My born again experience, at fifteen, launched me down a path that I will never waver from. This understanding of the otherness of God is the crucial way to move apostolically against the spirit of rejection out there in the world. So let's have an experience! Let's take this unveiling out into the world and watch God move mightily through His apostles.

Chapter Three Outline

"Unveiling the Otherness of God"

THE REPUTATION OF GOD

- God is the Father of love, yes, but He is just as much the Father of absolute authority, high and lifted up, holy unto Himself

- Apostolic anointing goes beyond the revelation of God as the Father of love but imparts a deeper understanding of the total authority of God

- John 10:10 – the God-kind of life is life in overabundance, stemming from that creative source that is the authority of God

- Apostolic anointing imparts this kind of life by revealing just how awesomely full of life and power God is

- Exodus 33:18 – we should desire above all else to know Him more completely, to know the perfection of His glory

- Reputation is an opinion of someone's worth. In Jesus' earthly ministry, He always manifested the Father's reputation into reality through His glory

- Apostolic anointing proves the trustworthiness of the Father's reputation through supernatural ministry

- God wants to cause His reputation, His worth, His weightiness to rest upon us

- Glory in Hebrew is translated as "weightiness" (kabod) – the heaviness of His limitless power

- Communicative glory (imminence) is that which He shares with His people, His closeness, His nearness (David Alsobrook)
- Non-communicative glory (transcendence) is that which He will share with no one else — He is high and lifted up (David Alsobrook)
- Apostolic anointing reveals a portion of His utter transcendence, the "otherness" of God
- If people truly had a revelation of His otherness in a transcendent experience, there would be no excuse not to worship Him as the one, true God
- We all need to have a transcendent experience, a brush with His otherness, to truly understand who He is

THE OTHERNESS OF GOD

- He is the Most High God, *El-Elyon* (Genesis 14:18-20; Psalm 78:35)
- "I am the Lord, that is My name; and My glory I will not give to another, nor My praise to carved images." (Isaiah 42:8)
- The only way we can truly be an apostolic, prophetic mountain-removing people, drawing the wounded into God's knowledge with lasting, magnificent results, is if we have a revelation of God's transcendence

- **The Supremacy of God**
- God is immutably sovereign, meaning He can do what He wants, when He wants, how He wants, and who He wants to use to do it through
- A revelation of God's love gives us an understanding of the Father's heart; it is Him in *expression*. But a revelation of God's person, His holiness, yields an understanding of God's *essence*
- Meeting God's authority creates a duty to worship, but above that it also creates a desire to be more godly and holy in our daily lives
- All of us, in one degree or another, have had a transcendent experience when we worship and praise Him

It Takes More Than Miracles
- What God the Father was doing, when Jesus was transfigured before the disciples, was showing them the *otherness* of Christ (Matthew 17)
- "Lord, You are the Christ, the Son of the Living God!" (Mark 8:27)
- He is the Christ [the Anointed One], the Son [the Disciplined One] of the Living God [the Creative One] (Chuck Flynn)
- The *anointing* comes upon you, so that you will *discipline* yourself, so that you can *speak creatively* to set the captives free
- Just because people have seen miracles, they don't necessarily change a person! Miracles aren't simply enough — the same

people Jesus was working miracles among still had Him crucified

It Takes Obedience

- So how do you know you've had a transcendent encounter with His glory? Afterwards, you want to obey Him. What else do you do with God but obey Him?
- Obedience is meeting authority, not just love
- Overcoming self-hatred and a lack of self-worth in wounded people goes beyond just sharing the love of Christ with them — it takes an encounter with His authority, and then they are forced to choose whether to obey Him or not
- Apostolic ministry comes from personal, ever-increasing experiences of a transcendent love encounter with the Father. Apostolic people give such pursuit for His glory presence, and their breaker anointing shows the weightiness of God which translates through their teaching and ministry expression
- "I have tried their works and have found out they [false apostles] are liars." (Revelation 2:2)
- All true apostles, prophets, evangelists, pastors and teachers who are mightily used by God have had a revelation of the otherness of God, a transcendent experience where they know Him in His love and His authority
- According to examples in scripture, these encounters often occur early in their ministries, but again not always

Chapter Four

Unveiling the Acceptance of God

HARRY'S STORY

I love my mom and dad deeply. My adoptive parents worked incredibly hard, and we were relatively affluent by 1960s standards. We had a nice home in a resort town up in the mountains near Palm Springs, California. Dad was a real estate agent. He sold properties in and around the mountain, some to famous people from Hollywood. I remember playing with the children of some of these actors while the adults golfed. Mom worked at a Tru-Value Hardware store that my uncle owned. She was a compact person, but let me tell you, she could handle that physical labor as much as any man twice her size! They instilled within me some valuable qualities: self-reliance, determination and grit, and a powerfully strong work ethic that I've endeavored to carry my whole life. I thank God that He used my adoptive parents to reveal aspects of His character throughout my childhood. I look back and see His supernatural hand at work even then.

Because Mom and Dad worked so much, they thought it would be prudent to have someone in the house to look after me and my Chinese-American adopted sister, Trish. That's when Dad's friend Harry became our *de facto* nanny and pretty much lived with us full-time for the next ten years. He was seventy-nine when I was nine, born in the late 1800s. He used to tell me stories of old-time life in the Midwest: how he once sat on a famous gunfighter's knee as a little boy. How he was one of the first people to buy a Model "T" or a Model "A"

Ford, or the expansion of electricity throughout rural America, things like that. He talked about the Great Ohio Flood of 1933, and how he'd lost friends and family in that deluge — the same one that claimed the life of William Branham's wife and daughter. My, my, Harry had so much to tell. I sure loved him dearly.

He taught me how to cook — of course, this was still the early '60s so everything was fried in lard. He created within me a love for the animal kingdom and nature. (For a time in high school I wanted to be a forest ranger, and in fact, I worked as a forest fire fighter briefly.) We built pigeon coops, chicken coops, and rabbit hutches. He was knowledgeable on just about every topic imaginable after nearly eighty years of living.

Harry wasn't saved, and he was possessed of a divided spirit. He could be incredibly kind and fatherly, and also filled with rage at times. Part of his problem was just old age. He began going blind, and it made him so angry to feel inept. I remember once he walked into the plate glass of the back door. It shattered and cut up his face pretty severely. I remember the blood, and Harry just sitting on the floor, weeping in pain, embarrassment, anger. I felt so disconcerted because there was absolutely nothing I could do for him. I was still a young boy. He was old, and he was dying. And I loved him.

I lay awake at nights just worried sick about his deteriorating physical state, almost to the point of nausea myself. I felt deeply for him, down in my guts; but because I had such a distorted view of myself and my understanding of God's acceptance of me was so limited, I had a lack of confidence in my daily life that would seem to paralyze me. I became despondent even at such a young age because I thought, *There's nothing I can do to help Harry out of this misery.*

Of course, I look back now and see that God was sustaining him even then. There were touches of God that I couldn't recognize at the time. Harry never went completely blind. The doctors couldn't explain it — he should have lost his eyesight altogether, but his eyes deteriorated to a point and then stopped. He could still see shapes, and I'm sure he attributed it to the witch hazel he poured straight into his eyes.... It seemed like I could hear them sizzle. He was a tough old fellow!

He told me a story of when he was much younger, back in the early 1900s. He was a bit of a troublemaker, a rabble-rouser, a rough guy back in those days. He was in Indiana with some friends of similar ilk when they heard of a traveling minister who was coming to town in a big tent revival. They decided to attend this evangelist's meeting to create a ruckus, stir up some trouble, so they went out to the tent ground and sat in the back.

Harry didn't know it at the time, but the Holy Spirit was convicting him, and while his friends would snicker and make rude noises from the back, he just sat silently and even found himself listening to the preacher now and again. The evangelist was a woman, and many years later, Harry was telling me something she said that had stuck with him his whole life. And since sharing it with me, it's stuck with me *my* whole life and has become a staple in my ministry.

She said, "Every time that you come to God and you pray, you can have confidence that He will hear you, and that He will answer your prayers in accordance to His wisdom." Knowing hardly anything about God, this simple statement slammed into me, and I know now that God was downloading an unveiling of His heart to me. Ever since that day, I have had such an incredible distaste for sickness and disease that it brings me to a point of almost righteous anger. I understand how God views the hurts of humanity — He's actually angered that people are getting ripped off. He created within me empathy toward people who were aching for His touch.

As I grew up and he grew older, Harry started having strokes. I'd have to hold him tight to me as he'd twitch and convulse throughout the night, muttering, crying. I felt utterly worthless, unable to help alleviate Harry's torment. It sickened me. Why couldn't I do anything to ease his suffering? I'd weep and silently beg God to help him out. I wasn't even entirely sure He was real, but I just felt like I should ask God for His intervention on Harry's behalf. That's what the evangelist lady had said decades earlier.

I suffered with Harry when he was in pain. Even though I had no real knowledge of God's heart, I would pray that He would help him because of what that woman evangelist said. See, a seed was sown then, and after Jesus came to me, and after a process of inner healing and restoration in Bible school that dealt with my warped view of God's acceptance, I now have a desperate passion to see people's pain alleviated. It is a motivating factor in my life that drives me to see the manifest presence of God operating in people's lives. And I am completely convinced it can be imparted in your life as well!

I know now that God spared Harry for my sake. Even with his corrupted nature, his dual personality, his bouts of anger and his depression at the seeming hopelessness of mortality, the Lord used Harry to unveil aspects of the Father's character to me, much like He used my adoptive parents. I learned things from him that help me in my ministry today. I'll never forget him telling me about what that "preacher lady" said....

Turns out that preacher lady was Maria Woodworth-Etter!

A woman possessed of an apostolic breaker anointing if there ever was one! I'm still astonished how God used Harry to teach me an apostolic truth — simple as it may have been — by linking me across the generations to someone of Woodworth-Etter's caliber. Amazing!

I led Harry to the Lord after I was born again, and then he moved out after ten years of living with us. He went on to live another four years after that — four very peaceful, lovely years. Harry died in 1977 at ninety-three years of age. I can't wait to see him again.

GARY'S BOY

Some years later, I was with a team of Americans over in India, and we came into a small village. At the edge of the village, we couldn't help but notice on opposite sides of the road were two temples: a Muslim place of worship and a Hindu place of worship. In the center of the village was a platform raised by steps for speakers so we congregated around this dais and began worshipping the Lord — a simple tactic to arouse the interest of the villagers. They began to gather around, and it was rather comical as they looked up to the sky to see whomever these white people were singing to. The platform was several feet high, flanked by steps, and one of the evangelists surrounding me on a step below was a friend of mine named Gary. This is a testimony of what happened to him.

Soon we had a gathering of a few hundred villagers, and it was plain to see that the Muslims gathered to one side, the Hindus on the other. I began to tell them how all the other gods they worshipped were false, and that my God, Jesus Christ, died for their sins to provide an ultimate way into heaven. After a simple plan of salvation, I proclaimed that in order to prove that Jesus was the one true God, and all others were false, they should bring up the sick and He would heal them. It's really the only way I know how to evangelize in foreign countries: proclaim the good news and let God back it up.

So the Dancing Hand of God began bouncing around among the people. And I noticed that God was moving strictly among the Hindus.

People began getting spontaneously healed, and several dozens of the Hindus came forward to receive Jesus. But I wondered why none of the Muslims were getting healed.

When the village elder of the Hindus (a man who had been blind for many years) suddenly had his eyes opened by the power of the Lord, the Hindus rejoiced greatly and nearly every single one came up for the altar call. It was a glorious day of soul winning, but inwardly I was concerned that so far the Dancing Hand of God had only moved among the Hindus. Not one Muslim had come forward. They all just stood back, frowning, angry that this new Jesus was touching the Hindus and not them.

Through the interpreter I told the Muslims, "Jesus is no respecter of persons; He will heal the Muslim and the Hindu the same. He loves you all equally. If He will heal this Hindu leader, He will heal you, too." So now I was silently praying that God would confirm my words. *Oh, Jesus, You better bail me outta this!* Great man of faith and power that I am....

Out of the corner of my eye I saw a Muslim mother shifting back and forth nervously. In her arms, she was holding her boy, and you could immediately see what was wrong with him. He was crippled. His little legs dangled like rubber bands, and he could only drag himself along on his elbows. The Muslim mom was now seriously agitated — she had seen all these Hindus getting healed, many of them converting to this new God, Jesus. And her eyes told me everything, no need for an interpreter. Why wouldn't God heal her boy?

I took a few seconds to ask God why the Muslims weren't being healed, and He revealed to me a slanderous spirit that many Muslims suffer under. *Devil* means "accuser, slanderer" — it is his highest form of attack to malign God's character to people, or their own characters to themselves. The revelation God shared with me in that moment concerning those dear Muslims is one of the most powerful unveilings I've experienced, and to God's glory and honor, I have used that revelation to see many Muslims swept into the Kingdom since. It's just amazing!

I'll share a little bit more about this slanderous spirit in a moment; but for right now, suffice to say that when I took authority over that veiled perception, it broke that spirit over those Muslims, and the mother decided to put Him to the test. I love it when that happens!

In her simplicity she assumed that this white man's God must be over there among the Hindus, so she slinked her way over to their side in an effort to catch this God's attention. The Muslims looked on at her disapprovingly.

Finally after a few fruitless minutes of searching for God among the Hindus she came to the foot of the raised dais and, without a second's hesitation, threw the little boy up at Gary. He staggered and caught the child in his arms; luckily he didn't drop him because we were about seven feet up in the air, he a few steps below me.

Now, the first thing that went through my mind was, *Thank God she gave him to Gary!* Great man of faith and power that I am....

This dear woman gave me a sharp look and placed a bony hand on her *sari*, and I could tell exactly what she was thinking: *Let's see if your God loves us Muslims the same as the Hindus.* Fresh panic now surged through us. Brothers and sisters, we began praying feverishly, let me tell you. I can only imagine what poor Gary must have been feeling!

Gary spoke life into those withered legs. He cast out. He broke off. He bound and he loosed. I think he might have even spit on the legs, I don't know for sure. He quoted a bunch of scriptures as they came to mind. I prayed in tongues under my breath and thought of every Smith Wigglesworth story I'd ever heard, all the meanwhile thanking God that she'd thrown the boy at Gary!

Nothing happened.

We prayed some more, harder this time, Gary looking down at the little boy's legs every couple of minutes to see if there was any change. There was none. Now I began pleading in my mind. *Oh, God, seriously! Help us out of this one! Do something!* Great man of faith and power that I am....

Oh, don't act like you've never prayed that way before! Come on now! This was serious.

So finally I got quiet enough to listen to the Lord. I stepped back while Gary was still cradling the boy in his arms. I thought, *Lord Jesus, You're just going to have to show me why he's not getting healed.* I had taken authority over this slanderous spirit, but for some reason, the healing was not coming.

Suddenly. I love that word. Suddenly. Say it with me, "Suddenly!"

Suddenly something *leapt up* in my spirit. This overwhelming sense of faith; this undeniable power to tackle any problem. It came right from the throne of God, I'm convinced. I always joke that it was like I went and changed clothes in a phone booth. Get it? I felt this awesome gift of faith still growing, rising up right out of my spirit.

Suddenly (there it is again!) it was as if I heard the voice of the Lord saying, "You tell Gary to throw that boy down to the ground. Right now!"

Um, OK. Gift of faith or not, that wasn't exactly what I wanted to hear, but never let it be said I'm disobedient, so in the calmest voice I could muster I said, "Gary."

Gary's eyes swam with relief. He looked up at me as if to say, "Oh, thank God! Help me out!"

So naturally, I helped him out. Sort of.

"Gary," I said, "drop that boy on the ground."

Right. The expression he gave me was of total shock. Had he misheard me? Uh, what? His eyes narrowed and he shook his head.

I spoke a little more authoritatively this time; that gift of faith was growing stronger. "Gary, I said, 'Drop that boy on the ground'!"

Gary probably thought I'd gone crazy. He stared up at me dumbfounded, wagging his head passionately *no*. He muttered through gritted teeth, "Uh-*uh*!"

By the third time, this faith had blossomed within me like an erupting volcano, and I shouted at him, "Drop him, Gary! You drop that boy *right now*!"

Now, I don't know if it was the fear of the Lord or the fear of James Maloney that caused Gary to let go of the boy, but as I bellowed "*Right now*!" Gary chucked the boy out of his arms.

Time seemed to slow down to a crawl.

But you know what happened!

As the boy came crashing down to the ground, in that split millisecond of time, the Lord instantly recreated his legs in midair. And he fell to the ground on two perfectly whole legs and went running and jumping into his mother's arms!

And nearly every single Muslim came to know Jesus that day!

DEATH OF AN EXPECTATION

Now what God showed me that day was a powerful revelation that has given me some great successes in seeing Muslims come to the Lord. Anyone who knows me knows that I have a passion for seeing the Muslims saved. This drive was birthed in my spirit early in ministry and really became white-hot when the Lord showed me this revelation.

Now, I will say this is not true in *every* case, with *every* Muslim. But quite often, I've seen it time and time again when evangelizing in Islamic countries. I guess I could call it the Ishmael Syndrome. Although that's probably an overgeneralization, but it's just to give it a name. Of course not all Muslims are direct descendents of Ishmael, I realize that. But it can be a curse that they come under, relating back to the Isaac/Ishmael dilemma. See, some Muslims can feel abandoned. Isaac was the one God chose to bring the Savior through, not Ishmael.

Yes, God loved Ishmael and took care of him (Genesis 21), but as spiritual descendents of Ishmael, a Muslim's view of God can be one of an angry taskmaster. They can inherit a warped opinion of God. Many feel that there is no hope in this life from Allah, that he is not a god of love. Many of them can feel unwanted, something like second-class citizens, left-behind children. Their view of God has become distorted by a lie from the enemy that they are not as important to God as others are — that God is a respecter of persons. He is just a vengeful, angry taskmaster. "Do this or face My wrath!" I believe this is one of the driving forces behind the Islamic extremists' fury against the Westernized "Christian" world.

What God showed me that day the Muslim mom's child was healed was that the devil has put a film over the eyes of many Muslims. He has warped their understanding, dulled their ability to view God as anything more than an angry, unloving deity. When the Lord showed me this veiling, I took authority over that spirit of confusion, and the breaker anointing crippled that falsehood in the Indian village, allowing the Muslims to see God as He really is. It was only after the special miracle of the boy being healed that the Muslims responded to God's love.

This veiling relates to *many* people out there in the world today, Muslim or not. It takes an apostolic, breaker anointing to shatter the misconception that God does not equally accept all. When they have such a warped view of His availability, they become disheartened and give up hope that life can be better than what it is.

Remember Jeremiah 8:21-22, "'For the hurt of the daughter of my people I am hurt. I am mourning; astonishment has taken hold of me. Is there no balm in Gilead, is there no physician there? Why then is there no recovery for the health of the daughter of my people?'"

Without this breaker anointing there are millions of people whose needs go unmet. I don't mean to be critical; we all fall short on occasion. But I'm tired of not seeing people receive the gospel that Jesus intended for them to have. Folks, if we were to be brutally honest with ourselves, wouldn't we agree that if the gospel preached today in a lot of churches was preached in Jesus' day, He never would have been crucified?

Think about it. That's a bold statement that rings true in a lot of churches.

The gospel should force people to make a choice. True Kingdom of Christ gospel creates a stir. "Whoa! That dude just threw down his crutches!" Or, "Wow! That lady's eyes were just opened!"

They're confronted, see? Is that truly God? And if it is, what must I do now that I know He's really out there?

For some, it can even be an offense to hear the good news. I've known some people that would just get downright *angry* when I shared the gospel with them. It's kind of sad that people can get so mad over something that you feel could revolutionize their lives, but there it is. The gospel should create a source of conflict — people must be forced to make a decision for Him, in what they believe and what they stand for. Either they must follow Him, or not. Because there it is. That dude just threw down his crutches. That lady's eyes were just opened. There really is a God, and He's expecting something from me.

This wishy-washy, mediocre preaching isn't cutting down to the root issues of people's lives. Most people out there in the world, especially in the more civilized countries, have heard that Jesus loves them. And they think that's nice. What a nice thing for a Person to do — die for our sins and all that. But what does the gospel really *do* for them? They read in their Bibles that Jesus went around healing thousands, restoring identity and purpose in an entire people group. Today they don't really see that as they should and it creates a warped, distorted view of God.

They have an expectation that if God is really God, that if He doesn't change at all, like His Word says, then why, oh why, aren't they seeing the things that the people saw 2,000 years ago?

And it's a valid question.

But since the question goes unanswered, since they aren't seeing the things that were seen in the past, the devil slanders God to them. He *has* changed, the foul being whispers. He loved *those* people more than you! You *aren't* godly enough to see miracles happen in your life.

And after a while, people begin to believe him. And their expectations die. They don't expect God to do anything for them.

Don't lose heart, my friends! It's a lie!

THE ALMOST EXPERIENCE

Apostles must be on a quest for greater miracles! Apostles must provide the Balm for the sickness in the Christian's life — let alone out there in the world. We have too many sick, wounded, hurt Christians that aren't living the dominion life God intended them to have. I mean, gentle readers, let's look at it from an unsaved person's perspective. I think we can see why many do not want to join our ranks if we're not offering them any more reality than the local psychic or some traditional religion. No wonder they don't want to join us when they see we're still dying of sicknesses, divorcing our spouses, splitting our churches, backbiting, arguing, bickering back and forth.

I'm not trying to beat people up; I'm trying to show them a problem and point out a better way.

We all have something to learn from this — myself most of all, since I'm the one making these statements. Please understand my heart. I hurt for these people, and I'm tired of hearing of these almost experiences.

"I almost kept walking with the Lord." "I almost quit drinking." "I almost got healed." "I almost heard from God." "You almost persuade me to become a Christian," King Agrippa said. (Acts 26:28) I want these *almost* experiences to be *complete* experiences. I believe God is raising up the apostles to combat this "almost" mentality in the Body of Christ.

John prayed, "Beloved, I pray that you may prosper in all things and be in health, just as your soul prospers." (3 John 2) The apostles need to bring a fresh, breaking anointing that creates a prosperous soul, a soul that is disconnected from the shame of the past. An anointing that breaks the yokes, bondages and limitations that have been dogging us for centuries. An anointing that changes the things in our health. Take a moment to see how Jesus healed the people He came in contact with.

He healed the vast majority of people *instantaneously*. There was very little progressive healing in Jesus' earthly ministry. Of course, some began to mend that very hour, and I don't want to minimize the importance of that. Divine healing is divine healing, whether it's instantaneous or a progression towards health. No way God heals is unimportant, and we're thankful each time He blesses us. But I think we need to begin moving toward more of these instantaneous miracles that allow for no doubt at all that God has intervened.

Secondly, Jesus healed *totally*. Generally, there was very little, if any, recuperation period; they were sick and then they weren't. And I believe we've shown scriptural reference — in the account of the single leper (Mark 1:40-42) — that Jesus healed all their infirmities at once, physical and otherwise. Imagine if every need in a person's life (spirit, soul and body) was taken care of without a prolonged time of warfare and then recuperation.

Don't misunderstand me, I believe in inner healing and counseling; I have a degree in counseling! But in so many cases, we've got people taking years and years to overcome weaknesses, when it should take weeks or months. Instead of becoming equipping grounds that release people into their own destinies, churches can become crutches to wounded people. Some attend deliverance classes, therapy sessions, counseling seminars, year after year but don't seem to overcome.

Friends, we are finite people. There's only so much of us that God has to renew. I believe we are moving into a time when an apostolic anointing is presented to people, and the Lord takes care of everything all at once. What an exciting potential!

Next, Jesus healed *everyone*. Every person who came to Him — even with flawed faith — was made whole. All they had to do was come to Him. Now shouldn't this be the case with His apostles? The excuses I hear: "Well, brother, you didn't walk out of that wheelchair because you didn't have the faith" just isn't cutting it for me anymore. I've heard people say, "Your wife is dying of cancer because she didn't pray hard enough." Well, she's in too much pain; she *can't* pray any harder. There has to be a new, apostolic anointing that supersedes our weaknesses or incomplete faith. My Bible tells me that Jesus was perfect in His earthly ministry; He saw 100% success, and that we are to be like Him. (Matthew 10:25) I ask myself the question, why do people two thousand years ago sometimes seem to have it better than we do today?

Now, don't shout me down. I recognize God is healing today. I'm a minister with a great desire to express God's healing power. I've been trying to do that for over thirty years, all praise unto Him. I desperately want to see Him heal people everywhere He sends me. Having Him heal the sick — through an empty, earthen vessel of clay — is what I endeavor to see God do all the time. I recognize God is moving just as powerfully today in certain parts of the world, through certain people. I know He is faithful and loving, just and compassionate. I don't want this to be construed as a "woe are we" crying session. No, I don't have all the answers to why some of the people that have cancer that I pray for get healed — and some do not. I don't always know why this person walked out of a wheelchair, and this person didn't.

In this day and age, we can't make excuses anymore. We cannot permit the enemy to create disillusionment so that we back away from the supernatural altogether. We cannot marginalize the interpretation of God's Word regarding healing and miracles because of what we have *not* seen, or because of extreme abuses of the supernatural perceived in the churches. I am calling all members of the Body of Christ, especially the leaders, to perform a heart-search. If necessary, we need to repent and return back to what the Word of God says.

It's one thing if someone in the Church has had little or no experience with the supernatural — they don't know any better. But I'm writing to some of you who used to operate in and honor the supernatural and, in the name of creating a friendly environment for the uninitiated or for the previously disappointed, have now moved away from the manifested presence of God. There are whole Charismatic churches with no healing, deliverance or prophetic operation. This must change!

I want to see the success that Jesus saw, and I'll do whatever it takes to allow God to use me in that capacity. I don't think it's wrong to expect Jesus to begin to use His people like He Himself ministered when He walked the earth, otherwise why are we called "little anointed ones"? After all, that's what the word *Christian* means – "a little Christ." It's not an arrogant statement; we are all simply grafted into Christ's accomplishments on the cross. We have nothing in ourselves, but when we come into Christ's household, we are His sons and daughters – His little ones. Because He was and is, *we* also become supernatural therapists to people.

There are simply too many people out there asking, "Is there no Balm in Gilead? Has Jesus changed in two thousand years?" I don't know about you, but I'm not taking that as a possibility. My God does *not* change. (Malachi 3:6) Full stop.

Therefore, the problem must be with us.

THE ROOT OF THE ISSUE

In Matthew 3:10, we see that, "'...Even now the axe is laid to the root of the trees. Therefore every tree which does not bear good fruit is cut down and thrown into the fire.'" And Proverbs 26:2 tells us, "Like a flitting sparrow, like a flying swallow, so a curse without cause shall not alight." The bottom line is there are root issues that always prevent someone from living life to its fullest. There is always a reason for a curse. And the anointing of an apostle is to seek out that root and cut it down with an axe, heave it into the fire, and toss those birds back up into the sky. We've got to recognize why people are not seeing the Balm of Gilead activated in their lives. People are not confronted with absolute, undeniable proof that God is a God of complete restoration.

One of the things I've noticed is that the majority of healings are taking place in the realm of the mind or in a functional capacity. They can sometimes leave doubt that God did indeed heal the ailing person. Let me clarify.

Medical doctors divide illness into three categories. They are *functional, organic* or *psychogenic* diseases. I want to give credit to author John F. MacArthur, Jr., for pointing out these categories as I read his book *The Charismatics: A Doctrinal Perspective* (Grand Rapids: Lamplighter Books, 1978: pp. 138-139.)

(As a side point here, it's my perception in reading his book that Dr. MacArthur is actually trying to *disprove* the Charismatic experience. I'm not afraid to read the material of people who believe differently than I do. I hope they'll take the time to read my book. Dr. MacArthur has some valid points here, folks. As a general rule, we *aren't* seeing God move on a level that leaves no doubt it is Him working through Christians to heal the sick of not only functional and psychogenic diseases, but organic as well. As a Charismatic traveling minister, I obviously disagree with Dr. MacArthur's stance toward Charismatic expression, but I believe a time of greater miracles is coming that will leave people with no doubt in their minds.)

Anyway, to continue, functional diseases occur when a perfectly good bodily system doesn't function properly. For example, lower back pain, headaches, heart palpitations, upset stomachs, breathing issues — these are all functional diseases. The system simply doesn't work right. Organic diseases occur when an organ or bodily system is destroyed, maimed or crippled — this can be a result of an internal pathogen or external forces, such as trauma. Infections, heart attacks, gallstones, hernias, cancers, broken bones, blindness and congenital deformities fall into this category. Lastly, psychogenic diseases are diseases that are processed in the mind — they don't normally occur in a physical state. So one could say it like this: a functional disease would be, "I have a sore arm." An organic disease would be, "I have no arm, or I have a withered arm." A psychogenic disease would be, "I *think* my arm is sore."

Dr. MacArthur is right: most miracle services *have* been in the realm of functional or psychogenic diseases. And thank God for that! It is no less spectacular for God to heal a person of allergies than to cause a tumor to disappear. We give glory and honor to Him for any of His wondrous deeds. But if we were to be truly honest, it's generally the organic diseases that keep most people plagued their whole lives with defeat, usually ending in a death before their time. I am firmly persuaded, and I hope you are too, that the apostles are being raised up with the keys to the Kingdom of Heaven; and as such, we will see more and more of these organic diseases being cut down to the quick and killed at the root. Praise God!

The breaker anointing seeks out the root of the curse and cuts it to the quick, exposing the deception or limitation, leaving no doubt that every infirmity — mental, physical or emotional — is subject to the power of God.

Isaiah 53:4-5, "Surely He has borne our griefs and carried our sorrows: yet we esteemed Him stricken, smitten by God, and afflicted. But He was wounded for our transgressions, He was bruised for our iniquities; the chastisement for our peace was upon Him, and by His stripes we are healed." Nearly every evangelical Christian in the world can recite that scripture — it's in the famous "Messianic Chapter." But even among Charismatic circles, the true nature of these verses has become lost.

It behooves us to study this passage in the original language for then we see that *borne* literally means "lifted up or off" and *carried* means "removed to a great distance." Also, we see that *griefs* is best translated "sicknesses" and *sorrows* reads "pains." We "reckoned" Him "struck down" by God — Jesus was "pierced" and "crushed" for our shortcomings and evil tendencies. He was "whipped" for our "well-being." And His stripes heal us — literally we *come to a state of euphoria,*" as taught by David Alsobrook.

If people could only have a true revelation of the depth of this passage of scripture, exactly what it is saying; and if we could couple that revelation with an apostolic anointing, there would be no reason in Christ not to redeem our traumas. Those greater, organic miracles would be a staple of Christian life. People would not go away disappointed and unchanged. Not only would their headaches disappear, but the root cause *behind* the headaches would be destroyed, too.

Apostles must realize that at the end of every disappointment, people can become vulnerable. So they harden their hearts to be saved from hurt a second time. There is nothing more destructive to the Body of Christ than the wounds of grief and sorrow. Redeeming traumas is found in the revelation of the Father's *heart* and in the revelation of the Father's *faithfulness.* It is the apostles that bring both to light.

THE WOUND OF GRIEF

I define *grief* as someone being "sick, weak, afflicted, faint of heart, diseased and wounded." Just like the Muslims in Gary's story a few pages back, the devil has slandered God's character to the world — they have a twisted view of His heart. They feel abandoned, illegitimate and parentless. They think God shows respect of persons. They feel they have no right to call on God to intervene on their behalves. Our ability to receive from the Lord is directly related to our perception of who He is.

Psalm 77:10 shows, "And I said, 'This is my anguish; but I will remember the years of the right hand of the Most High.'" The right hand is a symbol of God's power. Many people learn to believe that God's right hand has changed, like David was wont to misperceive, wistfully remembering things God did in the past, complaining about the current circumstances. People think somehow His right hand has ceased to move in power. Of course, this has not happened. Rather, people perceive incorrectly that He has changed. Let us be like David and remember that He is still the "God who does wonders." (Psalm 77:14)

When people are disappointed, time and again, they trade the truth for a lie by not holding on to what they *do* know. Verse 11 of the same Psalm should be their creed, "I will remember the works of the Lord; surely I will remember Your wonders of old." But they have forgotten His faithfulness. They have a warped view of His heart.

Apostles teach people to be honest with God. Most people don't pour out their hearts in the way they should; they don't deal with the root issue that causes them to be embittered. They don't release their disappointment. "God didn't heal me the first time; I won't be hurt again. It must be that He loves other people more than me." The apostolic anointing breaks this lie. Apostles reconstruct the perception of God through signs, wonders and miracles, showing that God is equally available to all who will come to Him with an expectation, with true faith (at whatever level of faith they possess) and with a sincere desire to be changed. Every apostle is going to have to find his or her own revelation keys to the miraculous that unlock the answers people are searching for.

Take a moment to study Psalm 137 and 138, and then Luke 21:1-13, especially verse 13, "'But it will turn out for you as an occasion for testimony.'" God is raising up apostles that will disarm disappointment. They bring encouragement, edification, comfort and confidence. They teach the people of God how to pray with expectation. God is raising up deliverers, individuals who are spiritually empowered to defeat Israel's oppressors. As the Church (Israel) cries out, they will be raised up. Let's not forget the power of tears! The apostles are answers to the prayers of the oppressed, and their ministry expressions will become a reward to people's faith, just as in the case of Nehemiah 9:27. "Therefore You delivered them into the hand of their enemies, who oppressed them; and in the time of their trouble, when they cried to You, You heard from heaven; and according to Your abundant mercies You gave them deliverers who saved them from the hand of their enemies." Judges 10:16 shows that "...His soul could no longer endure the misery of Israel." "'I have surely seen the oppression of My people... and have heard their cry... for I know their sorrows [pain]. So I have come down to deliver them....'" (Exodus 3:7-8)

I am reminded of a series of meetings I was at during a revival that was taking place in a denominational church in Missouri. What impressed me most about this move of the Spirit was how it responded to the intensity of the prayers among the youth. Their cries birthed an apostolic move that was unlike anything ever seen in that denominational setting. I considered myself blessed to have a part in the miraculous and prophetic move of God — something very few of them had ever seen before, and it all came about because the young ones were crying out in expectation of His visit. God will always answer people's expectations for a visitation of His grace if they cry out to Him. Their cries become the catalyst for divine intervention.

He doesn't just hear our prayers — He hears our cries! The Lord bears the misery of His people. He is never far from the plight of mankind. It's one thing to pray over a need; it's quite another to weep over it!

First Samuel 22:1-2, "David therefore departed from there and escaped to the cave of Adullam. So when his brothers and all his father's house heard it, they went down there to him. And everyone who was in distress, everyone who was in debt, and everyone who was discontented [bitter of soul] gathered to him. And there were about four hundred men with him."

When people are in captivity, many of them lose their song — that is, their desires, motivations and zeal. The people who came to David were emotionally *distressed*, materially in *debt* and spiritually *discontented*. Their hopes had been shattered because of Saul's iniquities. They possessed no strength, no resources and no motivation. They came unto David for renewing of a new vision, a new purpose and a new direction. David became a deliverer for them. Apostolic Davids will come in our paths to deliver us from disappointment.

The apostles restore hope among the people, causing them to anticipate something good, to look forward to something from God. Apostles shatter the disappointment that plagues many Charismatics. They are restoring to the Body healing, bringing revival and a fresh sense of God's greatness to the people.

BUT WE WILL BE TRIED

A pastor once chided me, "Why do you stir people up and awaken hopes? Why do you get people to believe they will be healed, delivered, revived when you know it won't happen? Why do you set them up when they'll only be disappointed?"

That bothered me... for about two seconds.

I then wanted to become a David to this poor, disenchanted pastor. I realized that's how God operates. He awakens hopes and desires within us that in the natural seem utterly impossible to be fulfilled. He makes us a promise and then permits circumstances to come out and try us. He blesses us and then tries us with a promise. The word *try* means "to purify and refine." As in Psalm 105:19, "Until the time that his word came to pass, the word of the Lord tested him." This is speaking of Joseph sold into slavery at eighteen. He had to wait twelve long years for the fulfillment of the word. He was tried by the word — by the promise. The very promise itself tried him as a person. The word refined and purified Joseph from impurities — it wasn't simply his circumstances. That's important to note. It isn't so much *God* trying us as the word itself that tries the people to whom it is given.

Lamentations 3:33 declares, "For He does not afflict willingly [from His heart], nor grieve the children of men." The apostles are called to ask a question: "Are you going to believe His words, or your circumstances?" One's circumstances simply say, "No, this won't work." But the promise of the Lord will try and test and refine, and then it *will* pay off. We have to separate these stages to avoid disappointment. As Luke 1:45 shows us, there will be a fulfillment of those things promised you by the Lord for those who continue to believe.

We must always realize that "'God is not a man, that He should lie, nor a son of man, that He should repent. Has He said, and will He not do? Or has He spoken, and will He not make it good?'" (Numbers 23:19) "The Lord will perfect that which concerns me; Your mercy, O Lord, endures forever; do not forsake the works of Your hands." (Psalm 138:8) An apostolic anointing can remind people that disadvantages don't disqualify the promises of God. We are not forgotten; we do not need to get angry. We need to take our bad situations and push them away, relying on God's trustworthiness — that He will prove Himself faithful.

Don't be like the woman who berated Elijah in 2 Kings 4:16. "Then he said, 'About this time next year, you shall embrace a son.' And she said, 'No, my lord. Man of God, do not lie to your maidservant!'" She was saying, "Don't deceive me! Don't awaken within me a longing that you cannot possibly fulfill." The question we must ask ourselves is: does God awaken or reawaken the greatest longing within our hearts only to let us down? The answer should obviously, emphatically be *No*!

Isaiah 10:27, "It shall come to pass in that day that his burden will be taken away from your shoulder, and his yoke from your neck, and the yoke will be destroyed because of the anointing oil." The word *yoke* means "to bow down, to press down, to lay a heavy burden." Many people suffer under a yoke of discouragement. They have been seemingly let down so many times that they have convinced themselves it will only happen again, so why believe in something? The breaker anointing that apostles have literally shatters that yoke. According to my friend and mentor, Dr. Chuck Flynn, the connotation in the scriptures is that the believer's neck will become so spiritually fat that the yoke will not be able to go around it. Oh, make our necks fat, Lord! I mean, spiritually speaking. Let us find our acceptance in You! Let us have an unveiling of Your true character!

You know, the devil has slandered God's character to people. He has veiled them in a wrong impression of who He is, as was in the case of the Muslim people in that Indian village. Many people's belief in God is based on a supposed expression of love (what He does for them), rather than His position of unchanging love for them (He will never stop loving them, but He still commands their worship) — ultimately, it's a distorted view of His love. They have reduced God to a meaningless experience, a half-truth, a formula. Many people want deeper truth but not a deeper relationship with Him. They want Him to do things for them without truly wanting to get to know Him in all facets. They try to "make" healing work for them — they fall under the power when there's no true power present. They formulaically try to connive prosperity or prophecy from God without a heart-felt decision to be with Him just because He is simply God. They don't want to share in the responsibility that comes from knowing Him. Their attitudes and their actions betray their true motives.

I've known many ministers that want the *charisma* of God rather than God Himself. They desire their ministries over Him. "But now you boast in your arrogance. All such boasting is evil." (James 4:16) Even the blessings of God can be a substitute for a living relationship with Him. Apostles are called to set the record straight. Just as Jesus rejoiced in His relationship with the Father way before He went about His earthly ministry, apostles are calling people on the carpet, so to speak, and demanding a true, vibrant relationship with Him before receiving His blessings.

Could this lack of relationship be the reason for failures, disappointments and discouragements in the Body of Christ? Our prayer should be that of Habakkuk's: "Though the fig tree may not blossom, nor fruit be on the vines; though the labor of the olive may fail, and the fields yield no food; though the flock may be cut off from the fold, and there be no herd in the stalls — yet I will rejoice in the Lord, I will joy in the God of my salvation." (Chapter 3:17-18)

We must recognize that God cannot fail — that love cannot fail. Hebrews 13:15 from the Amplified Bible states, "He Himself has said, 'I will not in any way fail you, nor give you up, nor leave you without support. I will not in any degree leave you helpless, nor forsake, nor let you down [release My hold on you], assuredly not.'"

Look, we will all go through the valley of the shadow of death (Psalm 23:4.) I call it "the Valley of the Shadow of Misunderstandings." Mario Murillo calls it "the dark night of the soul." But we cannot be afraid of hoping; we must maintain our joy. We cannot lose our motivation, our zeal, our desire; the spiritual momentum we have in the strength, authority and power of the Lord. No matter what we go through, what seems lost, what has deteriorated — it will turn out for us as an occasion for testimony! Let us not be so troubled by the false christs, wars, rumors of wars, earthquakes, famines, pestilences and persecutions that we forget God is still God. (Matthew 24:4-14) Let us cast off our griefs and bruising, our disappointments and discouragements.

THE MAN IN A WHEELCHAIR

I was in a meeting out in the Midwestern United States that the local church had advertised as a "Healings and Miracles Service." It was really quite humorous because they had actually placed it in the paper: "Come out – bring the sick, the infirmed, and the dead! Jesus will cleanse the sick, heal the lepers, and raise the dead!" Talk about being put on the spot! In these instances, all I can say is, "Well, Lord, You'll have to do it again!" It keeps a person really humble when one realizes there is nothing to offer an expectant people in oneself.

So I was up on the platform, facing the pastor and his congregation, a gathering of about two hundred people. I remember thinking how for being advertised as a healing/miracle service, there didn't seem to be a real sense of expectation and excitement among the people. It concerned me. I wondered why there was no spark among them – no anticipation of a move of God.

In the middle of praise and worship, a man in a wheelchair came into the church and wheeled himself up the aisle about halfway. We later found out that he was suffering from an advanced stage of multiple sclerosis, something he'd had for over fourteen years. He later said he had not walked in many, many years. It had gotten to the point that he couldn't even pick himself up on his elbows. People had to take him out of the chair to place him in the bath or in bed.

I noted interestedly that practically every eye in the place turned toward this man, and it was one of the rare times the Lord gave me insight into what they were thinking. It was as if I heard a hundred voices saying, "Oh no! Why did *he* have to come? Here's another person that's going to leave not healed, not delivered...." I was shocked at the unbelief of the attendees.

Anyway, I stood up to speak, and I found it very difficult to preach — like wading through thick molasses — when all of a sudden... the Holy Spirit decided to start healing people in the middle of the group... without me.

Which He is more than welcome to do any time He desires, I'd just like to say!

Many a well-planned sermon has been cut short when His hand starts to dance among the people. I've learned just to close my Bible and let Him do it.

He gave me a distinct word of knowledge about a lady who had a cancer underneath her arm in the lymph nodes and she was scheduled for surgery soon, but God was healing her. He caused the cancer to disappear.

There was a man who had been deaf for over thirty years — he did not even have an eardrum with which to hear! So God created one for him, and the man heard. Now to me, that was just about as exciting of a miracle as could happen!

But the people remained very muted in their praise.

A little girl had a deformity in her foot. She was right up in front. I could hear a *snap! crackle! pop!* as God fixed her. She came forward to tell of what He was doing, and several others that God was touching also came forward to testify. But even still, the atmosphere in the place stayed very placid and hesitant.

The man in the wheelchair just listened intently to them share. I gave a call for those who wanted to get saved to come forward, so then he pushed himself into the line and was swept into the Kingdom of God. I went down the line, ministering to people; and when I looked down at him, I thought it would be a foolish question to ask, "Now what else do you want the Lord to do for you?" Kind of obvious.

Instead, something rose up out of my spirit, and without any premeditation I said, "Sir, when would you like to walk out of that wheelchair?"

"Well, how 'bout now?"

He responded without any hesitation, looking up at me with an expectation in his eyes that even set *me* back. This guy had just been saved a couple of minutes at the most! It was just such a simple declaration, but you could hear the hush that fell over the congregation. It was like we all took a collective, sharp intake of breath.

So without any instruction from me, the man struggled to reach down and gingerly push the wheelchair pedals up. He then grasped his deadened legs and flopped them on the floor. The whole experience left him exhausted. He took a couple of deep breaths and then looked up at me.

"Well. Here goes."

Gritting his teeth, he pushed off the wheelchair with every bit of strength in his being. And as he struggled waveringly to his feet, God charged his body with life.

Now, I believe there's a principle that God will never ask you to do something that He will not give you the gracing to do. Like in the scripture where Jesus asked the man to stretch forth his withered hand (Matthew 12:13), obviously when the man purposed to do so, grace met him there, and he stretched forth his hand. This is why we need to operate in greater wisdom in knowing what God wants to do.

So under the inspiration of the Spirit, this man stood to his feet. He teetered a little bit, but he felt the power of God moving through him; so he said to me, "If I can stand — I can walk." And he began to take little baby steps. Probably twenty or twenty-five steps in one direction then turned around and came back. He flopped down in the wheelchair, just perspiring profusely, spent.

"Preacher," he said between deep breaths, "this is the first time I've felt pain in my legs in years! It's like ten thousand little needles pricking my legs. It really hurts. But in a good way."

You know, there is such a thing as a good pain!

You would have thought with all that the congregation had just seen, the place would've come unglued. There should have been an eruption of exuberant celebration, but there wasn't. Instead something was released into the crowd and people began to complain and grumble among themselves. Even a couple of people called out, "It's a set-up! This is a trick or something!" Voices all around were saying, "This isn't happening. This isn't real." I was utterly flabbergasted at their response.

But you see, there have been so many Charismatic meetings advertised as great healing and miracles services where nothing much has really happened, and so people become disenfranchised and disappointed. When there finally is a tangible move of God, the people suffer under such a veiling of dullness (something I'll address more fully in another chapter) they can't recognize when the Lord's hand is truly dancing. Apostles (and apostolic people) have got to throw off that veil, disarm that disappointment, that tool of the enemy. The anointing has to break that dullness off people's lives and permit them to see how readily available the Father is to showing off His power among them.

So back to the testimony, two weeks later I met the pastor of that church in the Midwest at a conference, and he said to me, "Do you remember that man with MS who walked out of the wheelchair?"

I said, "Yeah, of course."

"Well, he was totally healed, but I've got to ask you something. 'Cause we don't know what to do with this guy, Brother Jim."

"What do you mean you don't know what to do with this guy?"

"You know how there's a four-way stop sign in front of our church, and so motorists of course have to stop. Well, an hour or so before each service this guy stands out there by the stop signs, and when they stop, he raps on the window. Perfect strangers. They crack their windows, wondering what this guy wants — money or whatever — and the first thing that comes out of his mouth is, 'Do you have a pain in your body? Do you have a disease? Well, I did. I had multiple sclerosis, and I was in a wheelchair. But you see that church right there? I got healed in that church right there. So if you want to get healed, you should go there, too.'"

I kind of chuckled. Cool.

But the pastor wasn't laughing.

"Brother Maloney, we don't know how to turn this guy off! I mean, how do we get him to turn it off?"

"Why would you want to? You'd want to let him go — release him." Seemed like the obvious answer to his question.

"But you don't understand. He's making members of my congregation feel uncomfortable."

"What are you telling me?" I mean, I was thinking, *So what?* But I was trying to be tactful.

"They come up to me and say, 'How come this man who's only been saved a few minutes gets healed, and I've been waiting on God for my healing for years? How come God doesn't heal me? I've been a member of this church for years — I pay tithes."

Like they've earned it or something. But see, they have years of traditions and religious notions that they have to wade through. This man, so newly saved, didn't. He said he'd never been in a Charismatic church service in his life, so he didn't know what to expect. But every time they saw this man healed, it convicted them of their religious unbelief. They ended up giving this pastor an ultimatum. "Either he goes, or we go."

So I asked the pastor, "What was your response?"

He said, "Well, we just had to ask him to leave."

How sad it that? Here's this stunning miracle that possibly could have been used to revolutionize that area of the country, but they chose to stifle the man from influencing people to make it easier on themselves for not seeing God heal them. They used their financial clout to put pressure on the pastor to run out this poor guy.

The pastor went on to ask me, "What would you have done?"

I felt like telling him, *I would've pointed those folks to the door.* But instead I said, "Well, if you're asking me to choose between the money and the miracles... I'd choose the miracles."

Dear readers, we have got to disarm these people's disappointments. We've got to be like David and break this yoke of discouragement off God's Church. We cannot be intimidated by religiosity, and we cannot allow ourselves to become wounded, grieved and bitter, making excuses for ourselves when the Lord doesn't deal with us after the fashion we desire. We have got to position ourselves in this apostolic age with a right heart motivation that unlocks the by-product of God's power when we pour ourselves out for Him just because of who He is. We have to have a revelation of His availability as our ultimate Source for supernatural recharging.

THE SOURCE OF OUR STRENGTH

Look at Joshua in chapter 1, verses 1-5. He had just lost a friend and a leader. Joshua must have been grieving deeply. He must have been insecure and needing a formula for success. If anyone needed a word for direction, it would have been him. He had to fill Moses' shoes — he now had the awesome responsibility to lead the people of Israel into their land of inheritance. He needed to be seasoned; he needed to have wisdom. And God did not short him in the slightest. "'Have I not commanded you? Be strong and of good courage: do not be afraid, nor be dismayed, for the Lord your God is with you wherever you go.'" (Verse 9) Oh, how the apostles need to bring this word to the people in the Church — to the people in the world!

Joshua began to understand as the Lord spoke to him that Moses had a Source of strength: and that Source was God. "'...As I was with Moses, so will I be with you. I will not leave you nor forsake you.'" (Verse 5) God was saying, "I won't give up on you! You're more than just a servant to Me."

Many Christians, and many who are still lost, have a fear of hoping — it is the death of an expectation. Apostolically motivated people bring a revelation of His faithfulness, a correct view of the Father's heart. They bring about a knowing of God as Father to those willing to accept Him as such — this is the power of the gospel that His Spirit bears witness to in the apostles' acts. People begin to understand that He is their true, eternal Father. The apostolic anointing overcomes any lack of confidence, and people begin to understand their acceptance in Him. It is impossible to understand this with our lack of confidence, or with our disappointments, and so we must come into His confidence, casting off our grief. The answer is found in Christ. "He came to His own, and His own did not receive Him. But as many as received Him, to them He gave the right to become children of God, to those who believe in His name: who were born, not of blood, nor of the will of the flesh, nor of the will of man, but of God." (John 1:11-13)

Sometimes grief-stricken people are made mute, dumb. They cannot find their voice to express the emotional vacuum in their lives — it makes them unable to feel or to speak. They are locked out from emotional growth because they are in denial, or they are hurt and angry. People with wounded spirits are vessels that leak and cannot retain the acceptance of God. They turn out to be wasted lives. But the breaker anointing can release them! It can show them there is a healing Balm!

Jeremiah 30:17, "'For I will restore health to you and heal you of your wounds,' says the Lord. 'Because they called you an outcast saying, "This is Zion; no one seeks her."'" God will patch the outcast up with apostolic glue — the vessel will spring no more leaks. Jeremiah 31:25-26, "'For I have satiated [fully satisfied] the weary soul, and I have replenished every sorrowful soul.' After this I awoke and looked around, and my sleep was sweet to me." God will replenish every soul and give sweet sleep through the works of the apostles. Psalm 23 proclaims, "The Lord is my shepherd; I shall not want [lack anything]." Psalm 147:3 maintains, "He heals the broken-hearted and binds up their wounds [sorrows]." Song of Solomon 1:13 bursts forth, "A bundle of myrrh is my beloved to me...." Isaiah 61:3 shows Jesus "to console those who mourn in Zion, to give them beauty for ashes, the oil of joy for mourning, the garment of praise for the spirit of heaviness...."

There can be no doubt that Jesus felt deeply wounded by Judas' betrayal. It must have hurt Him so, even though He knew it was going to happen. But He is still our great Substitute — taking on all our miseries so we don't have to. The apostles must be anointed to reveal this truth to the people; otherwise the above verses are not being fruitful.

I said before that I didn't speak until I was four years of age. See, the first few years of my life all I ever heard was my unworthiness, my lack of any redeeming quality. "You'll never amount to a hill of beans!" I always felt I had to achieve acceptance by performance — I didn't have the building blocks for leadership correctly established in my life. I lacked the confidence on the inside to believe that I had the right to be loved unconditionally. I thought my actual genetic structure was corrupted. My view of God was slandered by the enemy, much like how many in the Muslim world see God today. But my transcendent salvation experience with the Lord made me believe I could feel that I was a child of great value. I knew then that I was accepted by God, with all my faults, and that He would work in me to turn those faults into strengths. There are some who believe I have been graciously gifted with a remarkable ministry, but in myself I certainly had nothing to offer the world — I couldn't even speak! Whenever I've felt pride pressing in after witnessing some fantastic miracle, I've been humbly reminded of how God's grace is the only reason I can even function as a human being today. God is my Source, and He must be yours as well. You must have an unveiling of God's acceptance.

You know, in the history of godly people who changed the world, very few of them had supremely high IQs, so they just related to the abilities they *did* possess in Christ. They linked their mighty deeds with their own *strong personalities, security* and *self-confidence*. I don't care who you are, how dumb you may think you are, how incapable you feel of finding your voice — the Lord is swiftly igniting His apostles and apostolic people with a mandate to lift the Church world out of its limitations and see themselves how God sees them — as children in His family and, friends... His family lacks nothing.

"Unveiling the Acceptance of God"

DEATH OF AN EXPECTATION

- Many people's view of God has become distorted by a lie from the enemy that they are not as important to God as others are — that God is a respecter of persons

- It takes an apostolic, breaker anointing to shatter the misconception that God is not equally available to all

- When people have such a warped view of His availability, they become disheartened and give up hope that life can be better than what it is

- "'For the hurt of the daughter of my people I am hurt. I am mourning; astonishment has taken hold of me. Is there no balm in Gilead, is there no physician there? Why then is there no recovery for the health of the daughter of my people?'" (Jeremiah 8:21-22)

- Without this apostolic, breaker anointing there are millions of people whose need for God's love and acceptance goes unmet

- The gospel must be an offense to the world at large. It has to create a source of conflict — people must be forced to make a decision for Him, in what they believe and what they stand for

- Today many people don't really see the miraculous, apostolic gospel as they should, and it creates a warped, distorted view of God

THE ALMOST EXPERIENCE

- Apostles must be on a quest for greater miracles! Apostles must provide the Balm for the sickness in the Christian's life – let alone out there in the world
- We must become fed up with the "Almost Experience"
- "I almost kept walking with the Lord." "I almost quit drinking." "I almost got healed." "I almost heard from the Lord." "You almost persuade me to become a Christian," King Agrippa said. (Acts 26:28)
- God is raising up the apostles to combat this "almost" mentality in the Body of Christ
- "Beloved, I pray that you may prosper in all things and be in health, just as your soul prospers" (3 John 2)
- Apostles bring a fresh, breaking anointing that creates a prosperous soul – a soul that is disconnected from the shame of the past. An anointing that breaks the yokes, bondages and limitations
- Jesus healed the vast majority of people *instantaneously*. There was very little progressive healing in Jesus' earthly ministry
- Jesus healed *totally*. He healed all their infirmities at once, physical and otherwise

- Jesus healed *everyone*. Every person who came to Him — even with flawed faith — was made whole. All they had to do was come to Him

The Root of the Issue

- "'...Even now the axe is laid to the root of the trees. Therefore every tree which does not bear good fruit is cut down and thrown into the fire.'" (Matthew 3:10)
- "Like a flitting sparrow, like a flying swallow, so a curse without cause shall not alight." (Proverbs 26:2)
- Apostolic anointing seeks out the root and cuts it down with an axe, heaves it into the fire, and tosses those birds back up into the sky
- Medical doctors divide every illness into three categories: *functional, organic* or *psychogenic* diseases (John F. McArthur, Jr.)
- Functional diseases occur when a perfectly good organ or bodily system doesn't function properly (lower back pain, headaches, heart palpitations, upset stomachs, breathing issues.) "I have a sore arm"
- Organic diseases occur when an organ or bodily system is organically destroyed, maimed or crippled, through internal or external circumstances (infections, heart attacks, gallstones, hernias, cancers, broken bones, blindness and congenital deformities.) "I have no arm, or I have a withered arm"

- Psychogenic diseases are diseases that are processed in the mind – they don't normally occur in a physical state. "I *think* my arm is sore"
- Most miracle services have been in the realm of functional or psychogenic diseases. And thank God for that!
- But it's generally the organic diseases that keep most people plagued their whole lives with defeat, usually ending in a death before their time
- Apostolic people are being raised up with a greater anointing to see the organic diseases healed!
- "Surely He has borne our griefs and carried our sorrows: yet we esteemed Him stricken, smitten by God, and afflicted. But He was wounded for our transgressions, He was bruised for our iniquities; the chastisement for our peace was upon Him, and by His stripes we are healed." (Isaiah 53:4-5)
- *Borne* means "lifted up or off" and *carried* means "removed to a great distance." *Griefs* means "sicknesses" and *sorrows* reads "pains."
- We "reckoned" Him "struck down" by God – Jesus was "pierced" and "crushed" for our shortcomings and evil tendencies. He was "whipped" for our "well-being." And His stripes heal us – which can be transliterated, "we come to a state of euphoria"

THE WOUND OF GRIEF

- *Grief* is when someone is "sick, weak, afflicted, faint of heart, diseased and wounded"

- The devil slanders God's character to the world – people have a slighted view of His heart. They feel abandoned, illegitimate and parentless, thinking God shows respect of persons. They feel they have no right to call on God to intervene on their behalves

- Our ability to receive from the Lord is directly related to our perception of who He is

- "And I said, 'This is my anguish; but I will remember the years of the right hand of the Most High.'" (Psalm 77:10) The right hand is a symbol of God's power, but many people have come to believe that God's right hand has changed

- When people are disappointed, time and again, they trade the truth for a lie by not holding on to what they do know

- Apostles teach people to be honest with God. Most people don't pour out their hearts in the way they should; they don't deal with the root issue that causes them to be embittered. They don't release their disappointment

- Apostles reconstruct the perception of God through signs, wonders and miracles, showing that God is equally available to all who will come to Him

- God is raising up apostles that will disarm disappointment. They bring encouragement, edification, comfort and confidence. They teach the people of God how to pray with expectation. God is raising up deliverers, individuals who are spiritually empowered to defeat the Church's oppressors

- "Therefore You delivered them into the hand of their enemies, who oppressed them; and in the time of their trouble, when they cried to You, You heard from heaven; and according to Your abundant mercies You gave them deliverers who saved them from the hand of their enemies." (Nehemiah 9:27)

- "...His soul could no longer endure the misery of Israel." (Judges 10:16)

- "'I have surely seen the oppression of My people... and have heard their cry... for I know their sorrows [pain]. So I have come down to deliver them....'" (Exodus 3:7-8)

- God will always answer people's expectations for a visitation of His grace if they cry out to Him. Their cries become the catalyst for divine intervention. He doesn't just hear our prayers – He hears our cries! The Lord bears the misery of His people. He is never far from the plight of mankind. It's one thing to pray over a need; it's quite another to weep over it!

- "David therefore departed from there and escaped to the cave of Adullam. So when his brothers and all his father's house heard it, they went down there to him. And everyone who was in distress, everyone who was in debt, and everyone who was discontented [bitter of soul] gathered to him. And there were about four hundred men with him." (Samuel 22:1-2)

- When people are in captivity, many of them lose their song – that is, their desires, motivations and zeal. The people who came to David were emotionally *distressed*, materially in *debt* and spiritually *discontented*. Their hopes had been shattered because of Saul's iniquities. They possessed no strength, no resources and no motivation. They came unto David for

renewing of a new vision, a new purpose and a new direction. David became a deliverer for them

- Apostolic Davids will come in our paths to deliver us from disappointment. The apostles restore hope among the people, causing them to anticipate something good, to look forward to something from God. Apostles shatter the disappointment that plagues many Charismatics. They are restoring to the Body healing, bringing revival and a fresh sense of greatness among the people

BUT WE WILL BE TRIED

- God awakens hopes and desires within us that in the natural seem utterly impossible to be fulfilled. He makes us a promise and then permits circumstances to come out and try us. He blesses us and then tries us with a promise
- The word *try* means "to purify and refine"
- "Until the time that his word came to pass, the word of the Lord tested him." (Psalm 105:19)
- It isn't so much *God* trying us as the word itself that tries the people to whom it is given
- "For He does not afflict willingly [from His heart], nor grieve the children of men." (Lamentations 3:33)
- "'God is not a man, that He should lie, nor a son of man, that He should repent. Has He said, and will He not do? Or has He spoken, and will He not make it good?'" (Numbers 23:19)

- "The Lord will perfect that which concerns me; Your mercy, O Lord, endures forever; do not forsake the works of Your hands." (Psalm 138:8)
- An apostolic anointing reminds people that disadvantages don't disqualify the promises of God. We are not forgotten; we do not need to get angry. We need to take our bad situations and push them away, relying on God's trustworthiness – that He will prove Himself faithful
- "It shall come to pass in that day that his burden will be taken away from your shoulder, and his yoke from your neck, and the yoke will be destroyed because of the anointing oil." (Isaiah 10:27)
- The word *yoke* means "to bow down, to press down, to lay a heavy burden." Many people suffer under a yoke of discouragement
- The breaker anointing that apostles have literally shatters that yoke. The connotation in the scriptures is that the believer's neck will become so spiritually fat that the yoke will not be able to go around it. (Dr. Chuck Flynn)
- Many people's belief in God is based on a supposed expression of love, His position of love for them – but it's a distorted view of His love. They have reduced God to a meaningless experience, a half-truth, a formula. Many people want deeper truth but not a deeper relationship with Him. They want Him to do things for them without truly wanting to get to know Him in all facets

- Even the blessings of God can be a substitute for a living relationship with Him
- Just as Jesus rejoiced in His relationship with the Father way before He went about His earthly ministry, apostles are calling people to a true, vibrant relationship with Him before receiving His blessings
- Could this lack of relationship be the reason for failures, disappointments and discouragements in the Body of Christ?
- "Though the fig tree may not blossom, nor fruit be on the vines; though the labor of the olive may fail, and the fields yield no food; though the flock may be cut off from the fold, and there be no herd in the stalls — yet I will rejoice in the Lord, I will joy in the God of my salvation." (Habakkuk 3:17-18)
- "He Himself has said, 'I will not in any way fail you, nor give you up, nor leave you without support. I will not in any degree leave you helpless, nor forsake, nor let you down [release My hold on you], assuredly not.'" (Hebrews 13:15 *Amplified*)

THE SOURCE OF OUR STRENGTH

- Many Christians, and many who are still lost, have a fear of hoping — it is the death of an expectation
- Apostolically motivated people bring a revelation of His faithfulness, a correct view of the Father's heart. They bring

about a knowing of God as Father to those willing to accept Him as such — this is the power of the gospel that His Spirit bears witness to in the apostles' acts

- The apostolic anointing overcomes any lack of confidence, and people begin to understand their acceptance in Him — He becomes their Source of strength
- "He came to His own, and His own did not receive Him. But as many as received Him, to them He gave the right to become children of God, to those who believe in His name: who were born, not of blood, nor of the will of the flesh, nor of the will of man, but of God." (John 1:11-13)
- "'For I will restore health to you and heal you of your wounds,' says the Lord. 'Because they called you an outcast saying, "This is Zion; no one seeks her."'" (Jeremiah 30:17)
- "'For I have satiated [fully satisfied] the weary soul, and I have replenished every sorrowful soul.' After this I awoke and looked around, and my sleep was sweet to me." (Jeremiah 31:25-26)

Chapter Five

Unveiling the Burden of God

THE LONG BEACH MIRACLE SERVICE

It was August of 1973. I was a receiver for my high school football team in Hemet, California. I loved track-and-field and baseball, too, but American football has always been my favorite sport. I mean, sports were my life. I wanted to play football for Jesus at Notre Dame University. Hey, I was seventeen, all right? I dreamed of wearing a Fightin' Irish gold helmet, but I was also pursuing a few probable scholarships from various colleges around the country. It ended up being that I received a coveted Congressional appointment to attend the Naval Academy in Annapolis, Maryland, and I was to play ball for the United States Navy. So my mind was made up. I was going to win souls for the Lord, fly fighter jets and work my way to the NFL.

Then I met Animal.

That's what was stenciled across his helmet: "Animal." He was a mountain — just a huge defensive tackle from a rival high school team that was beating me to a pulp during one game. If memory serves, he hit me so hard once that my helmet flew off. The refs weren't calling any penalties against him — they were probably scared!

I jumped up to catch the ball, made the reception, and there was Animal, grunting and hollering. He picked me up out of midair and slammed me back down to the turf. My whole career flashed before my eyes in that instant before I was knocked out. A three-inch rock protruded out of that particular corner of the field, overlooked by the groundskeepers. All of Animal's weight came crashing down on me as that rock jammed into the middle of my spine with a sickening *crack!* I went completely numb.

A dislocated shoulder and severely messed up ankles were bad enough. But I suspected that I had fractured a vertebra. My career was over – my life was over. I was in excruciating pain for months, hobbling around on my ankles, nursing my cracked back.

I was in need of a tremendous healing miracle. I could barely function, let alone play football. A sister in the Lord called me one day concerning a miracle service out in Long Beach being held by a young minister named Brant Baker, who had been strongly influenced by the late Kathryn Kulhman. At around twenty years of age, Baker started holding meetings; and in a matter of a year or two, there were thousands attending these miracles services, getting healed in droves.

This friend of mine called to say that she felt I needed to attend one of these services. So she, another friend and I drove to Long Beach. I remember sitting in the back of the car in incredible pain. But I just kept speaking to myself and the Lord that I believed this was to be my time of encounter with Him. I drew up an expectation and a resolve that I would not leave that miracle service until I had met with God and was healed.

People had to get to the service about an hour and half before it started because if they didn't, there weren't any seats left. It was an auditorium for about a thousand people, but it seemed like there was twice as many people trying to find room to stand. Thankfully, I think we got the last three available seats in the whole auditorium. The pain in my body prohibited me from standing for too long.

Before the service took place, what utterly amazed me was this sense of awe that the people had. The tangible touch of God was so strong that people were sobbing and giving their lives to the Lord, and the preacher wasn't even on stage yet! That, in and of itself, was an amazing experience. The Lord was already stirring my spirit, and I was beginning to enter into a heightened sense of God's manifest presence. It was as if there was a fog that had settled in the auditorium. As I was looking through this fog, I was literally caught up in a transcendent type of experience. I sat there, one part of me in excruciating pain, the other part of me spiritually raptured into the presence of God.

Something like a two hundred-voice choir lined up and started singing powerfully. The music was supercharged with His glory. Every note seemed electrified by this fog. After they finished, Baker stepped onto the platform. I was amazed at how young this guy was and how mightily God was using him.

I learned that night that age has nothing to do with how God wants to use us. We can become spiritual fathers and mothers at any age. I know now that God was preparing me for that particular type of life ministry.

I honestly don't remember what he preached about at all — I'm sure it was good. But at the end of the message, it was as if someone just flicked a light switch on in his head. His eyes brightened up, and he pointed down in my general direction.

"About the eighth row back, seventh or eighth person over, there's a lady that has a cancer in your stomach. Stand up! You're being healed."

The woman stood up and screamed, "How did he know my condition?" She ran forward to the stage and was tremendously touched by the power of the Holy Spirit.

At the time, I didn't know what he was doing because I'd never been in a healing service before, but he began to call people out with various words of knowledge, pointing to different sections of the auditorium.

"There's a person over there that has leukemia. A person over here with an ear problem — uh, you can't hear in your right ear." This went on and on, and people began to stream forward to the front.

Although I was shocked by the new experience and caught up in this foggy weight, I was still struggling with a dull feeling in my spirit. I was in immense pain, crying out to God. It never would have dawned on me that the Lord would actually speak back to me that night, but a thought just popped into my head suddenly: God was going to speak to me then and there.

No more had the thought crossed my mind when the preacher pointed down at me and said, "There's a young man down there being healed of his ankles — but in particular his back — due to injuries sustained in high school sports."

Now, I had only been saved a couple of years. I was so spiritually naïve that I turned around and asked three or four people, "Do you have my condition? Hey, who's got my condition? Is that you? That's amazing. I have the same problem." I couldn't believe that He was speaking to me personally and so specifically.

Finally my friend touched me on the shoulder and said, "Uh, I think he means you."

"Oh. Right."

So in that fog, I gingerly moved out of my seat and hobbled down to the front, still in agony, and stood with the people whom God was dancing among. The minister was just strolling down the line, and as he walked past people, he would gently touch them on top of their heads. They would instantly become overwhelmed by God's presence and collapse to the floor. It was the first time I had ever seen anybody "slain in the Spirit" or "fall under the power" as Charismatics call it.

I was so ignorant of His ways; I thought they were actually being *killed*, because they would just lie there, immobilized — some for hours.

Then I realized this preacher must have some *real* power because after awhile, some of these dead people got up again! I thought to myself, *This guy's amazing! He kills people and then raises them from the dead! They're killed and then raised up, killed and raised up. Wow!*

I suddenly became very aware that I didn't want to be killed and raised from the dead, so I said to the Lord, *Look, I want to be healed, but I don't wanna fall.* A split second after I made this dumb statement, Baker, who was standing a few people down from me, turned and gave me this innocent smile and a little chuckle. He strode over and lightly tapped me on the head.

It was like falling on a bed of pillows....

I woke up several minutes later under the baby grand piano, looking up at all this pink bubblegum that someone had stuck up there. It was such a spiritual setting! I just lay there, feeling this warmth float through my body. I couldn't move. Finally someone was kind enough to drag me out from under the piano and stand me to my feet. I staggered around in a drunken, Holy Ghost stupor (something else I had never experienced before) and wobbled over to the side of the stage.

A sister in the Lord came up to me and asked, "What was it that you were healed of?"

My tongue didn't seem to work right, so I sort of thickly mumbled, "I don't know." I was blubbering like a child.

"Well," she said, "just stand there and let God speak to you."

Soon people began to go up to the platform and testify of what God had done for them. The thought came to me that I'd told the Lord I had purposed in my heart I wasn't going to leave the service unless He healed me. So I said to myself, *I'm just going to believe that this touch from You, this encounter I've had with You, is a sign that You've set me free from my condition.* At that moment I felt no physical manifestation I had been healed.

I decided to step forward in faith and went back up on the platform to give testimony of my miracle. All of a sudden, I began to sense this heat, this anointing, that touched my ankles first and then rose up into my back. When the time came for me to give my testimony, I realized I was totally healed.

As I was testifying about what God had done, Brant came over to me. I'll never forget what he said as he was looking at me, "There's just something about this man — the presence of God that's all over him! I can't even touch him because the Lord's all over him." I began to sob uncontrollably. He turned to walk away but stopped about four steps later and came back toward me.

He touched me on the head and said, "Lord, this is Your empty vessel. Use him!" Once again, I was slain in the power of the Holy Spirit, and several minutes later I was "resurrected" and stumbled back to my seat. There was still about forty-five minutes left of the service, so I began to just thank the Lord and rejoice for my healing. I remember saying, "Thank You, Lord, that You've healed my body! I just want to glorify You! When I go to the Naval Academy, I'll praise You by playing the best that I can!"

I felt a voice rise up out of my spirit, and the Lord spoke to me. "I have another plan for your life. You know I do." I didn't want to hear it. I was going to play football. But He kept saying the same thing over and over again. Then this voice said, "Will you make a covenant with Me? Will you sacrifice your desires and your life for My sake?"

THE COVENANT-MAKERS

I didn't even know what the word *covenant* meant. It wasn't until some months later I found out that a covenant was scriptural. I came across this passage found in Psalm 50:3-5: "Our God shall come, and shall not keep silent; a fire shall devour before Him, and it shall be very tempestuous all around Him. He shall call to the heavens from above, and to the earth, that He may judge His people: 'Gather My saints together to me, those who have made a covenant with me by sacrifice.'"

Some of you may not know what a covenant means. Allow me to elaborate. In the Old Testament, there were two Hebrew words for "covenant": *berith* (Strong's #1285) and *karath* (Strong's #3772.) *Berith* means "to cut asunder," and *karath* means "to divide or cut in two." In the New Testament, the Greek word for covenant is *diatheke* (Strong's #1242), meaning "a testament or a will."

There are some principles to know regarding covenant standings. One, the death of the testator, or the writer of the will, was required before the conditions and the effects of his testament could be realized.

Two, a basic covenant was a pact, or a promise, between two parties in which each pledged to the other all his possessions and strength. The covenant was then sealed with the shedding of blood; they cut prized animals in halves and passed between the parts, thereby sealing their covenant with one another. (Genesis 15:9-17; Jeremiah 34:18)

Three, covenants were permanent, binding contracts, perpetually reestablished from generation to generation. Lastly, covenants were fair as each participant pledged the same to the other. Now, God's covenant is a matter of grace and mercy on His part. (Psalm 89:28)

In the Bible there are eight covenants between God and man. Take a moment to study them. Read Genesis 6, Genesis 15, Exodus 24, Psalm 89, 2 Chronicles 29, 2 Chronicles 34, 2 Kings 11 and Luke 22.

So now back to Brant's meeting. I was wrestling in the spirit with this voice that kept asking me to make a covenant. I vaguely recalled all these people going up to the stage to testify of the various diseases they had been healed of: crippling diseases, blindness, deafness, internal organs that weren't functioning correctly. Some of the people had been to the service a week or two earlier and were now testifying with doctor verification that they'd been healed of any number of diseases. Cancers had disappeared, blood had been cleansed. People, who'd been in wheelchairs for months if not years, were totally healed and walking around again.

This didn't even touch the salvations. We know that salvation is the greatest miracle. So in this meeting, when the altar call was given, hundreds of people literally rushed forward to turn their lives over to the Lord. It was this awesome open-heavens experience where people couldn't *wait* to get right with God.

As I watched these things, arguing with this voice, I began to realize that there was so much more that God had in store for my life than being a football star or going to the Naval Academy and flying fighter planes. God was wanting me to make a covenant with Him by sacrifice. He wanted me to give up the things that I most dreamed of in order to fulfill His purposes. He was on a manhunt for a laborer to do His bidding.

GOD'S MANHUNT

The fire of God is His burden and His zeal. Follow me here for a bit, and I'll more fully explain what that statement means. See, it is His will that He will accomplish, plain and simple. In His infinite wisdom, He has decided to share that burden with His children. So one could say that He is on a manhunt, if you will, looking for men and women who will covenant with Him to work out His plans on the earth. His people must be stirred into action.

Apostles assist in this stirring; they bring the people to a point of confrontation that demands others to alter their current path. This is part of the reformation that apostles help bring to the Church — to help wake up the people, to let them know they have a work to do! The people in the world are confronted with God's demand that their lives belong to Him because He has something for them to do. An apostolic spirit confronts spiritual apathy.

Elijah was used to bring about this kind of confrontation. Remember in 1 Kings 18 the story of the prophets of Baal? Here's the prophet, in his typically agitated fashion, confronting the children of Israel on their indecisiveness. Verse 21, "How long will you falter between two opinions? If the Lord is God, follow Him; but if Baal, follow him." Seems simple enough really. What else does one do with a God but follow Him? Of course, the Israelites are not convinced by his stirring admonishments, so he decides to put on a little test.

Read the story if you're unfamiliar with it. Elijah challenges the 450 prophets of Baal to a showdown, or a barbecue of sorts. Two bulls are cut into pieces and laid on some wood. So then Elijah says, "...Call on the name of your gods, and I will call on the name of the Lord; and the God who answers by fire, He is God." (1 Kings 18:24)

That's important to note — God answers by fire. Remember, His fire shows His burden and His zeal for people to do His bidding.

So the prophets of Baal whoop and holler, dance around like fools, from morning until midday. And nothing happens. So Elijah, the well manicured man that he is, starts to make fun of them, probably kicking back under a shade tree, drinking some iced tea.

"So where's your god, fellas? What's up? Is he sleeping? On vacation? Perhaps he's brushing his teeth!" (I'm paraphrasing here, but the gist is the same.)

He taunts the prophets into another fit of foolishness from noon until about three o'clock. They start cutting themselves with knives, blood gushing out all over the place, working themselves up into a frenzy. And nothing happens. I love what is says in verse 29, "...No one paid attention." How funny is that?

Finally, Elijah stands up, takes his bull, cuts it into pieces and lays it on an altar of twelve stones made in the name of the Lord. Then to add insult to injury, he digs a big trench around the altar, has water poured on the covenant sacrifice three times and then fills the ditch up with water just for good measure. (Remember, it hadn't rained for three years, so we're talking about a lot of water here.)

After all of this preparation, after a whole day of the prophets of Baal whipping themselves into a panic over their inattentive god, Elijah utters a sixty-three word prayer (count them) and the fire of God consumes not only the sacrifice, but the wood, the dirt and the stones. And it licks up the water in the trench.

"Now when all the people saw it, they fell on their faces; and they said, 'The Lord, He is God! The Lord, He is God!'" (Verse 39)

Wouldn't you?

That's what I call an all-consuming fire! It's a burden that goes beyond the norm – God's passion is to have His people obey Him, and He will do whatever it takes to complete His designs. The fire of God is His burden and His zeal, and we need that kind of fire to fall today! The kind of unquenchable, Holy Spirit blaze that consumes the entirety of our covenant sacrifice. We need apostolic people who are going to stir us to a point of change because, whether Christians want to admit or not, we are all called to confront.

"The world is wrong by believing in a God and not obeying Him. But we're wrong by believing in a God and not instigating a confrontation." (Mario Murillo) These types of "fire miracles" are always quite confrontational. Let me give an example.

THE CROSS-EYED BOY

In a retirement community in California, I was asked to minister at a particular church where the pastor himself was in his seventies. He had been advertising a couple of weeks before that I was coming to hold a miracle service on Sunday morning. Bring the sick out, it said, bring the afflicted. Brother Maloney is going to share his testimony. If anyone needs baptism in the Holy Spirit, come on out. The power of God will be here.

Once again, no pressure.

Of course, he later told me that God had not really powerfully moved in the church for many, many years, so there was hardly any expectation for the miraculous among the elderly congregation of about one hundred people.

I actually found it quite comical as we were sitting on the platform that fine Sunday morning. The dear pastor turned to me and whispered, "Brother Maloney, we're so appreciative that you're here, and we've been advertising the last couple weeks. We want to give you plenty of opportunity for ministry. We want miracles and healings, but we also want to hear about your testimony. So take a few minutes and share that 'cause there's some unsaved people here — they're all pretty old, and many of them don't have too many years left. Several need the baptism in the Holy Spirit, so can you minister to them for that as well?"

"Sure." I smiled. "Of course."

"Now, we're gonna turn the service over to you about 11:20, but you'll need to be done about ten after noon, OK?"

I chuckled. "That's absolutely impossible — how can I do all of that in less than an hour?"

"Well, you got to realize that at ten after twelve, it doesn't matter who's preaching — I mean, Jesus Himself could be on the platform — they're going to get up and walk out on you."

"Why?" This suddenly wasn't sounding too good.

"Because they're elderly, and they don't move too quickly, and they have to beat the Sunday crowds down at Wyatt's Cafeteria."

I just shook my head as the pastor got up to start praise and worship. Sure enough, at 12:10... *halfway through my testimony*... about three-fourths of the people stood up and began to walk out. The pastor was thoroughly embarrassed.

How rude! I felt a flash of anger whiff through me, and I'll admit it wasn't the righteous indignation of God, you know? It was me. I was just mad. I've repented since then....

Now, the only thing that saved me in this situation was that a lot of them had walkers and canes, so they moved very slowly toward the exits. But there was no way I was going to minister to anybody, so I shut my Bible and sat down. I was just fuming. The pastor was muttering apologies. The elderly people were still shuffling toward the foyer.

One of the few people remaining seated in the service was a boy about ten-years-old. He and his younger brother were the only children in the whole church. I found out later their unsaved parents lived up the road and just to get rid of them for a few hours on Sunday morning told them to find a church — didn't matter which one — and go to Sunday school. The boy and his little brother happened to walk into this church several weeks earlier and became the entire youth program. They were the only two kids in Sunday school class, so the elderly people got them saved and baptized in water, and they just loved on those boys like prized possessions.

But the oldest boy was just as crossed-eyed as cross-eyed could get. I mean, it was so bad that when you looked into his eyes, your eyes went crossed, too! He heard the pastor saying this coming Sunday, Brother Maloney will have a healing/miracle service, so come out expecting your miracle. When I sat down in disgust, he thought his opportunity was passing him by. Without anyone asking him, he came forward and just stood there, right in front of the pulpit, not saying anything, just staring at me and the pastor.

After a few seconds, I figured I better find out what he wanted, so I got up and leaned over the pulpit to see him better. He looked up at me — his eyes were crossed; my eyes went cross and started to water. I asked the most ridiculous question a minister has ever asked behind a pulpit before.

"What would you like Jesus to do for you?"

"Well, what do you think?" He stared at me. "I wanna see straight."

At first I didn't feel any anointing because I was still angry at the people leaving, but I remember stepping down off the platform; and he shut his eyes, eagerly awaiting his miracle. Compassion suddenly flowed out of my spirit, and I prayed for him about thirty seconds. When he looked up at me, his eyes were as straight as they could be!

Now, I can be a little spiteful sometimes — and I can't say that I was being led by the Lord here, but I spun that kid around and yelled, "All of you stop! Turn around! Look at what God did for this little boy in spite of you!"

I'm convinced it was the only time that church came together in one mind and one accord. Everyone stopped and turned in unison, staring. Just dead silence with gaping mouths. It was hilarious.

Then, out of the corner of my eye, I see this walker go flying in the air and land on the stage; on the other side, this cane went spinning.

And like little children, they all began to cry out to God and started *running* to the front. "Jesus! Jesus! Jesus!"

We were there until about a quarter to three that afternoon. We had a good, old-fashioned Pentecostal revival meeting, complete with tremendous miracles and healings. God danced among His people for hours. Hey, forget about Wyatt's Cafeteria!

Now, what do you think the parents must have thought when those little boys went back home? "Mom! Dad! Look what Jesus did for me!"

I wish I could tell you they softened their hearts and said, "Let's go find out about this preacher and about this Jesus." But the pastor told me a few months later, from that moment forward, those little boys were not permitted to step foot into any church again. How terribly sad! It pains me to say that this was a confrontational miracle, but, my friends, I won't apologize for it. In God's eyes, there is no middle road – you're either for Him or against Him. And it is the apostolic spirit that flies in the face of the spiritually indifferent, forcing them to draw lines for what they believe.

WE NEED FIRE MIRACLES

It's not a very popular subject, but we need these kinds of *fire miracles*, dear readers. The kinds of miracles, like what Elijah witnessed, that provoke a confrontation. "How long will you falter between two opinions?" We need the totally consuming zeal of the Lord and the rod of authority that proceeds out of Zion. (Psalm 110) These are the apostolic miracles that leave no room for confusion in the minds of people, confronting society with the rude awakening that there's a God in heaven, and He is demanding something from them. This is a primary purpose for signs, wonders and miracles (which, as I said before, I'll give concrete definitions for those in a later chapter.) To confront the disbelievers out there in the world. Imagine an atheist being confronted with a creative miracle where his own wife walks out of a wheelchair. He'll be forced into making a decision – that's either her mental ability giving her physical strength, or that's God. And if God makes her walk out of the wheelchair, he had better be prepared to worship Him. The miraculous demands a response. For more teaching on fire miracles, read *Heaven Fire* by David Alsobrook.

Of course, all of God's miracles reveal His compassion and mercy, but in that revelation, there are certain kinds of miracles that apostolic people operate in to create a confrontation. It behooves the apostolic person to press into that realm of the miraculous signs and wonders where God's love is revealed, and those around are provoked to a response. Now, it's true; that that kind of ministry is not popular. There seems to be an extreme majority of some big churches that don't flock to confrontational, supernatural expression – that's just a fact. (And of course, as always, there are exceptions, I know.) But see, apostolic people have to be willing to forget about whatever kind of reputation they're attempting to gain by man's standards.

I know I have no reputation to maintain within religious society; I'm already a marked man in the current level of ministry the Lord has given me. This book'll probably just make it worse! Doesn't bother me – I just want to be open to the supernatural.

See, the apostles are being stirred, and a passion is being born within them. They are the covenant-makers, moved to change. God is looking for an apostolic person that has a hunger, a consuming passion so intense that he or she will pay any price God requires to have the supernatural. They must have a burden for the nations and a faith to proclaim what God wants to accomplish in those nations. They must make a deliberate, intentional choice to live for the worship of Jesus among the nations.

In Isaiah 7:2, "...It was told to the house of David, saying, 'Syria's forces are deployed in Ephraim.' So his [Ahaz's] heart and the heart of his people were moved as the trees of the woods are moved with the wind." We are to be moved by the Spirit for the purpose of reaching every nation. Our greatest dream is to be that Jesus will be praised in earthly languages never before heard in Heaven. The whole earth is to be covered with the glory of God. He is longing for His Son to be glorified in the nations.

Apostolic people are called to cultivate a passion — a radical abandonment, if you will: an apostolic focus in decision-making and strategies, apostolic praying that is completely committed to spreading His glory throughout the earth — even to the point of death. There is no other reason for living. The word "passion" comes from the Old French, and ultimately from the Medieval Latin *passus*, meaning "to suffer." Passion is what a person is willing to suffer for. Apostles are willing to pay whatever price. They are continually asking themselves the question, "Does my faith stand for something?"

Acts 4:33 says, "And with great power the apostles gave witness to the resurrection of the Lord Jesus. And great grace was upon them all." As you may or may not know, the Greek word for "witness" is *marturion* (Strong's #3142), where English-speakers have coined the word *martyr*, a person who witnesses for their God by their death. Not every act of witnessing requires death, but whatever is needed to get the point across — that's all right with them.

While he might not remember it, I was blessed to have a few moments with Reinhard Bonkke a few years back. Now, he'll be the first to admit that he's an intense individual — this firebrand in the hand of the Lord eats, sleeps and breathes souls, to which the continent of Africa can attest. Some members of his team were once shot at while out ministering to the masses. They were seeing healings and miracles, and somebody was taking potshots at them! To say their lives were being put in grave danger for the sake of the gospel would be an understatement!

I asked Brother Bonkke what he thought about that — I mean, could he really face that kind of intense persecution? Possibly even dying?

Without hesitation, he flashed me one of the most intense stares and growled, "If I have to die bringing the gospel to them, then, Jim... today... is a *good* day to die."

I tell you what; goose bumps crawled up and down my arms as I read the passion in his eyes. That single statement has stuck with me since, and I now feel that I can agree with him without any false sense of bravado. I am convinced that apostles are witnesses of His resurrection with great power and great grace, no matter what.

Apostles have a revelation of the *zoe* kind of life — life that goes beyond regular, physical life. It's an understanding of the God-kind of life that permeates every facet of existence. When you have that kind of life, giving up this one doesn't seem too bad if it's for a worthwhile cause. And what could be more worthwhile than executing the orders of your God? A fellow minister, Gary Black said, "You know you have it [passion], when you are deeply disappointed that God hasn't called you to leave your home and get out among those who have never heard the Name — only those who long to express His glory to nations, have a right to." I would also add only those who have a passion to *go* have a right to *stay*. This is what I mean: apostolic people must have a desire forged within them to go, but they also have to be willing to stay. Don't take the previous paragraphs out of context. I'm not saying we're supposed to rush off and stupidly throw our lives away without the call from God. I recognize that many apostles are called to stay in their own area — that is where they are sent. But the point is: affect a change, wherever you might be, and be willing to give whatever it takes to affect that change.

.This call to change originates deep within the Father's heart. In John 20:21, Jesus says, "As the Father has sent Me, I also send you." The world will be changed when the Church is transformed into a company of apostolic people — sent ones with a mission that will succeed no matter what. We will *not* fail!

In his book *The Gift of the Apostle*, David Cannistraci wrote something to the effect that, "to assure we are a part of this apostolic move, we must see that anyone who is sent by God is apostolic." Makes sense to me. He goes on to show beautifully that God uses ordinary men and women in very apostolic ways. I say that we are now being separated into an apostolic company. And I think I have a fine definition for *apostle*, if I do say so myself: "to be sent, to be set apart, to be set off by a boundary — to draw a clear boundary line and establish a definite territory within which apostolic people are meant to operate with full authority."

We must find our positioning, making a commitment to the land we are currently in or where we are sent, that this territory belongs to God. It's worth repeating: God is on a manhunt for a people who are willing to make a covenant with Him based on sacrifice. This is what God was dealing with me about in Brant's service all those years ago; He was challenging me to be stirred, to be changed, into a person of passion. I've committed my life to seeing the fire of God's blessing burning in the heart of man.

In 1 Kings 18, God answered by fire. What makes us think He would not do the same today? We are being *stirred to confront*. We are being *stirred to prepare*. The spirit of John the Baptist is stirring our cities to prepare the way of the Lord. "Repent, for the kingdom of heaven is at hand!" We are to be "the voice of one crying in the wilderness: 'Prepare the way of the Lord; make straight in the desert a highway for our God.'" (Isaiah 40:3)

We must make a commitment to the land we are in to bring the fire of God — to confront people with the reality of God's zeal and to prepare the way of the Lord to see that zeal consume the people. To me, that is a pivotal point of apostolic ministry: to see God answer by fire. That to me is the essence of an apostolic revival.

I think Mario Murillo has some powerful thoughts on a stirring to revival — some keys to preparing the way of the Lord: "The key to revival is whether or not we're going to venture out and discover the secrets to uprooting Satan's strongholds. Revival is launched from heaven but must find a landing pad in the hearts of man. It takes a covenant of God's will with man's preparation to bring revival."

God always creates changes within His people by making them promises — and then asking something back from them. It's as if God is saying, "I'll give you all of Me, if you give Me all of you." Remember, there is no halfway with God. All of you gets all of Him. (Psalm 103) Now, who do you think gets the better end of that bargain? Let's see, all of Him gives us salvation, deliverance, healing, peace, joy, purpose, identity, reputation, glory and passion. And, oh boy, what does He get in return? *Drum roll...*

Us.

Doesn't seem like a very good deal for Him, does it? I'm being humorous here, but God's purposes are completed when we come out on top. He wants to give us all of Himself, in all His wondrous splendor, but He wants something in return.

God is asking each one of us to make a covenant with Him by sacrifice. I remember a message from Mario Murillo (see why he's my favorite preacher?) where he puts it as if God is asking you, "Are you willing to give up something permanently that is of ultimate joy to you, never desiring to retrieve it again?" The burden of God costs you something.

Take a look at the first chapter of First Samuel. Barrenness was a great reproach in the Hebrew culture — considered to be a curse from God as in "...the Lord had closed her womb." (1 Samuel 1:5) And while Elkanah loved his wife Hannah, she would weep and not eat, year after year, during the time of sacrifice because she had no child. It would be the pinnacle of her existence if she could just give birth. There was such a driving force behind her desire to have a child that it consumed her entire being.

"...'Hannah, why do you weep? Why do you not eat? And why is your heart grieved? Am I not better to you than ten sons?'" her husband would ask. (Verse 8)

So Hannah goes to the tabernacle, in bitterness of soul, and prays to the Lord, weeping in anguish. Then she does something absolutely incredible.

She makes a vow to the Lord. "...'O Lord of hosts, if You will indeed look on the affliction of Your maidservant and remember me, and not forget Your maidservant, but will give Your maidservant a male child, then I will give him to the Lord all the days of his life....'" (1 Samuel 1:11)

This woman of God made a vow in a selfless act. "I need a son; if You give me one, I'll give him back to You." See, Hannah recognized that God was in desperate need of a prophet for the land of Israel. She perceived that her heartbreak for a son was not as great of a heartbreak as God's need for a prophet. Yes, she was weeping because of her lack, but she understood a vital truth that God can always out-weep His people. That, indeed, God needs something from His people.

"Covenant is born of the sorrow of heaven mingling with the sorrow of earth." (again, Mario Murillo)

Let the apostolic people across the world recognize God's needs for His people. Let them rise up to say, "Give it to me, and I will give it back to You!" Let them praise Him and remember His burdens. That's what apostolic people are: a generation of men and women who work out the burdens of God in constant praise and sacrifice. Take a moment to meditate on Psalm 50 — you'll see what I mean.

So here I am. Sitting in this service in Long Beach, California, watching Brant be used of God in the most tremendous fashion I'd yet seen. Here were people giving testimonies that would blow your mind. I myself just healed of a crippling condition, wrestling with this concept that God needed His servant to complete something in His name. There is no more humbling of a moment when you realize the God of all creation has asked for your services.

And finally, I gave in. I released the un-renewed, self-centered dreams and desires I had been clinging to.

Sighing, I muttered under my breath, "If I do this, Lord — if I give up everything I've ever dreamed and desired for Your sake, I want You to make me a promise. I want You to promise me that everything I've seen tonight in this guy's ministry, every healing and salvation, every dynamic touch — I wanna see that in the ministry you entrust to me." I wasn't being covetous or demanding — it was under the unction of the Holy Spirit that the Lord was orchestrating this burden in my heart.

It was silent for a few seconds, and then the voice responded. It just seemed the voice was almost audible, although only to me.

"Yeah... I'll take you up on that," He said.

I've found that God doesn't always speak in the King James English, you know?

I won't lie to you. I still get a stirring in the pit of my stomach every time I watch the Dallas Cowboys (they're God's team, after all) march onto the field, helmets glinting in the scorching Texas sun. But I wouldn't trade my life for a second. Just one miracle has been worth it all.

I'm not saying that I see everything that I want to see in my ministry; I'm always pushing for a greater revelation of His heart to release a greater experience of His power, but every time I witness a healing or a sign and wonder, I know that I've become a covenant-maker with God.

And He always keeps His end of the bargain.

I found that in releasing my supposed heart's desires and surrendering my will to the Lord, I came into a greater understanding of what were my true desires and dreams for life. It turns out my Creator knew my desires better than I did! The Father wants to fulfill *your* desires, too, as your heart is changed and you fully yield to Him.

Recall Brant's simple prophetic declaration over me, "Lord, this is Your empty vessel. Use him!" It was at that precise moment that destiny was put within my spirit. A prophetic word conveys the burden of the Lord and makes it real for the recipient.

I love signs and wonders and miracles. I love prophecy, too. To God's glory and honor, He has blessed me to be able to minister in both flows — I think they all go hand-in-hand really. The prophetic breeds the miraculous. One of the greatest joys I get out of being in the ministry is to give someone a personal prophetic word and watch the power of God hit them, seeing the burden of the Lord for their lives downloaded into their spirits. They look changed. They look invigorated. It's just awesome!

I teach a lot on the prophetic, and there are some wonderful truths and insight I could go into here about how prophetic ministry conveys the burden of the Lord and releases destiny, but I suppose it's not entirely within the scope of a book on the apostolic. So who knows? Maybe I'll just have to write another book!

Suffice to say for now, in my prophetic classes, I teach in the Old Testament that when a prophet knew it was time to speak the word of the Lord, he felt the hand of God press down upon him. It was God's burden that He placed upon him, and he couldn't help *but* to speak. See Isaiah 8:11, "... a strong hand." These are the Hebrew words *yad chezqah* (Strong's #3027, #2393), literally meaning "a powerful, directing force."

It's as if when God lifted His hand off the prophet, He placed the impression of His burden and His word upon the people. It was then their responsibility to release the word and seek out its fulfillment. This is prophetic destiny. When Brant laid his hand upon me, it was symbolic of the Dancing Hand of God pressing His burden down upon me, not only healing me, but releasing destiny. Apostles have got to be people that operate from this perspective. A prophetic word of destiny can change a person's life and release the burden of God. Let me give an example.

THE GIRL IN LONG SLEEVES

There was a young lady, who had been saved just a few weeks before, in this meeting I was at in Colorado. The word of the Lord came upon me when I looked at her. I felt the hand of God impress deeply upon me, and I sensed a burden for this woman. I called her up, and she stood in front of me. I found out later she had never received a prophetic word before.

I opened my mouth to release this burden and said, "Four years ago you attempted to take your life."

That's a very bold statement, I know. Normally when I have a word of this nature, something that specific about a person's problems, I usually keep it quiet until I can share it with them privately so as not to embarrass them in front of people. But in this case, I felt the Holy Spirit gave me liberty to share the word publicly because most of the people knew who she was and knew her testimony.

I had never met her before, but I continued, "You tried to take your life because your father committed incest against you." It was graphic, but it just began to roll out of my spirit. I described the picture I saw in my mind. "You took a razor blade and slit your wrists several times. You were in the bathroom, and your parents came home in the nick of time to wrap your wrists and rush you to the emergency ward. You've spent the last four years in drug addiction, living in a crack house."

Friends, how many know when you give a word that specific, you're either right or you're wrong! She began to sob, and the people around her began to weep because they knew her.

"But just a couple of weeks ago a friend of yours," (who happened to be standing next to her), "led you into the saving knowledge of Jesus. And you've learned that if Jesus has forgiven you of your sins, you also have had to forgive your earthly father of his sins committed against you. And so you made that conscious decision to forgive him not too long ago. The Lord wants you to know that He is going to restore that sense of esteem in Christ – that all of the hurts and all of the wounding will be healed. You will be able to look back without pain. And the Lord says, 'And I will remove *all evidence* of the reproach of what you went through!'"

When I said that, she felt the power of God move through her wrists. She was wearing a long sweater because it was rather cold there in the Rockies, but it didn't matter what time of the year it was. She always wore long-sleeved shirts or sweaters because she had several huge, puffy scars on each wrist. Obviously she was embarrassed because she knew that if people saw the scars, they would instantly know they were self-inflicted and that she had tried to commit suicide. Those kinds of precise gashes on a wrist don't come accidentally.

But spontaneously now, she pulled up her sweater sleeves and stuck her wrists out in front of everyone. We all stared at these horrible gashes, symbols of the reproach in her life. They were unnerving to look at until....

Instantly... in front of everyone's eyes... the scars vanished!

Pandemonium broke out; people began to sob and weep. That young lady was released from her past; she had a glimpse of just how much God thought of her. She was important to Him. He needed her, and He wanted her made whole.

See, a prophetic word can release destiny when God's hand dances over you, pressing that burden down upon you.

You need to make an agreement with Him! God is waiting for the apostolic people to make a covenant with Him by sacrifice. Dear readers, we need the fire of God to fall! We need those kinds of fire miracles, and we're not going to get them until the burden of the Lord is experienced. This is one of the great keys to apostolic release.

"Unveiling the Burden of God"

THE COVENANT-MAKERS

- "Our God shall come, and shall not keep silent; a fire shall devour before Him, and it shall be very tempestuous all around Him. He shall call to the heavens from above, and to the earth, that He may judge His people: 'Gather My saints together to me, those who have made a covenant with me by sacrifice.'" (Psalm 50:3-5)

- "Covenant" in Hebrew is *berith* or *karath*, meaning "to cut asunder, to divide or cut in two"

- "Covenant" in Greek is *diatheke*, meaning "a testament or will"

- Principle I: The death of the testator, or the writer of the will, was required before the conditions and the effects of his testament could be realized

- Principle II: A basic covenant was a pact, or a promise, between two parties in which each pledged to the other all his possessions and strength. The covenant was then sealed with the shedding of blood; they cut prized animals in halves and passed between the parts, thereby sealing their covenant with one another. (Genesis 15:9-17; Jeremiah 34:18)

- Principle III: Covenants were permanent, binding contracts, perpetual from generation to generation.

- Principle IV: Covenants were fair as each participant pledged the same to the other. Now, God's covenant is a matter of grace and mercy on His part (Psalm 89:28)
- Eight covenants between God and man: Genesis 6, Genesis 15, Exodus 24, Psalm 89, 2 Chronicles 29, 2 Chronicles 34, 2 Kings 11 and Luke 22

GOD'S MANHUNT

- The fire of God is His burden — it is His will that He will accomplish, plain and simple. He has decided to share that burden with His children. He is on a manhunt, looking for men and women who will covenant with Him to work out His plans on the earth. His people must be stirred into action
- Apostles assist in this stirring; they bring the people to a point of confrontation that demands others to alter their current path
- "How long will you falter between two opinions? If the Lord is God, follow Him; but if Baal, follow him." (1 Kings 18:21)
- "...Call on the name of your gods, and I will call on the name of the Lord; and the God who answers by fire, He is God." (1 Kings 18:24) God answers by fire. His fire shows His burden for people to do His bidding
- God's passion is to have His people obey Him, and He will do whatever it takes to complete His designs

- Apostolic people stir us to a point of change because, whether Christians want to admit or not, we are all called to confront
- "The world is wrong by believing in a God and not obeying Him. But we're wrong by believing in a God and not instigating a confrontation." (Mario Murillo)
- In God's eyes, there is no middle road — you're either for Him or against Him. And it is the apostolic spirit that flies in the face of the spiritually indifferent, forcing them to draw lines for what they believe

WE NEED FIRE MIRACLES

- Fire miracles are the apostolic miracles that leave no room for confusion in the minds of people, confronting society with the rude awakening that there's a God in heaven, and He is demanding something from them
- The miraculous demands a response
- All of God's miracles reveal His compassion and mercy, but in that revelation, there are certain kinds of miracles that apostolic people operate in to create a confrontation. It behooves the apostolic person to press into that realm of the miraculous signs and wonders where God's love is revealed, and those around are provoked to a response
- Apostolic people have to be willing to forget about whatever kind of reputation they're attempting to gain in religious society
- God is looking for an apostolic person that has a hunger, a consuming passion so intense that he or she will pay any

price God requires to have the supernatural. They must have a burden for the nations and a faith to proclaim what God wants to accomplish in those nations

- "...It was told to the house of David, saying, 'Syria's forces are deployed in Ephraim.' So his [Ahaz's] heart and the heart of his people were moved as the trees of the woods are moved with the wind." (Isaiah 7:2)
- We are to be moved by the Spirit for the purpose of reaching the nations. Our greatest dream is to be that Jesus will be praised in earthly languages never before heard in Heaven. The whole earth is to be covered with the glory of God. He is longing for His Son to be glorified in the nations
- Apostolic people are called to cultivate a passion – a radical abandonment, an apostolic focus in decision-making and strategies, apostolic praying that is completely committed to spreading His glory throughout the earth – even to the point of death
- Passion is what a person is willing to suffer for. Apostles are willing to pay whatever price. They are continually asking themselves the question, "Does my faith stand for something?"
- "And with great power the apostles gave witness to the resurrection of the Lord Jesus. And great grace was upon them all." (Acts 4:33)
- The Greek word for "witness" is *marturion*, where English-speakers have coined the word *martyr*, a person who witnesses for their God by their death. Not every act of witnessing

requires death, but whatever is needed to get the point across — that's all right with them

- "You know you have it [passion], when you are deeply disappointed that God hasn't called you to leave your home and get out among those who have never heard the Name — only those who long to express His glory to nations, have a right to." (Gary Black)
- Apostolic people must have a desire forged within them to go, but they also have to be willing to stay
- Affect a change, wherever you might be, and be willing to give whatever it takes to affect that change
- "As the Father has sent Me, I also send you." (John 20:21)
- A definition for *apostle*: "to be sent, to be set apart, to be set off by a boundary — to draw a clear boundary line and establish a definite territory within which apostolic people are meant to operate with full authority."
- We must find our positioning, making a commitment to the land we are currently in or where we are sent, that this territory belongs to God
- We are being *stirred to confront*. We are being *stirred to prepare*
- "The voice of one crying in the wilderness: 'Prepare the way of the Lord; make straight in the desert a highway for our God.'" (Isaiah 40:3)
- "The key to revival is whether or not we're going to venture out and discover the secrets to uprooting Satan's strongholds. Revival is launched from heaven but must find a landing pad

in the hearts of man. It takes a covenant of God's will with man's preparation to bring revival." (Mario Murillo)

- God always creates changes within His people by making them promises — and then asking something back from them. God is saying, "I'll give you all of Me, if you give Me all of you."
- Hannah recognized that God was in desperate need of a prophet for the land of Israel. She perceived that her heartbreak for a son was not as great of a heartbreak as God's need for a prophet. (1 Samuel 1)
- "Covenant is born of the sorrow of heaven mingling with the sorrow of earth." (Mario Murillo)
- Apostolic people are a generation of men and women who work out the burdens of God in constant praise and sacrifice (Psalm 50)
- A prophetic word conveys the burden of the Lord and makes it real for the recipient
- An Old Testament prophet knew it was time to speak the word of the Lord when he felt the hand of God press down upon him.
- When God lifted His hand off the prophet, He placed the impression of His burden and His word upon the people. It was then their responsibility to release the word and seek out its fulfillment. This is prophetic destiny
- A prophetic word of destiny can change a person's life and release the burden of God

Chapter Six

Unveiling the Glory of God

THE GOLDEN CANDLESTICK

After my healing at Brant Baker's miracle service, and my subsequent covenant with God to be one of His workers, life for me in my hometown of Idyllwild, California, became... *strange*, to say the least. We have reached a point in my story that is the core of all that I have seen in my ministry, to God's great glory and honor. This singular event, this one defining moment, is the place in history I can draw back to in my mind and say, "That's when it all started."

Again, I want to share this story with you not to puff myself up. There is nothing special in myself that you can't enter into yourselves, at least in some similar measure. That is why I am sharing this story: to show you that these experiences are for the entire Body of Christ. Whatever encounters I've had have always been for the edification of others. I share them so that *you*, dear friend, can enter into your own encounters and experiences with the Lord. I'll just have to ask you to trust me on that.

It has only been the last few years that God has permitted me to speak publicly about this experience at all. That shows me that we are approaching a time of great power and glory being added to the Church. Even still, I am very guarded when I share this with churches, only under an extreme mandate of God when He is desiring to unveil a new attribute of His glory that consistently amazes and humbles me.

It holds *that* special of a place in my heart, and I am moved to the brink of tears every time I share this story.

Before we get into it, let me say I am so very thankful and deferential that God would desire to use someone of so little consequence to share this experience with you. Humbly allow me to introduce to you some of the finest people God ever placed on this earth: a group called the Golden Candlestick.

I was seventeen. I had come down from my home higher up the mountain into the town village to collect the mail. As I was leaving the post office, an elderly lady accosted me, just out of nowhere, materializing in front of me, wagging this bony, crooked finger up in my face.

"You're the young man!" she croaked.

Ice poured down my back. I looked around, bewildered. I thought to myself, *Oh, great! What have I done now? I can't get away with anything in this dinky, little town!* There was this strange feeling that emanated off of her — it unsettled me greatly.

Now, the town I lived in was one of the major centers for mysticism and the occult in Southern California. Being a Jesus Freak wasn't that big of a thing. The Hippies living up in the woods, the transient backpackers hiking around, the seclusion of the area lent itself to the "weirdoes" who wanted to escape the oppression of Los Angeles city living.

The town was a stronghold for the metaphysical sciences. And there were these really strange groups of people who'd walk around the town in white robes and long hair. Don't really know what *they* were all about. Oh, and it was a congregating point for the Hell's Angels bikers, so you can imagine what *that* was like!

Spiritism and New Age philosophy were highly prevalent, as well as satanic ritualism. Supposedly this area was some vortex or nexus point of special power or some other such junk — the point is, the Force was strong with this town....

It wasn't uncommon in that situation, living under the tyranny of the occult, to see and hear weird things. Sacrificed animals out in the woods, people dressed like witches and warlocks who would walk by you with this far-off look in their eyes and proceed to "prophesy" over you, tell you what you were thinking, read your mail. You get the idea.

I was buffeted constantly by the demonic. There were times in my life that I had seen fully formed apparitions. They'd float in and disappear. You know, it's interesting to note that not always is a demon ugly and grotesque. Some of these had the ability to appear quite beautiful. (Hence, their ability to lure people into a false sense of peace.) Still, they'd move chairs, open up drawers, throw out knives, forks and spoons, scratch on the walls, pound on the doors. It was a terribly vexing, frightening way to grow up.

(Thankfully I never participated in the occult or got involved with the mystics — it was just the saving grace of God that kept me from that oppression. But living in that saturated environment has burned within me sensitivity to mysticism and the occult; something that has aided me throughout my ministry. I have a well-developed discernment when something is of a familiar spirit, versus a true manifestation of the Lord.)

"Yes, you're the one. You're the young man," this lady crooned, still waggling that crooked finger up at me. I was unnerved by her statement, but I didn't get that same sense of "ookiness" that I got from the witches and warlocks in the village. There was something *different* about her.

I remember sidestepping this woman, muttering something to the effect of, "Lady, you got the wrong guy." I hotfooted it out of the post office, and thankfully the elderly woman didn't follow me. I half-expected that whole night for some phone call to my parents about some ancient prank I'd pulled on that lady's flower garden or whatever. I kept wracking my brain, thinking, *What did I do?* I fell into a fitful sleep that night, tossing and turning, beating my pillow, with this emblazoned image of that bony crooked, wrinkled finger wiggling under my chin. *It's you! You're the young man!*

Several days later, with that nagging image still tickling my mind, a friend in the Lord phoned me up, saying I should go over to such-and-such place at such-and-such address this evening. "There are some great people there I'd like you to meet." So on her advice, I went.

Turns out this place was a house out in the sticks. *Oh, brother, where is she sending me?* I thought. I knocked on the door and waited for a few seconds, wondering what had I gotten myself into. When the door opened, guess who was standing there, beckoning me to come in?

Yep. That little lady with the bony finger.

It figures....

"Come in. We've been expecting you."

Huh? Expecting me? But I screwed up my courage and followed her into the living room. There were about two dozen people (some men, mostly women) staggered around the place, looking at me expectantly. I had no idea what I'd walked into.

The lady (I found out later her name was Frances Metcalfe) began to tell me what it was they were all doing here. I'll put this in quotes, even though I don't exactly remember the order of her words, but she did say all these things in the course of her explanation.

"We call ourselves the Golden Candlestick, and there were about forty-five or fifty of us in the beginning. Some have gone home to be with Jesus now. Forty or more years ago, we were all students in seminary, preparing to go into our various ministries, when the Lord spoke to each of us and told us He had another plan for our lives. He told us that if we gave up all aspirations for public ministry and just continuously gathered together to worship Him in the high praise and deep intercession ministry..." [What we would commonly term today as the "harp and bowl" ministry; see Revelation 5:8] "...that He would take care of our physical needs, and He would use our intercessions to birth tremendous moves of His power throughout the earth. So, since then, all of these years, four or five nights a week, from six until whenever — sometimes one or two in the morning — we just gather here and worship the Lord. Some of us work, and the Lord has permitted thousands of dollars to flow through us into the Kingdom, to support missionary works all over the world. We praise Him, we war in the spirit against demonic powers, and we share strategies from heaven to people to further His goals. We're a chosen covenant group."

She said it so simply, just stating the facts.

"Wow," was all I could stupidly offer in response.

Mrs. Metcalfe nodded and continued. "Several years ago, in a time of great intercession, one of us called out to the Lord — not in anger, but under His guidance — calling Him to remember that we had sacrificed so much, that we had given up our own ministries for this calling. We were always praying for other people, other ministries, other issues; but in all this time, we've only asked one thing just for ourselves in return from Him: that someone, a person from our hometown, would be sent forth into the world with a ministry that would inherit all of the prayers and supplications we have offered to Him. That this person would enter into all of the ministry expressions we gave up in order to minister to Him — an anointing to open His heart to the world. We had a vision of a fireball rolling down our mountain and splashing into the world around us. That's what we asked for: just one person to be that fireball."

Electricity sparked through my entire being as tears welled up in her eyes. She began to weep and stuck that finger out at me one more time.

"Jim," she cried, "*you* are that young man!"

Ladies and gentlemen, I want you to know, as she said these words, my knees slammed into the carpet, my face dropped into my hands, and I wept. This overpowering anointing smeared over me. I couldn't move; I couldn't speak. The humbleness of that moment is not something I am equipped to describe on the printed page. I have no words, and I am not artistic enough to tell you what was happening to me. This was the defining moment of my life. Everything that had happened to me had led me up to this one moment. It's the most astounding feeling in the world to know you are not worthy of such a calling; there is nothing in yourself that is "good enough" to receive such a grace gift. But here I was, crying like a child, while these men and women prayed over me, prophesying things I would do years and years later. Dreams and visions they had had for themselves that God would credit them for my works.

So now you know why I am the way I am. See, I can't go back now. I can't turn away from the supernatural. I don't do this for me; I do it for the Lord and to honor the Golden Candlestick. They receive their continued treasure and reward for my actions here on earth. In a way, I entered into *their* ministries. You have no idea how truly humbling that is. I never want to be the cause for their sadness.

After awhile — I don't know how long really — I heard Mrs. Metcalfe speaking to me. "There's a Bible college in Dallas that's undergoing tremendous revival. You're supposed to go there, to Christ for the Nations. God has some things He wants to work on you there."

"Yes, Ma'am," I muttered through the sobs.

I have kept up with the people of the Golden Candlestick throughout the years, telling them how this and that came to pass. The highlights of my ministry with the Lord — the things they prophesied over me. (And, no, not all of them have yet come to pass.) They met my wife. They met my children. They were my friends.

To the best of my knowledge, they've all passed on now. One of the last of that great ministry went home to be with the Lord several years ago. Her name was Dora. She was eighty something years of age. I was preaching at a church in California, and she came out to anoint me with a vial of oil — and I mean a whole *vial!* It ruined my expensive suit!

She blessed me, told me some things I won't share (it's personal) and then said, "Now I can go home and be with the Lord. Be faithful, Jim! Be faithful to impart our anointing to this generation as well as the next." Then she turned to walk away. She died just a short time later, peacefully in her sleep.

See, up until that point in time, I did not have the revelatory concept that the anointing of the Golden Candlestick was to be reproduced in the next generation of ministers. I had just simply walked in their anointing in my own ministry up until then. They were my inheritance.

But it's just been in recent years the Lord has conveyed to me that there is an apostolic impartation that's to go to this generation and the next. That is the motivation behind this book: that *you* would be released in this anointing! Dora and the Golden Candlestick challenged me to give their anointing to the next group of world-changers. I want *you* to have it! I hope that thought excites you as much as it excites me, dear friends!

I can't even begin to stress to you how important this recollection is. If the Holy Spirit does not bear something to your spirit, I'm not sure if you will be able to understand its intent. As the Golden Candlestick reproduced a measure of their anointing in me, I have been commissioned to reproduce a measure of that anointing in others, if they want it. That's why I'm writing this book. This experience is for you — to unveil an attribute of God's glory — to birth within you a sense of destiny that God has something for you to enter into. There is a level of experience with Him that He is just waiting to share, if you'll press into it. This is not about me; this is about you! I don't know what your calling is. I don't know if you're a plumber or a lawyer or an evangelist. But each of us is as important as the Golden Candlestick; each of us has a level of experience that we are to enter into and share with the world.

I learned from the Golden Candlestick that they were used by God to create a habitation of His presence, a hole in heaven, as it were, for God to visit them continuously, to share in their lives on a daily basis, not for just a season of time. That mountain in California was blessed for their sakes, in spite of all the witchcraft concentrated in that area. Like Jacob's Ladder in Genesis 28, there was a permanent link in that geographic area between heaven and earth. I believe the Father wants to establish more and more of these open-heavens all over the place. It comes from a revelation of His glory; it comes from Him building a habitation among His people.

CREATING A HABITATION

Get ready. This chapter, I think you will find, is rather "meaty." Like I said before, some chapters will be more inspirational. Others will require a bit of homework on your behalf; but if you'll plug in,

I'm convinced you'll find the next several pages very powerful in the formation of the apostolic spirit. So take a few moments to clear your head, grab a cup of coffee (or a soda, if you prefer) and open your hearts and Bibles to unveil further the glory of God.

The word *veil* comes from the Greek *kalupsis*, meaning "to hide, cover up or wrap up." The word *revelation* adds the Greek prefix *apo* to *kalupsis* (Strong's #602), thus implying "an unveiling or an unearthing." As in the Book of "Revelation" — or the "Apocalypse" — neat, huh?

This chapter will deal with unveiling the glory of God, revealing His greatness to the world. It comes partly when He builds a habitation among us, when an open-heavens is established. I am always thankful for visitations from God because I recognize it is His working with us to build a more permanent dwelling place among His people.

The long, very hard-to-spell Greek word *katoiketerion* (Strong's #2732; don't even *ask* me how to pronounce it!) means "abode" or "habitation" — a dwelling place. It's found in Ephesians 2:18-22 (remember the bit about the Householder's Anointing?)

From *katoiketerion*, we can extrapolate the following definition: "we have identified the talents and motivations in our lives, and the Holy Spirit has armed us with His fruit and His gifts, so that we go out into the world and reflect Jesus, as if He Himself was there ministering to people."

So what does that mean? Well, try this on: what you have *seen*, what you have *heard*, what you have *discerned*... you become like. You reflect Jesus and the way He ministered.

See why it's important to create a habitation for His presence?

Isaiah 66:1-2, "Thus says the Lord: 'Heaven is My throne, and earth is My footstool. Where is the house that you will build Me? And where is the place of My rest? For all those things My hand has made, and all those things exist,' says the Lord. 'But on this one will I look: on him who is poor and of a contrite spirit, and who trembles at My word.'"

God is posing some questions to us today. "Where is My habitation? Where is My place of rest? I am looking for a place to rest among you, so that I might express Myself to you. I want to give you My fullness; I want My favor upon you."

Remember the glory of the Lord is His favor, His reputation, resting upon us. It is the face of God turned toward us; we are accepted by Him and are found favorable in His sight. It is the Hebrew word *barak*, meaning "to be blessed" (Strong's #1288.) In the Book of Genesis whenever it says, "And God blessed them," that's the word that's used.

We are blessed by His glory. For an example, most of us know the Hebraic covenant compound name *Jehovah-Rapha* (*Yaweh-Ropheka.*) We translate that name for God as "I AM the Lord Who Heals You." (Exodus 15:26) It can be rendered "I AM God your Doctor/Physician." The notion of a doctor, to me, conveys a concept of one who waits on a sick person, nursing him back to health. Couldn't we just picture a doctor sitting by the bedside of an infirmed person, serving him until he recovered?

I believe we would be within the bounds of the scripture, then, to render *Jehovah-Rapha* as, "I, the Lord, will kneel down and extend healing to you," or "I will serve you with healing." The name takes on a slightly different meaning in that light, doesn't it? The point is that's blessing; that's favor. He will kneel down to serve us (in this case with healing.) That's His glory resting upon us.

We are to be made complete (Colossians 2:10) in His fullness of glory so that we might recover the fullness of the testimony of Jesus (See 1 Corinthians 1:6.) God is desirous to construct a permanent dwelling place for His glory among the apostolic people.

But I think we could all agree we are not experiencing His fullness in our current level of relationship with Him, right? It's not a depressing observation, but it does show us our need for a greater unveiling of His glory. An unveiling that provides a full measure of the manifestations of who He is, what He is all about. The better news is that we are being surrounded in the *circle* of God's deepest glory — the Apostolic Reformation is creating an unshakeable habitation of His presence among the people. There is a breaker-anointing coming forth to rend the veil between His home in heaven and ours here on earth.

His habitation comes from truly knowing who He is and having faith to know He is a keeper of His word. Faith can only operate when there is a revelation of God's true Person. A breaker anointing creates an environment for people to learn to believe His promises right out of their spirits, to discern the barriers before them and break them down.

I call this the *Parrhesia Principle*. This is the Greek word for "boldness" found in Acts 4:31. We'll share more about boldness in a later chapter. But for now, it is the opposite of cowardice, forged only from an unveiling of God's true glory freely given to His sons and daughters, not His slaves and illegitimate children. When the apostolic anointing tears that veil away from disbelieving people, they have a stunning recognition of their rightful place by His side, in Christ, where they have boldness to access the very Throne of God (Ephesians 3:2) and ask of their generous Father their inheritance and His unfettered blessing. *Selah.*

In Numbers 14, Moses' intercession on behalf of the iniquity of the people solidified his zeal in protecting the reputation of God — he was determined to show He is as good as He says He is! And we see in Verse 20 that He pardoned their sin, but there was still a cost — "You won't see My glory." You see, the sin may be forgiven, but if the problem is not corrected, it comes at the sacrifice of His dwelling among us. People can be forgiven, but it doesn't mean God is in their midst in the level He desires.

First Corinthians 16:13, in the original King James, contains one of the strangest phrases in all of scripture for our modern language. It says, "Quit ye like men." The new King James provides the translation, "Be brave." I thought about the original phrase for quite a bit. "Quit ye like men." What in the world does that mean?

It's as if God is saying, "Hey, don't pull your shoulder back from Me." Come on, act like men! Don't back away out of cowardice; be brave! Don't recoil. Like God is saying, "When I reach out to touch you, don't jerk back away from Me." Quit ye like men. I like that!

Do not allow your relapses into disbelief to keep you from the liberty that is found in God's touch. He is not some angry Taskmaster setting His hand to your shoulder to push you into heavy burden — it is with a Father's love that He is pulling you into a glory embrace. Don't pull away from Him. Quit ye like men!

Matthew 11:28-30 proclaims, "'Come to Me, all you who labor and are heavy laden, and I will give you rest. Take My yoke upon you and learn from Me, for I am gentle [meek] and lowly in heart, and you will find rest for your souls. For My yoke is easy and My burden is light.'" It is easy to carry His ark. His tasks are not too difficult to bear. Yes, He has something for you to accomplish, but it is with His hand on your shoulder all the way.

But Jesus needs you to respond properly; God can't use you if you pull away, as the Israelites had done, and our carcasses will be left in the Wilderness of Unfruitfulness, just as theirs.

I've found that some people only want to experience the supernatural upon death, like it's something out of their control, because to experience the supernatural here on earth demands a response. Let us not be one of these people.

LET NO ONE VEIL YOUR FACE

A key to apostolic anointing coupled with prophetic intercession can be found in Isaiah, "And He will destroy on this mountain the surface of the covering cast over all people, and the veil that is spread over all nations." (Isaiah 25:7)

In Exodus 34:29-35, we see that whenever Moses was in the presence of the Lord, his face would shine because of the glory, but when he spoke to the children of Israel, he would place a veil over his face. Why is this? Wouldn't they *want* to see the glory of the Lord revealed?

Paul gives insight into the matter in 2 Corinthians 3:12-18, "Therefore, since we have such hope, we use great boldness [there's that word again!] of speech — unlike Moses, who put a veil over his face so that the children of Israel could not look steadily at the end of what was passing away. But their minds were blinded. For until this day the same veil remains unlifted in the reading of the Old Testament, because the veil is taken away in Christ. But even to this day, when Moses is read, a veil lies on their heart. Nevertheless when one turns to the Lord, the veil is taken away. Now the Lord is the Spirit; and where the Spirit of the Lord is, there is liberty. But we all, with unveiled face, beholding as in a mirror the glory of the Lord, are being transformed into the same image from glory to glory, just as by the Spirit of the Lord."

I should just quote Paul for the rest of the book — that man was a genius in his speech!

My point, although not as earth moving as Paul's, is this: Don't let anyone veil your face! Don't let anyone's fear or religious doubts hinder you from responding to His glory. The traditions and institutions of men can bring us into religious bondages — it can be a source of control, and people fall under a curse of veiling.

There was a rather ugly altercation between Peter and Paul in Antioch, recorded in Galatians 2, because Peter hypocritically associated with Gentiles when no Jews were present, but reverted back to portions of the Law when Jews arrived. Paul, the well-manicured man that he was, called him on the carpet for it. Not so much out of spite, but because he knew that if Peter continued to allow the legalists to stifle his liberty, it would be at the expense of the glory that inhabited Peter's very shadow! (See Acts 5:15.)

The very next chapter of the same book (Galatians) shows more of Paul's wonderfully couth argumentation skills. We'll flesh out this subject more fully in a later chapter, but for now, read this scripture: "O foolish Galatians! Who has bewitched you that you should not obey the truth, before whose eyes Jesus Christ was clearly portrayed among you as crucified? This only I want to learn from you: Did you receive the Spirit by the works of the law, or by the hearing of faith? Are you so foolish?" (Galatians 3:1-3)

Nice! Apparently he didn't have to worry about being invited back to the church in Galatia the following year!

I'm writing in levity, but I want to point out seriously the word "bewitched" here. See, the Galatians were actually under a curse; they had been smitten with an Evil Eye of Substitution. This is the glazing of indifference to His presence that I mentioned earlier. The question you have to answer is, "Have I been bewitched? Have I veiled my face?" Just give it some thought. We'll talk more about bewitchment later on.

For now, do not let others' fears or religious doubts hinder you from responding or reacting to a manifestation of the Lord! We *need* His presence, completely unveiled, in order to know unquestionably the Living Word. Malachi 4:2 says this: "But to you who fear My name the Sun of Righteousness shall arise with healing in His wings; and you shall go out and grow fat like stall-fed calves."

Again, I researched that unusual epithet for the Messiah – the Sun of Righteousness – and discovered the Hebrew word *shemesh* (Strong's #8121.) *John Wesley's Explanatory Notes* points out shafts, or beams, of light; the rays of the Sun that have healing grace in them. So I pondered on that idea and came to render the phrase "healing in His wings" as connoting those beams, that when they shine out, they shine out in God's perfect, divine harmony, yielding a remedy or a cure to the sickened person. The Sun restores people back to healthy standing. The point is – other than I think it's a pretty cool concept – is the implication that anything in discord with God will be brought back into equilibrium and harmony when the Sun rises on the people.

Natural law desires homeostasis with every particular in the environment. In other words, there is a specific balance and order between every living thing. That's why politicians and scientists are concerned with ecosystems and global warming – other than for your vote or your money. These are manifestations that the environment is in discord. Now I won't comment on global warming or other such matters – they are not in the scope of this book. But I wanted to use these concepts to create a picture in your mind that just as in the natural, also in the spiritual. (See 1 Corinthians 15.) The point is our *spiritual* ecosystems can also fall out of alignment.

The enemy comes in to knock these particulars out of whack. This can range from physical diseases to mental or emotional deficiencies to financial depravation. Whatever it takes to knock the people out of alignment.

Apostolic people must recognize the need for harmony in their churches. But, as we are all painfully aware, so many churches are far from harmonious. The key is the healing rays of light that emanate out of the wings of the Sun of Righteousness — the glory of God manifested on the very floors of these discordant churches. Unity is only truly restored in the glory! I have a pretty good message on unity, if I say so myself. I'll highlight that a bit later on in the book.

But see, this is why we need the glory — the weightiness of God displayed! His glory brings conviction, permits a permanent change upon the people, as they yield to that weightiness. We are forged together in harmony, with one single purpose of mind. We enter into His presence; we pray, we worship, and He answers. A *change* comes in that encounter! The things that are out of order in our spiritual systems come into place.

Be wary of the accusations of the devil. One of his greatest ploys is to convince you that you'll never change. You're out of whack and you always will be. "Your daddy was a drunk and a hypocrite — so will you be! You'll always be inferior; God can't change you!" Don't allow a veiling on your personality to prohibit you for calling Him a God of His Word, incapable of lying. If He says He will change you from glory to glory in encounters with Him, you can be well-assured He means what He says.

But the moment you veil the glory, your mind becomes blinded, your heart becomes shrouded.

Now here's the statement that will cause no small stir... In this time of apostolic reformation, I believe the Lord has purposed that ministers who refuse to allow the glory to manifest, who prohibit the people from entering into those changing times with God, will fall dangerously against the will of Him and will come under the correction of the Lord. Eventually, those who still jerk their shoulders away from Him may be removed from their positions of authority altogether — I'm speaking of those who know what the better way is and still stifle it, not those who know no better.

Remember Revelation, where the Lamb speaks about removing their candlesticks? Where He tested their works and found out they were liars, false apostles? (Revelation 2:1-7) Apostles must demonstrate the glory of God — they cannot be lukewarm concerning His acts.

We, as leaders in the Spirit-filled Church, cannot allow any veiling to come upon our charges, lest we incur the displeasure of the One we serve. I'm preaching to myself as much as to anyone else — let us be admonished in the knowledge that God's glory will be manifested... with or without us.

Isaiah 40:5 says, "'The glory of the Lord shall be revealed, and all flesh shall see it together; for the mouth of the Lord has spoken.'" God is the only Being that can boast in Himself without the sin of pride. The revelation of the glory is God permitting Himself to show off to the world. I know that rings a few religious bells. But stay with me here.

God boasts in Himself when He unveils His character and His heart to all flesh — in essence, He "brags" of His greatness to the world. It's a rather strange concept to prideful people, but in all the existence of creation, who but the Creator has the right to sing His own praises? If You were the Source of all life, it would not be arrogance to revel in Your creations. Does that make sense?

See, God wants to show Himself off to you, to display His great worth among His prized possessions. He takes pride in His creations, and His glory descends to dance among us to boast of His greatness, but also to bring that which is out of order into synchronization as we work with Him.

We know the glory of God is His *kabod* — the resting of His reputation upon us. He desires to bear His weight down upon you. It's as if He's saying, "I'll bring down My worth upon you all." For God to be not only willing, but desirous, of bestowing such an honor must show that He holds His people in great favor.

"And they shall call them The Holy People, The Redeemed of the Lord; and you shall be called Sought Out, A City Not Forsaken." (Isaiah 62:12) See, we are a favored people, highly prized, and sought out.

I think we could say that God might define *glory* as, "My face is unveiled, and My heart is exposed, or revealed, to you." That is to say, His face is turned toward us in favor. The Greek word *doxa* (Strong's #1391 and #1380; recall the *Gloria Patri Doxology*: "Glory to the Father, Son and Holy Ghost...") means the honor of God placed upon a good opinion – His glory. In other words, God represents His reputation to the world through us. That's favor. We know from Chapter Three that God's glory is His reputation placed upon us. We know that Jesus in His earthly ministry manifested that reputation into reality. (See John 14.)

It bears repeating the question again: **Will you allow God's reputation to be seen upon you?** This is the crux of apostolic ministry. Will you be one of the Holy People, highly favored, with your God's face always turned toward you? Has His *doxa* found a person in which to reside?

"And it came to pass, when Moses entered the tabernacle, that the pillar of cloud descended and stood at the door of the tabernacle, and the Lord talked with Moses." (Exodus 33:9)

How highly favored!

Apostolic people desire the same level of favor in their lives and ministries. They say to themselves, "Boy, if I can just get under that cloud, anything and everything can happen! That's what *I* want!" The pillar of cloud represents the glory of God, come down to talk to His friends. "So the Lord spoke to Moses face to face, as a man speaks to his friend...." (Exodus 33:11) The key to the miraculous — what *we* want — is that favor of God found in His cloud of glory, where He speaks to us as friends!

Let's just simplify this all into one phrase most Charismatics are now familiar with: we want an open-heavens above us. I'll give an example of what I mean.

THE LOW-DESERT VISITATION

It was 1979 in the low desert of Southern California near my hometown that I had a major experience with an open-heavens. Of course, at that time, I don't think anybody was using the term "open-heavens"; but now that I look back on it, that's obviously what it was. I had been invited by a church to conduct a series of meetings for eight days, Sunday through Sunday.

The pastor was a dear man of God, but he had a piece of garbage car. I mean, friends, trust me when I say this automobile was fit to be taken behind the shed, shot in the head and buried. Time for an upgrade.

First off, I'm a tall guy — 6 foot 5, according to my driver's license — and this teeny tiny itty-bitty, little car was definitely prejudiced against taller people. It was about the size of a soup can. Maybe.

The pastor picked me up, and I thought, *There is* no way *I'm fittin' in that!* But somehow I folded up and *squeeezzzed* myself in. It was like one of those mini-cars that pull up in a circus and fifty clowns jump out, you know what I mean? So here I was — send in the clowns! Picture a Yugo, but not as classy. My knees were in the dash and under my chin at the same time. I suddenly became a contortionist.

The pastor thought it was funny. I didn't think so.

Well, so here we are, puttin' along at, like, seven miles an hour. I think the stupid car tried to die on us at least twice — and it's just *hot*. Low desert California — hot. The air conditioner coughed and sputtered, the engine whined, the dashboard hurt. Just not a spiritual setting at all. I'm praying over the car that it gets us in one piece to the church. *Come on, Betsy, you can make it!*

As we approached the facility, I notice this smoke start billowing up from the floorboard where my feet would have been, if I could've seen them. *Oh, great!* I thought. *The car's on fire. Perfect. We're gonna blow up out in front of the church!*

Let it never be said that James Maloney is always thinking on spiritual matters....

But it wasn't smoke — at least, not from the car. I was instantly caught up in the presence of God. Now, I don't know if the pastor saw the smoke. I didn't think to ask. But as we were coasting along, we both felt this incredibly enveloping glory of God fill the car. This smoke rolled upward filling the car, so much so that I could barely see out of the windshield. It was *that* thick.

I turned to look at him and asked, "Are you sensing this, too?"

He nodded. "Yeah." He had this huge grin on his face, and the car kind of weaved a little bit on the street. I rolled down the window, trying to get the smoke to dissipate, but it wouldn't waft away. I had a quick thought as we swerved along, *What if a cop sees all this smoke and the car weaving on the street? He's not going to know it's God. He's gonna think it's something* else! You know what I mean.... Luckily, no police saw us.

I don't know what the pastor's transcendent experience was, but I'm sure the Lord was ministering to him as well. The anointing and fragrance of the Lord were rolling thickly in with this smoke. We were both caught up in the anointing together.

The car puttered to within a couple hundred yards of the church building, and miraculously the smoke cleared just enough for me to see out the windshield. I looked at the church building directly ahead, and I had a vision.

This huge purplish, mushroom-looking cloudy pillar splashed down on the domed building. You may think that's weird, but that verse from Exodus 33:9 popped into my head. And I heard a voice speak from behind me.

I remember thinking, *Huh. That's weird. My face is in the windshield, this car's the size of a shopping cart, I have no idea how we even got the luggage in the trunk... how can this voice be coming from* behind *me? Lord, how can You fit in here?* I know, it's not a typical thought when one hears the voice of God, but it just came into my head. Sorry. I wish I could say I thought something really clever and spiritual. You know, "Speak, Lord, Your servant listens!"

Nope, instead I'm like, *Whoa, there's no way He can fit in this car! Where is He sitting?*

If the Lord caught onto my stupid line of thinking, He didn't make fun of me for it. Instead, He said, "For the next eight days, I am going to cause this place to become a habitation for My Spirit. And anyone who makes the attempt in faith to come under My resting will be saved, healed and delivered. No exceptions."

Verbatim, just like that. The voice was audible to me; I don't think the pastor heard it — he was caught up in his own experience.

Anyway, we didn't wreck, and the car actually made it to the church, so the services went on as planned.

It would take pages and pages of this book to describe what we saw over the course of the next eight days of meetings. It was more than just a visitation — it was a *habitation*. God dwelt among the people. See, all visitations are to lead to a habitation of God's Spirit, a true, established open-heavens. It was just an amazing, dramatic experience! There had been very little advertisement of the meetings, but it seemed like hundreds of people poured through those doors during the week.

It didn't really matter what a person was in need of. If they made the effort to enter the church, they were just simply healed. I remember there were several people healed of all manner of muscular dystrophies, cerebral palsies; missing organs were replaced; crippling conditions were reversed, teeth were filled. It was as if people just *blossomed* into their miracles — they just exploded into their healings. There were angelic encounters; the fragrance of the Holy Spirit could be smelled at times. Many people, when they were slain in the Spirit, would be out for two or three hours at a time. We just piled them over in the corner. It got to the point that people didn't want you even to lay hands on them because they didn't want to be slain in the Spirit and miss out on seeing what God was doing.

I recall one particular lady with grotesquely deformed feet. There was a group of Vineyard teenagers and young people that gathered around her, and as they ministered to her, a three inch by two-inch beam of light would flick on an area of her feet and then wink off after fifteen seconds. Where the light tracked, it left behind perfectly formed feet. Then it flicked to another section of her feet, and that area became whole. It was mind-boggling!

People with crushed, mangled limbs were made whole. Deformities were corrected with an audible *snap!, crackle!, pop!* I remember one lady whose elbow was twisted around the wrong way, sitting on top of her arm. It moved back to its proper position in front of everyone's eyes!

Another person was afraid to have her teeth pulled, but they were rotting away. So the Lord replaced them with brand new teeth. In fact, many people had their teeth filled, not with gold or silver, but with entirely new teeth. That's a strange sight to behold!

I saw Jesus appear in the room once, just to receive the worship and praise of His saints. Angels came and went on a few occasions. There was this sensation of falling rain in the sanctuary — like you were getting wet, but you weren't. Everything was so creative. People would sob and laugh, sit in utter silence and humility, praise God with a loud, boisterous voice. It all happened during that eight-day period. It was just an open-heavens.

I told the people that anyone who made an attempt in faith to enter into His habitation would be saved. One couple took my statement to heart. Their teenage son had placed locks on his bedroom door at home. So, they went upstairs and broke down the door, hog-tied him, gagged him, threw him in the back of the car, chucked him into the foyer of the church, untied him and ran off.

He came tearing into the sanctuary, bellowing, "I'm gonna kill this preacher!"

I remember chuckling to myself, 'cause he was, what, five-foot nothing, 140 pounds soaking wet? Yeah, OK. You know I'm six-five and I weigh....

Well, I won't tell you what I weigh....

Suffice to say, I was a lot bigger than him. I thought, *Kid, you ain't gonna kill me; I'm gonna squash you with my thumb!*

But I didn't need to squash him. He ran up to the front and got KO'd by the Spirit. He started spittin' and sputterin', these demons screaming out of him. Then he came to and got saved. It was what I call one of those "snotty conversions." You know the kind I mean, where the person's blubbering and asking forgiveness, wiping their nose on their sleeve.

It was just that kind of week.

Anyway, at the end of the eight days, the cloud lifted. I went on to my next set of meetings thinking, *I have arrived!* But the services, while still good and the Lord moved among the people, they just weren't of the same caliber. I became concerned and went into prayer to ask the Lord how come that desert experience wasn't the norm.

I mean, since that time I have been blessed to be a part of seasons like that. Throughout the years, there have been periods — two, three, four weeks at a time — where the habitation of God's Spirit stayed in that measure; where it seemed that everyone was healed, everyone was saved, everyone was delivered. But after a time, it would lift.

And after that first visitation in California, I became worried something was wrong, but the Lord spoke to me and said, "There will come a time that My habitation will become a regular occurrence, not only in your ministry, but in My Church as a whole. The people are being prepared for this type of resting of My presence. It is coming."

I hope that this book will facilitate that habitation, that it encourages the people to expect the beginning of that time of His resting. The apostolic people are starting to understand the authority and power needed to see that kind of visitation on a regular, consistent basis. It's an exciting time to be in the Lord's house!

THE PILLAR DREAM

Here's another encounter relating to an open-heavens. I had a very vivid, supernatural dream from God a few years ago. Keep in mind, it was a dream. I don't have them very often, but when they do come, I can always tell it's more than just a normal dream. My spirit leaps within me; everything is crystal clear and vibrant. And I immediately awaken from the dream, praying in tongues, and I can remember it exactly, as if I was watching a movie in my mind.

Anyway, in this dream I'm standing in a church of about 300 people (I don't think it's a real church I'll be in, but rather more of a symbol) and as I often do, I step down among the people to minister.

You'll have to realize, my ministry is conducted with love; but it also confrontational because many times I'll call people to step out as an act of faith, to create an expectation to receive. Because I'm a big guy, and I tend to intimidate people, I have to minister in a very natural, often humorous, way. It disarms them and allows them to hear what God is saying. It's something I've learned over the years.

In my early days, I'd put on these spooky, prophet's eyes — you know, like that one astronaut from the old *Outer Limits* episode who lives in the cave? *Those* eyes. I found it just freaked people out. Folks would scamper out the back door. You know, being serious all the time, whipping my head around, tiptoeing up and down the stage steps.... *What is God revealing to me about you now? Mwahaha!*

Thank God I've grown a bit since then, eh?

He taught me just to be myself, act naturally. So I started telling jokes while I was preaching, having a bit of fun. Because it should be fun. God's a pretty fun Person, if you think about it.

I mean, He made you, right?

Moving right along.

I believe a word of knowledge or wisdom or a prophecy can create an environment of faith for the other people in the congregation to receive as well. So I make an example, as it were, by calling certain people forward. Obviously, if I know nothing about the person called forward, and the Lord is sharing specific details about their situations, it creates faith in others to receive their miracles with or without my influence. A lot of the miracles we've heard about come from people entering into their own encounter with the Lord apart from me. And that's just fine. Saves me the time and energy!

If I'm in a room with a couple thousand people, there is no physical way for me to lay hands on them all. So I'll call out fifteen or twenty or more with unique or specific words, and this sends out a breaker anointing over the entire congregation, then the Spirit moves in a mega way among them all.

OK, so back to my dream. I stepped down into the people and called one lady forward, placing my hand on her forehead, like I often do. I heard a voice behind me — I don't know why it's always speaking behind me — but anyway, the voice said, "Look up, My son."

I looked up and I saw this golden pillar of anointing descend down upon both me and this sister in the Lord. What was so neat about this pillar was it wasn't hollow. It was thick, not like a tube, but like a roll. It didn't just cover us, it went through us. Everyone else in the congregation disappeared because the pillar was so thick. The thought came to me that there was nothing from the outside that could penetrate this cloud to distract me; and because it was going through me, there was nothing from the inside that could inhibit its flow. I had this sensation that I was so under the control of the Spirit that whatever would flow out of my spirit, whatever words that bubbled out, I could speak with confidence and know it was from God. I felt incredibly bold.

So I began to share with this dear lady what her condition was, where she was from, what had traumatically happened to her several years earlier (it was a car accident.) It was the most specific word I'd ever given, and it just rolled out of my spirit for about a minute or so. She was weeping, and things were breaking off of her, and she was set free.

As soon as all of that was exhausted out of my spirit, the pillar lifted. We were both glowing. She returned to her seat, praising God. I then called out a man, and the exact same thing happened again. The pillar came down, crashed through both of us, I gave this powerfully specific word, he was set free, and then the pillar went back up.

I came out of this dream and asked the Lord what it meant. He responded — behind me again, "There will come a time in your ministry with Me that this will be normal. Once you are prepared for it, My reputation and glory will rest upon you like the pillar, but you have to know Me."

One of the premises of this book is that any visitation, dream or revelation I have had with God can be translated into something for anyone else to understand and experience for themselves, at least to a certain extent. These moments with God can be released, transferred, reproduced or imparted to the Body on a corporate level. I don't believe God gives supernatural experiences for just that one person only, with no expectation that at least some level of the experience can be shared by all saints. I am convinced this level of God's anointing is for all people who are properly prepared to know Him on the deepest levels. I know that you can expect to pursue a similar, if not exact, encounter on your own, if you want to. There is a need for discipline, and there is a price to pay, but I promise you it's worth it.

THE OPEN-HEAVENS ABOVE JESUS

Understanding a habitation as a key to the miraculous can be found in the ministry of Jesus on this earth. John 1:51 quotes Jesus as saying, "...'Most assuredly, I say to you, hereafter you shall see heaven open, and the angels of God ascending and descending upon the Son of Man.'"

Nearly everyone can quote John 3:16 — we're all so familiar with it, but look at it from this light: God so loved the world that He gave His Son, resplendent in His favor and glory, to reveal His [the Father's] reputation to the world. Wherever Jesus walked, the heavens were opened above Him — He was in constant communication with

His Father. It was not until His crucifixion that Jesus ever knew a moment of separation from His Father in heaven — the time in which God poured all sin upon Jesus' body and looked away. It was only at this moment that Jesus cried out, "My God, My God, why have You forsaken Me?" (Matthew 27:46, Mark 15:34, Psalm 22:1) The key to the miraculous is to have the heavens opened above us, where we delight in constant communication with the Father, and His angels descend and ascend upon us, just as Jacob dreamed of the ladder in the sky. (Genesis 28:12) This is the principle of the open-heavens, and Jesus is our great Example.

The purpose of salvation, of Christ coming down from heaven, was not only just for everlasting life after we die. Don't misunderstand, that *is* the main purpose for Christ's coming — to restore righteousness to people and to restore communication with the Father. But it was also to create a permanent link between heaven and earth for those who were saved by Christ's descending and ascension. It was His crucifixion and resurrection that provided saving grace, but His coming and going to and from heaven showed an example of heaven being opened to all who were in Him. Does that make sense?

John 3:13 records a very strange declaration of Jesus'. "'No one has ascended to heaven but He who came down from heaven, that is, the Son of Man who is in heaven.'"

Uh, excuse me, what? Huh? Have you ever read that? How is it that Jesus can say He came *down* from heaven... Who *is* in heaven? It's as if He was saying, "I'm standing here on earth, and I'm also standing in heaven." How could He be in two places at the same time? Because Jesus was always standing under an open-heavens. His Father was constantly revealed to Him; there was no veil separating Him from God. So He was in heaven, standing on earth. That's why He only did what He *saw* the Father do *in heaven.* (John 5:19) He came down to earth and was in heaven. Wherever He went He took heaven with Him.

When Jesus ministered on the earth, the heavens that for centuries had been closed by mankind's rationalization of the supernatural, his religiosity, his legalism and apostasy, were opened once again. Do any of these hindrances to an open-heavens sound like things you might have heard of in your church today? I'm guessing so.

So Jesus went around, handing out heaven. What an amazing thought! Heaven was like a cloud that came down and encircled Jesus; everywhere He went it was opened to Him, so He handed it out to others. Jesus spoke out of heaven; He healed out of heaven; He ministered to the needy out of heaven. The glory of God that was reserved for the heavens (remember Chapter Three?) was doled out to the earth, through Jesus the Conduit. And, then, are we not to follow after Jesus?

"And I heard a loud voice from heaven saying, 'Behold, the tabernacle of God is with men, and He will dwell with them, and they shall be His people. God Himself will be with them and be their God.'" (Revelation 21:3) By aligning ourselves with Christ, we have access to an open-heavens, where God Himself is with us; and He brings great favor and glory with Him.

The purpose of the apostolic spirit, in my mind, is to recover the miraculous first and foremost. I trust that I've shown throughout the course of this book, that apostolic people are much more than just miracle-workers, but it is one of the most sorely unused attributes of apostolic anointing. The point of this entire book is to present keys to the Kingdom of Heaven, dominion tools of power that unveil the fullness of God's character.

In that passage of scripture that reveals Christ as the anointed Son of God, He commends Simon — renamed Peter — for allowing his spirit to receive that unveiling from the Father. He rewards the disciple for his revelation. "'And I will give you the keys of the kingdom of heaven, and whatever you bind on earth will be bound in heaven, and whatever you loose on earth will be loosed in heaven.'" (Matthew 16:19)

Thayer's definition of "heaven" in the original Greek *ouranos* (Strong's #3772) speaks of *heavens*, in the plural. So one could extrapolate literally the keys of the heavens, implying that there are deeper levels of the Spirit we are to uncover. Indeed, levels of heaven. I think that's kind of neat to ponder for a bit.

Jesus was saying, "Whatever you prohibit on this earth, I will back you up and prohibit it in heaven; and whatever you permit on this earth, then I'll open the heavens to you and send it down." There are two very powerful keys to the Kingdom presented here: binding and loosing.

Charismatics, as a whole, are very familiar with binding. We bind just about everything. The power behind binding is to tie up the operations of the enemy, making them of no consequence. We gum up the works, as it were, of the devil by paralyzing his activities in a particular situation. If you've ever been in a Charismatic service for any length of time, chances are you've heard a minister say, "We bind you in the name of Jesus," while praying over a person's illness. And that's awesome in the proper context of use!

The victory that Jesus won on our behalves permits us to operate in His kind of power to bind the strongman and plunder his house — we cannot neglect this facet of ministry, but remember that *two* keys (binding and loosing) were presented to us in tandem. Binding must also be combined with the loosing of the Spirit — this breeds the miraculous. As a rule, Charismatics have stressed too much on the binding and not enough on the loosing. This attitude does not permit a dominion mentality to be cultivated in the Church as a whole. The movings of the Spirit (loosing) are found in apostolic reformation so that the binding might become complete.

The bottom line is we need more loosing! That's where the apostolic people come in.

Often, we harp on the binding and neglect the loosing. We need both operating in perfect unison, one as much as the other. Jesus' ministry heralded a profound sense of binding the enemy but also loosing the Kingdom among the people. Follow Him!

Again, 1 Corinthians 1:6 speaks of confirming the testimony of Christ. The apostolic movement has come to recover the fullness of that testimony in not only binding the enemy but loosing the Spirit over the people. Revelation 19:10 says, "…'I am your fellow servant, and of your brethren who have the testimony of Jesus. Worship God! For the testimony of Jesus is the spirit of prophecy.'"

What does that mean, "spirit of prophecy"?

The testimony of Jesus is that "now!" word — relevant right *now*, this moment, today — spoken now and energized to confirm the fullness of God in His signs, wonders and miracles. Prophecy yields Holy Spirit-inspired activity (acting in boldness), calling forth the loosing of God. Speaking forth, proclaiming our rights. Prophecy releases the Dancing Hand to minister to the people. It is the testimony of Jesus in expression — the pinnacle of the apostolic release. Prophecy is an important aspect of apostolic ministry.

Without it, the Church is plagued with incomplete victories, half-wins. We bind, but there is no loosing. It is the loosing that administers the Spirit to the needy, the Spirit who works miracles on the people's behalves. Remember the church in Galatia, smitten with the "evil eye" of bewitchment — they were experiencing a mirage, a glazing of indifference based on a legalistic, religious apathy toward the movings of God, which yielded a substitute for His anointing. They were bound and not loosed.

We can, each of us, probably think of churches with similar motivations today. These poor churches, while meaning to be completely sincere, can sometimes quash the loosing of the Spirit by replacing the Spirit of Prophecy with a spirit of religion, maintaining the "status quo" through a spell of enchantment that discourages people from breaking into Christ's freedom and the activities of God (the miraculous) and ultimately fails to meet the people's needs. Wow! Now that's an *awesome* statement, if I do say so myself....

It may be a strong statement, but hopefully one that wakes the people up to see our inequalities in implementing the keys of the Kingdom. The apostolic anointing exists to push people into a greater move of the manifestations of God's glory. We all need an unveiling of the need for His weightiness to press down upon us! We need the proof of His authority revealed to us!

THE *DUNAMIS* PRINCIPLE

I call it the *Dunamis* Principle. *Megadunamis* (Strong's #3173 and #1411) is a compound word for "great power" — being found in Acts 4:33. Think of *dynamic, dynamo, dynamite*. We should all recognize the prefix *mega*, as in mega-detergent, megavitamins, mega-churches, mega-bucks. *Megadunamis* is explosive power — excessive energy. More than enough to complete the job. It is power that has the ability to reproduce itself, to make *more* power. *Dunamis* in function is the expression of a release of authority. It is the release of a measure of influence or rule over a particular situation. It is the power to command. For example, if you say you have a healing ministry, then you exercise the *dunamis* to minister healing to the sick. Or, say, prophecy; you claim to have a prophetic ministry and then back it up with prophetic power. The same can be said of apostolic ministry.

Look at Elisha in 2 Kings 2. Here his predecessor, Elijah, is about to be taken up to heaven in a whirlwind. Elijah asks Elisha to tarry in Gilgal, for he must go on to Bethel. Of course, Elisha refuses, and they go together. The same thing happens again when Elijah must go to Jericho, but Elisha demands to come with him. Then a third time, at the banks of the Jordan River, Elijah asks Elisha to remain behind. The answer is the same; and when the two prophets reach the river, Elijah takes his mantle, smacks the water with it and the two cross over on dry land. Then Elijah asks a very pertinent question of his successor.

"Ask! What may I do for you, before I am taken away from you?"

To which Elisha deftly replies, "Please let a double portion of your spirit be upon me."

"You have asked a hard thing. Nevertheless, if you see me when I am taken from you, it shall be so for you; but if not, it shall not be so." (Verses 9-10)

That translation of "hard thing" is somewhat vague. Literally, Elijah replied, "You have asked for a *rare* thing...." (See *John Wesley's Explanatory Notes* and *John Gill's Exposition.*) The word really means a "stiff-necked" thing (Strong's #7185.) He wasn't chiding Elisha for asking for the double portion, just merely stating, "Hey, that's a great thing to ask for, but a lot of people don't get it..." Concerning that phrase, Matthew Henry in his *Concise Commentary* says, "Those are best prepared for spiritual blessings that are most sensible of their worth and their own unworthiness to receive them." In other words, it was between Elisha and God if Elisha was to receive the double portion. It wasn't up to Elijah; it was up to Elisha.

I wrote all of that because I've heard some say "hard thing" is proof that the anointing is not for everyone. But in reality, the hard thing is an *essential* thing we need to ask for, and we have to be willing to do what it takes on our end to receive it from God.

Anyway, we know how the story goes: Elisha does indeed see Elijah snatched away in a whirlwind to heaven. He then retrieves the mentor's mantle, goes to the Jordan banks again, smacks the water and with great authority, rhetorically asks, "Where is the Lord God of Elijah?" The water splits, and he crosses over again on dry land.

Elisha inherited a rare, but essential, thing — a double portion of authority, what apostles might call *megadunamis*. The apostolic spirit dwells in this expression of great power. We, too, must persevere as Elisha did, not tarrying, but pressing on to the waters of Jordan, desiring to receive the mantle of God's authority. Remember 2 Corinthians 12:12; the signs of the apostles are signs, wonders and mighty deeds with all perseverance. This is a great concept, but let's take a look at the flipside. So if one claims an apostolic unction but has no *dunamis* to back it up, are they not of questionable authority? I'll let that one settle in a moment.

OK, I'm back. Have I lost anyone yet? I hope not. I'm not trying to attack anyone's sincere beliefs here — we are all striving towards the mark of the highest calling. No one has achieved perfection yet; and me most of all, I can honestly say, because I *live* with myself, so I would know! But it doesn't negate the standard that God is raising up for us to congregate around. The apostolic anointing must be given free rein to exercise power and authority in the miraculous — it is the only way to bind and loose completely, releasing the keys of the Kingdom of the Heavens and unveiling the glory of God.

So anyway, back to Peter's revelation of Christ as the anointed Son of God (Matthew 16:13-19.) I want you to note upon what *rock* Christ will build His Church — what foundation this entire movement called Christianity is supposed to be based upon. I know we all read it as meaning Peter, the founder of the "Church" (even the first Pope for the Catholics.) His name does indeed mean "little stone" (*petros*), but Jesus substituted *petra* (BIG rock) for *petros* (a fragment of rock) when talking about the foundation of His Church. So Peter is just one part. We also take it to mean Jesus referring to Himself, as the Rock of the Church. And that's true as well. But read Jesus' conversation with Peter in its whole context.

The rock of the Church is the revelation that Jesus is the anointed Son of God, right? Upon *this* rock — "You are the Christ, the Son of the living God" — is what Jesus builds His Church upon. Remember Chuck Flynn's teaching that I mentioned in Chapter Three? "The *anointing* comes upon you, so that you will *discipline* yourself, so that you can *speak creatively* to set the captives free." It is *this* revelation of the anointing upon Christ that Peter had.

What did Jesus give to Peter, the very next sentence after "on this rock..."? The keys to bind and loose. It is the revelation of the rock that gives the keys to the Kingdom. It is as if Jesus had said, "You have revealed My anointing. I have given you the keys to release that anointing on the earth." This is the apostolic spirit found in the fullness of God's glory. This is the miraculous.

Now, it has been taught that miracles can be placed into four main categories: *mega, notable, diverse* and *special*. We talked a bit about mega and special miracles earlier, but now is as good a place as any to delve a little bit deeper. These four types of miracles are staple attributes of an open-heavens. That doesn't mean they can *only* happen in an open-heavens, but if you see these kinds of operations, they generally relate to an open-heavens. It's worth talking about apostolic miracles and their functions.

Mega miracles come from the word *megadunamis*, which we defined earlier. It means miracles on a mega scale. Simple enough, huh? *Megadunamis* means excessive power, great power, power and then some more power, so much so that it spills over to other people. So, we could say that if one miracle is recorded in scripture and *megadunamis* is used, it could mean there was enough power and authority present in that one miracle to heal dozens, hundreds, even thousands. That's not too far of a leap, right? I mean, the miracles that Jesus worked were mega. If He healed one person of blindness, then a hundred could potentially have been healed, right? There would be no way to itemize all of Christ's miracles in one book, so the authors of scripture often used *megadunamis* to describe His works. It can speak of mass healings. If you've ever been to a miracle service where, say, dozens of crippling conditions were healed at once, that's mega miracles.

Notable miracles can be found in Acts 4. These are miracles that catch the attention of the media, of the opponents of truth, the critics. The kinds of miracles that don't leave any room for nay saying. "Thirty seconds ago, I didn't have an arm, and now I do." That's notable. The secular people stop and take note of what just happened. Get it? Take note — notable.

Next are diversities of miracles. The New King James translates it as "various miracles" in Hebrews 2:4. It falls under the "diversities of gifts" in 1 Corinthians 12:4. Just as God is many-sided in His nature, capable of an infinite range of emotion and expression, His miracles are diversified like the colors of a rainbow, each bleeding into the other with varying degrees of articulation.

I have heard it taught before that to come in contact with diversities of miracles creates an astonishment among the participants. That these diverse miracles create a celebration atmosphere, an excitement at God's wondrous, varied nature. People whoop and holler when they see them. I think that's a pretty neat concept.

Could we go one step farther and say "diversities of gifts" creates a sense of outrageous joy and festivity? Perhaps it's not too far of a stretch to say "diversities of gifts" is a party with God in miracles.

Bet you that slays some religious cows there, doesn't it?

But think about it, is that not what occurs when God's hand dances among the people? Are they not moved to frivolity, merriment, and fiesta-ing? I know that's not a word, but you get the point. I was at a Spanish miracle service that was called *Noche de Celebracion* (Night of Celebration.)

It's the same as diversities of tongues found in the Book of Acts, chapter two. The people who saw the faithful come down from the Upper Room thought they were drunk. It wasn't just what they heard, it's what they *saw*. The indwelling of the Holy Spirit created an intoxication wherein the apostles and those gathered with them were celebrating God's presence, partying in tongues. That's diversities of miracles, people jamming in the streets in celebration of God's wondrous acts. You probably hear that Lionel Richie song from the '80s playing in your head, don't you?

Lastly, and probably most significant to the mark of an open-heavens, are special miracles. In Acts 19:11-20, God wrought special miracles (translated as "unusual" miracles in the New King James) by the hand of Paul that tore down the seductive spirit surrounding Ephesus. Special miracles are the covering of God in a local area. As Dick Mills said in *A Word in Season, Volume One,* "The thing stressed here is the geographical location involved." (page 67; Harrison House, Tulsa, Oklahoma, 1986)

The Greek words *ou* and *tugchano* (Strong's #3756 & #5177) translate as "special." It's interesting to me because *ou* is a double negative, as in "absolutely no, most certainly not." *Tugchano* can imply "happening by chance." So *ou-tugchano* means "absolutely no, certainly not happening by chance." I've heard it rendered "extraordinary, extraordinary." Therefore, "special" or "unusual." That's powerful in the Greek, isn't it?

In Acts 19, the word "special" applies to a specific, geographic location: Ephesus. You have to understand that Ephesus, in that time, was laboring under a very seductive, enchanting spirit due to the people's worship of a goddess called Diana. This pagan goddess required acts of idol worship in the form of perversion, debauchery, lasciviousness, sexual immorality. They were used to "feeling" things in the flesh, if you catch my drift. It was a spirit that created a false image of God, leading to faulty worship. Thus, it took something special to break that enchantment off of them, something truly powerful to rise above the noise, if you will, of that town.

Something was extended in the local proximity or vicinity of Ephesus that was beyond measure. Special miracles are those which are taken to the people. I might define them as miracles that "obtain or secure a region" or perhaps "object to and end a particular spiritual regime."

Thayer's Greek Definitions, #2181, defines the word "Ephesus" as meaning "permitted." A Greek legend says that Hercules "permitted" the Amazons to reside in the city, although that's probably not from where the city literally took its name. But it's interesting to think that from a spiritual standpoint, Ephesus could mean "dealing with strongholds" or rather "what is and what is not permitted." The special miracles wrought by Paul did not "permit" the enchantment of Diana to stand.

It was the manifestation of the supernatural acts worked by God through Paul that succeeded in breaking the hold off the people of Ephesus. The key to note here is that it was the *miracles* themselves that were used as weapons of warfare against the Diana spirit. The supernatural encounters themselves awakened the people into an awareness of God's true authority over some idol. They literally *felt* something happening under the hands of Paul — a manifestation of true virtue that was translated into their warped five senses and brought clarity.

The people could physically feel some dramatic sign and wonder, a presence, a breaker anointing that spawned deliverances. I believe it *shocked* the people into spiritual understanding. Acts 19 goes on to show that they brought their amulets, charms, various articles and books and burned them at the feet of Paul. Something was unveiled, and they understood. There was something established there, a covering of God.

Now, Paul tells us to mimic him as he mimicked Christ. (1 Corinthians 11:1) Should we not also be used of God to bring about special miracles? What if special miracles happened in your town? Would Chicago become an Ephesians church? How about London? Or Tokyo?

See, the Golden Candlestick, in the midst of the great perversion surrounding that mountain town, stood as an open-heavens against the demonic. What made them so unique and so effective were the special miracles they were used to bring about. These were miracles for that specific geographic location that broke the stranglehold of the occult and quite literally punched a hole into the heavens, as it were. A spiritual Jacob's ladder was established over my hometown, and the effects (read blessings) of those miracles still reverberate there to this day.

The town is blessed, in spite of its gross darkness, not just only on the Golden Candlestick's behalves; but also because of the continuing work of another dynamic ministry that has purposed to enter into all of the fullness of the open-heavens that God desires. Dear friends of mine, Kristine and Wade Bandelin, head up Shiloh Ministries there in my hometown. They're a valuable asset to that community, and they've been very faithful to seeing God move in that area. If you ever take a vacation up there, make sure you stop in and say hello!

In Genesis 28, Isaac blessed his son Jacob and charged him to return to the place where Abraham first called upon the Lord, Bethel. When Jacob returned to that specific geographic area, he triggered something that had already been established by his grandfather. It was here he had the dream of the hole in heaven and the ladder ascended into the place of God.

It's not just that everywhere we go, we take God with us. Of course that's true. We know that we have the right to call upon His name wherever we are, and He will intervene on our behalves. But there is also a concept of a specific location that marks a special place for God to come down to earth, in a fashion.

Something can be established, something special, like what occurred through Paul in Ephesus. That congregation became one of the most revelatory churches in Asia Minor, alongside some of the others, obviously.

Even though Paul was ministering to individuals, something was happening to the culture of the town. People were seeing some kind of manifestation under his hands that when each individual was delivered, when the demon power was broken off of them, it did warfare in the atmosphere and famished the gods those people worshipped. (See Zephaniah 3.) The gods were starved of the worship that fed their satanic influence. It threw down the powers of the air and purged the heavens, opening them up.

Dear readers, it's the miracle manifestation through the breaker anointing of the apostle and apostolic people that opens up the heavens!

It's not just binding the stronghold through things like prayer mapping and prayer walks. Don't misunderstand, I think those are needed, too. But allow me to share a word of caution about them: be extremely wise and careful that you are mandated by God to, say, go stand on a mountain in Nepal and bind the spirit of that land. That's a very special calling, to have that kind of authority and power. One needs a *rhema* word to go do something like that. If you are not under the protection and unction of the Lord, you can become a target for powerful spiritual beings you were never meant to deal with in the first place. I have seen it cause severe problems for some people.

I'll be honest here; there's not a whole lot of scriptural precedence for that kind of binding. Notice that Daniel didn't deal with the principality of the kingdom — he simply focused on the Lord in prayer and fasting. It was the archangel Michael who fought the Prince of Persia. (See Daniel 10.) I'm just saying, put more focus on establishing an open-heavens in your area rather than picking a fight with a ruler of darkness in a wicked place. Wisdom. Be more concerned on loosing the Spirit over a people group! The power of God is inherent simply in preaching the gospel. Just preach the gospel of the Kingdom, administer healing in a breaker anointing and God will confirm His Word — and *He'll* deal with the big demonic rulers as He sees fit. I'm convinced this is where the emphasis should be: in preaching the gospel, seeing the miracles and that will cast down the principalities.

Anyway, back to the point; there is a biblical principle in special miracles creating an open-heavens in a particular place. I believe there will be many places all over the world that will be praise and worship centers — like the Golden Candlestick — with harp and bowl intercessors, people that are established in the watch of the Lord. (Isaiah 62:6) Through their intercessions, high praise and devotions to God the Golden Candlestick established a special link in that mountain community that even today sensitive people can sense the residual anointing effects of their ministry.

Special miracles create an open-heavens, a window, a door or a portal, if you will, opened in that area where God is doing something very singular. It's not just the binding, but it's the loosing that is the emphasis of the miraculous — that is what is used as weaponry to cripple the forces of darkness. Look at Exodus 7-11. We call these the Ten Plagues of Egypt, but really they're special miracles.

It took those plagues to break the enchantment of that spirit off the Egyptians. Let's be realistic. God could have killed Pharaoh the first time he denied Moses the freedom of the Israelites, right? But each of those ten miracles was used to pull down and strip bare the gods the Egyptians worshipped. See, He was dealing judgment against the demons that the Egyptians deified. For instance, the Egyptians worshipped frogs. So God was saying, "You wanna worship frogs? OK. I'll give you frogs. I'll give you frogs up to your armpits!"

Special miracles.

Again, it's the operation of the miraculous that opens the heavens. I don't want to sound mystical here — it's not always just for a specific place. Remember, you can call upon the Lord anywhere for you are the people of God, and He is with us wherever we go. But I want to stress that it takes the apostolic ministry to realize open-heavens kinds of miracles. This is why the apostles have to move in a breaker anointing, to punch a hole, if you mind, through that canopy of darkness and let the heavens be revealed. (See Isaiah 25.)

ANOTHER JESUS?

All apostolic miracles deal with the veilings of deceptions. They are gifts given as extensions of who God is to overcome the distorted views of deceived people; they are given to unveil the Personage of God. The enemy attempts to veil Jesus as the Christ. It attempts to suppress the revelation of the breaker anointing and limit an experience in Him. It tries to convince the people that Jesus has changed. That He is another Person. But "Jesus Christ is the same yesterday, today, and forever." (Hebrews 13:8)

Verse 9 goes on to say, "Do not be carried about [away] with various and strange doctrines...." Thus implying it is *strange* and *variant* to say Christ has changed. Beware of this doctrine! Any doctrine that tells you Christ was one way in the past but is not that way now is a strange doctrine you are *not* to be carried away with. If He healed 2,000 years ago; He heals today. If He cast out demons 2,000 years ago; He casts them out today. It's as simple a premise as that.

But that is the work of the enemy — the veilings of deception: that there is another Jesus, or another gospel, or another spirit.

"But even if our gospel is veiled, it is veiled to those who are perishing, whose minds the god of this age has blinded, who do not believe, lest the light of the gospel of the glory of Christ, who is the image of God, should shine on them." (2 Corinthians 4:3-4)

"But I fear, lest somehow, as the serpent deceived Eve by his craftiness, so your minds may be corrupted from the simplicity that is in Christ. For if he who comes preaches another Jesus whom we have not preached, or if you receive a different spirit which you have not received, or a different gospel which you have not accepted — you may well put up with it!" (2 Corinthians 11:3-4)

It takes a manifestation of the truth — a truth that exhibits a virtue — to unveil this deception. Second Corinthians 4:2 states, "But we have renounced the hidden things of shame [iniquities], not walking in craftiness nor handling [adulterating] the word of God deceitfully, but by manifestation of the truth commending ourselves to every man's conscience in the sight of God."

"'And you shall know the truth, and the truth shall make you free.'" (John 8:32)

A lack of the supernatural creates a vacuum wherein the truth is not manifested, and a wrong concept of God emerges — it is a "form of godliness." (2 Timothy 3:5) But in reality God is not heard and seen as how He truly is. There is no proper demonstration of God — He *is* love, He *is* peace, He *is* joy, He *is* healing, etc. This form of godliness can potentially become idolatry, dear readers! Demons distort and change the image of God, so that the deceived worship *it* instead of *Him*.

"...Because, although they knew God, they did not glorify Him as God, nor were thankful, but became futile in their thoughts, and their foolish hearts were darkened... and [they] changed the glory of the incorruptible God into an image made like corruptible [perishable] man — and birds and four-footed animals and creeping things... [They] exchanged the truth of God for the lie, and worshiped and served the creature rather than the Creator, who is blessed forever. Amen. And even as they did not like to retain God in their knowledge, God gave them over to a debased mind, to do those things which are not fitting...." (Romans 1:21, 23, 25, 28)

This is the doctrine of the Pharisees, which is still prevalent today in the concept that somehow Christ has changed. It takes the signs of an apostle to present the truth in manifestation that Jesus cannot, will not, change! The glory of God is unveiled in the proving of His unchanging word through the miraculous. The glory of God is unveiled through the open-heavens that go wherever apostles and apostolic people go.

All right, that's enough. This chapter is too thick as it is. There's a lot of information here to absorb. Let it settle for a bit.

Now, the next chapter dovetails nicely into this one. In fact, it used to be all one chapter. But I've decided to break them into two chapters because this one runs a little long, and I believe it's "meaty" enough as it is. So take a quick break, and let's move onto unveiling the rule of God.

Chapter Six Outline

"Unveiling the Glory of God"

CREATING A HABITATION

- "Veil" comes from the Greek *kalupsis*, meaning "to hide, cover up or wrap up"
- "Revelation" adds the Greek prefix *apo* to *kalupsis*, thus implying "an unveiling or an unearthing"
- "Dwelling Place" comes from the Greek *katoiketerion* (Ephesians 2:18-22)
- Isaiah 66:1-2, "Thus says the Lord: 'Heaven is My throne, and earth is My footstool. Where is the house that you will build Me? And where is the place of My rest? For all those things My hand has made, and all those things exist,' says the Lord. 'But on this one will I look: on him who is poor and of a contrite spirit, and who trembles at My word.'"
- God is posing some questions to us today. "Where is My habitation? Where is My place of rest? I am looking for a place to rest among you, so that I might express Myself to you. I want to give you My fullness; I want My favor upon you."
- Apostolic anointing creates an unshakeable habitation of His presence among the people

LET NO ONE VEIL YOUR FACE

- "And He will destroy on this mountain the surface of the covering cast over all people, and the veil that is spread over all nations." (Isaiah 25:7)

- Exodus 34:29-35: whenever Moses was in the presence of the Lord, his face would shine because of the glory, but when he spoke to the children of Israel, he would place a veil over his face

- "Therefore, since we have such hope, we use great boldness of speech — unlike Moses, who put a veil over his face so that the children of Israel could not look steadily at the end of what was passing away. But their minds were blinded. For until this day the same veil remains unlifted in the reading of the Old Testament, because the veil is taken away in Christ. But even to this day, when Moses is read, a veil lies on their heart. Nevertheless when one turns to the Lord, the veil is taken away. Now the Lord is the Spirit; and where the Spirit of the Lord is, there is liberty. But we all, with unveiled face, beholding as in a mirror the glory of the Lord, are being transformed into the same image from glory to glory, just as by the Spirit of the Lord." (2 Corinthians 3:12-18)

- Don't let anyone's fear or religious doubts hinder you from responding to His glory. The traditions and institutions of men bring us into religious bondages — it is a source of control, and people fall under a curse of veiling

- "O foolish Galatians! Who has bewitched you that you should not obey the truth, before whose eyes Jesus Christ was clearly portrayed among you as crucified? This only I want to learn from you: Did you receive the Spirit by the works of the law, or by the hearing of faith? Are you so foolish?" (Galatians 3:1-3)

- The Galatians were under a curse; they had been smitten with an Evil Eye of Substitution – the glazing of indifference to His presence
- The question you have to answer is, "Have I been bewitched? Have I veiled my face?"
- "But to you who fear My name the Sun of Righteousness shall arise with healing in His wings; and you shall go out and grow fat like stall-fed calves." (Malachi 4:2)
- "Healing in His wings" connotes shafts, or beams of light, that when they shine out, they shine out in perfect harmony, yielding a remedy or a cure to the sickened person
- Apostolic people must recognize the need for harmony in their churches
- Don't allow a veiling on your personality to prohibit you for calling God what He is – a God of His word, incapable of lying. If He says He will change you from glory to glory in encounters with Him, you can be well-assured He means what He says
- "'The glory of the Lord shall be revealed, and all flesh shall see it together; for the mouth of the Lord has spoken.'" (Isaiah 40:5)
- God is the only Being that can boast in Himself without the sin of pride. The revelation of the glory is God permitting Himself to show off to the world

- God proves Himself sovereign when He unveils His character and His heart to all flesh — He "brags" of His greatness to the world
- God wants to show Himself off to you, to display His great worth among His prized possessions. He takes pride in His well-manufactured creations, and His glory condescends to dance among us to boast of His greatness, but also to bring that which is out of order back into synchronization
- "And they shall call them The Holy People, The Redeemed of the Lord; and you shall be called Sought Out, A City Not Forsaken." (Isaiah 62:12)
- God might define *glory* as, "My face is unveiled, and My heart is exposed (revealed) to you." Literally, His face is turned toward us in favor
- *Doxa* means the honor of God placed upon a good opinion
- "And it came to pass, when Moses entered the tabernacle, that the pillar of cloud descended and stood at the door of the tabernacle, and the Lord talked with Moses." (Exodus 33:9)
- Apostolic people desire the same level of favor in their lives and ministries. They say to themselves, "Boy, if I can get under that cloud, anything and everything can happen! That's what *I* want!"
- "So the Lord spoke to Moses face to face, as a man speaks to his friend...." (Exodus 33:11)
- The key to the miraculous is that favor of God found in His cloud of glory, where He speaks to us as friends

The Open-Heavens above Jesus

- "...'Most assuredly, I say to you, hereafter you shall see heaven open, and the angels of God ascending and descending upon the Son of Man.'" (John 1:51)
- Wherever Jesus walked, the heavens were opened above Him — He was in constant communication with His Father
- The key to the miraculous is to have the heavens opened above us, where we delight in constant communication with the Father, and His angels descend and ascend upon us, just as Jacob dreamed of the ladder in the sky. (Genesis 28:12)
- "'No one has ascended to heaven but He who came down from heaven, that is, the Son of Man who is in heaven.'" (John 3:13)
- How could He be in two places at the same time? Because Jesus was standing under an open heavens. His Father was constantly revealed to Him; there was no veil separating Him from God
- "And I heard a loud voice from heaven saying, 'Behold, the tabernacle of God is with men, and He will dwell with them, and they shall be His people. God Himself will be with them and be their God.'" (Revelation 21:3)
- This is our great salvation, by aligning ourselves with Christ, we have access to an open heaven, where God Himself is with us; and He brings great favor and glory with Him
- "'And I will give you the keys of the kingdom of heaven, and whatever you bind on earth will be bound in heaven,

and whatever you loose on earth will be loosed in heaven.'"
(Matthew 16:19)

- Jesus was saying, "Whatever you prohibit on this earth, I will back you up in heaven; and whatever you permit on this earth, I'll open the heavens to you"
- The power behind binding is to tie up the operations of the enemy, making them of no consequence. We gum up the works of the devil by paralyzing his activities in a particular situation
- But binding must also be combined with the loosing of the Spirit — this breeds the miraculous
- The movings of the Spirit (loosing) are found in the apostolic reformation so that the binding might become complete
- "...'I am your fellow servant, and of your brethren who have the testimony of Jesus. Worship God! For the testimony of Jesus is the spirit of prophecy.'" (Revelation 19:10)
- The testimony of Jesus is that "now!" word — relevant right *now*, this moment, today — energized to confirm the fullness of God in His signs, wonders and miracles. Prophecy yields Holy Spirit-inspired activity, calling forth the loosing of God. It is the testimony of Jesus in expression — the pinnacle of the apostolic release

THE DUNAMIS PRINCIPLE

- *Megadunamis* is explosive power — excessive energy. More than enough to complete the job. It is power that has the ability to reproduce itself, to make *more* power

- *Dunamis* in function is the expression of a release of authority. It is the release of a measure of influence or rule over a particular situation. It is the power to command
- "Ask! What may I do for you, before I am taken away from you?" "Please let a double portion of your spirit be upon me." "You have asked a hard thing. Nevertheless, if you see me when I am taken from you, it shall be so for you; but if not, it shall not be so." (2 Kings 2:9-10)
- Elijah replied, "You have asked [the] *essential* thing...."
- Elisha inherited the essential thing — a double portion of authority, what apostles might call *megadunamis*. The apostolic spirit dwells in this expression of great power
- If one claims an apostolic unction but has no *dunamis* to back it up, are they not of questionable authority?
- The apostolic anointing must be given free rein to exercise power and authority in the miraculous — it is the only way to bind and loose completely, releasing the keys of the Kingdom of Heaven and unveiling the glory of God
- Matthew 16:13-19
- The rock of the Church is the revelation that Jesus is the anointed Son of God. Upon *this* rock — "You are the Christ, the Son of the living God" — is what Jesus builds His Church upon
- It is the revelation of the rock that gives the keys to the Kingdom

- It is as if Jesus had said, "You have revealed My anointing. I have given you the keys to release that anointing on the earth."
- Miracles can be placed into four main categories: *mega, notable, diverse* and *special*
- Mega miracles come from the word *megadunamis*. It means excessive power was present, so much so that it spilled over to other people. If one miracle is recorded, there was enough power and authority present to heal thousands. It speaks of mass healings
- Notable miracles catch the attention of the media, of the posers of truth, the critics. The kinds of miracles that don't leave any room for nay saying. "Thirty seconds ago, I didn't have an arm, and now I do."
- Diversities of miracles create an astonishment among the participants, creating a celebration atmosphere, an excitement at God's wondrous, varied nature. They carry outrageous joy and festivity; it is, "to party with God in miracles"
- Acts 19 — "God wrought special miracles by the hands of Paul in Ephesus"
- Special miracles are for a specific geographic location (i.e., your hometown) that breaks off the enchantment of the people, revealing God's supreme authority and love for them
- Miracles themselves can be weapons of spiritual warfare

- "Special miracles" (Acts 19) means that something happened underneath the hands of Paul that those people could physically feel, a breaker anointing that spawned deliverances. It *shocked* the people into spiritual understanding
- People were seeing some kind of manifestation under his hands that when each individual was delivered, it did warfare in the atmosphere and famished the gods those people worshipped. (See Zephaniah 3.) It threw down the powers of the air and purged the heavens, opening them up
- An open-heavens was established in that geographic location because of special miracles

ANOTHER JESUS?

- "Jesus Christ is the same yesterday, today, and forever. Do not be carried about [away] with various and strange doctrines...." (Hebrews 13:8-9)
- Any doctrine that tells you Christ was one way in the past but is not that way now is a strange doctrine you are *not* to be carried away with
- "But even if our gospel is veiled, it is veiled to those who are perishing, whose minds the god of this age has blinded, who do not believe, lest the light of the gospel of the glory of Christ, who is the image of God, should shine on them." (2 Corinthians 4:3-4)
- "But I fear, lest somehow, as the serpent deceived Eve by his craftiness, so your minds may be corrupted from the simplicity that is in Christ. For if he who comes preaches

another Jesus whom we have not preached, or if you receive a different spirit which you have not received, or a different gospel which you have not accepted – you may well put up with it!" (2 Corinthians 11:3-4)

- It takes a manifestation of the truth – a truth that exhibits a virtue – to unveil this deception
- "But we have renounced the hidden things of shame [iniquities], not walking in craftiness nor handling [adulterating] the word of God deceitfully, but by manifestation of the truth commending ourselves to every man's conscience in the sight of God." (2 Corinthians 4:2)
- "'And you shall know the truth, and the truth shall make you free.'" (John 8:32)
- A lack of the supernatural creates a vacuum wherein the truth is not manifested, and a wrong concept of God emerges – it is a "form of godliness"
- Demons distort and change the image of God, so that the deceived worship *it* instead of *Him*
- "...Because, although they knew God, they did not glorify Him as God, nor were thankful, but became futile in their thoughts, and their foolish hearts were darkened... and [they] changed the glory of the incorruptible God into an image made like corruptible [perishable] man – and birds and four-footed animals and creeping things... [They] exchanged the truth of God for the lie, and worshiped and served the creature rather than the Creator, who is blessed forever. Amen. And even as they did not like to retain God in their knowledge, God gave

them over to a debased mind, to do those things which are not fitting...." (Romans 1:21, 23, 25, 28)

- It takes the signs of an apostle to present the truth in manifestation that Jesus cannot, will not, change! The glory of God is unveiled in the proving of His unchanging word through the miraculous

Unveiling the Rule of God

OUT OF ORDER

Something is out of order in the structure of the Church at large — we are not seeing the greater miraculous moves of God on a continual basis. I understand there are timings involved, *kairos* moments of visitation; but I am convinced that the miraculous should not be an exception to the norm when so many people need a touch from God *today*. Those seasons of blessing, I believe, are to be even greater saturations of the supernatural on a national, or even global, level. I refuse to believe that, as Christ cannot change, the first-century Church simply had it "better than we do." He blessed them with great power and great grace; He wants to bless us with great power and great grace as well. If this is truly His desire, then the fault lies with us, not Him.

So what is missing from our present day Church that the people of Acts had? Something is out of order in the foundation of the church structure. Thankfully, He is raising up an apostolic company to address these issues and put the Church back into order. Then we will see His works, and greater, in operation.

We need a paradigm shift in our thinking concerning "church order." Now, don't misunderstand me when I say, "Things are out of order." That doesn't necessarily mean *wrong* or *sinful*, just incomplete. The apostle is not the end-all, be-all of ministry expression — it takes the entirety of the five-fold to keep the Church on track. Just because the apostolic is the new buzz of evangelical Christianity does not negate the other branches of saint-equippers. I am not pro-apostle to the exclusion of every other expression; the Lord has graciously moved in powerful ways in thousands of ministries throughout the world, through pastors, evangelists, teachers and prophets. But I do believe there needs to come a wineskin change in the collective culture of the common believer.

Normally, they have been neglecting the office of the apostle, perhaps because they think of the apostle as a "one man show," some Lone Ranger cowboy who comes into a church and starts spouting governmental decrees with no true tie to the land itself, and no supernatural unction to back up his claims. Hey, I know this has happened, and it leaves a bitter taste in many churchgoers' mouths. There is a concept change that needs to occur in viewing apostles as "God's men" when in reality, they are one facet of a larger group — but they *are* the foundational facet. They are not better, but they are still as vital in today's Church as they were when Ephesians 4:11 was written. It's not a strict hierarchy; I don't believe in a formulaic pattern for every church. But I believe many churches — I'd even hazard to say more often than not — have ignored or, at the very least, lessened the influence of the apostle.

The fact still remains that "...God has appointed these in the church: first apostles, second prophets, third teachers, after that miracles, then gifts of healings, helps, administrations, varieties of tongues." (1 Corinthians 12:28)

Let me digress here for just a moment, please. Some people might say pastors/teachers are synonymous, therefore, a "four-fold" expression. Ephesians 4:11 does not provide a comma between "pastors" and "teachers." This can be semantics, really. While I *do* know people who travel around as roving teachers, and I believe they do stand in the office of a teacher, I believe *every* teacher should have signs and wonders *backing up* what they are teaching — a breaker anointing that goes beyond what they are saying.

I believe it's the same for any five-fold (or four-fold) minister. I'm not convinced that God ever intended people to say, "I am a teacher" or "I am a prophet" or "I am a pastor" and not have some kind of visible tangible, supernatural anointing backing them up. I think it's great to teach a really catchy, thoughtful sermon, but I always want the Lord to exhibit some sort of virtue that *proves* that what I'm teaching is truly from His Word. I never want to be in a conference, say my three-point, eloquently homiletic message (and I think I often do fairly well, thank you very much!) and then just sit down. I want the people to *see* something that backs up what I just shared.

So with all that being said, I don't think it's wrong to say pastors and teachers are the same. I think prophets are to teach. I believe apostles are to teach. And I know they're all supposed to teach with an anointing and some kind of signs and wonders following after them. It may not be a very popular opinion, and I'm not trying to overthrow anyone's philosophies; but it is something to ponder on. Something to digest.

Oh, and incidentally I personally am of the opinion that "miracles" in the 1 Corinthians 12 passage above speaks of evangelists, as in using the miraculous to reach the unsaved.

Back to the main point of 1 Corinthians 12:28. I've heard "apostle-phobes" (yes, it's a made up word, but you get the point) say that the word "first" is simply a numerical list. One, two, three in a series, not order of importance. And I can understand that philosophy, with a proper attitude to the entirety of the five-fold (or four-fold) operating in harmony. Yes, the apostle is just one of many in a series of items. But according to the Law of First Things (check out some Biblical hermeneutics websites or textbooks for a further definition) – one thing must come first fully to release the next.

So, one could equally argue *"first* apostles, *then* prophets, etc." In fact, the word "first" is the Greek *proton* (Strong's #4412), as in *prototype*, implying a building block for an atomic release of molecules designed of first protons, then neutrons, then electrons. The initial building of God's Church is rooted in the foundation of apostles and prophets for the dynamics of Church-life, with Christ being the chief Cornerstone. (Ephesians 2:20) In other words, the Law of First Things dictates that the apostolic and prophetic function in a church must first be established fully in order to facilitate the release of the other expressions. This was the way it was in the early Church, and as God is restoring, it is to be released in these days, too. But currently how many of you dear readers can think of one church in your area that is not built on a foundation of apostles and prophets? Then could something be out of order or incomplete? Quite possibly.

For the most part, we've just had pastoral and evangelistic churches, especially in the United States. Take a look at the early Church in Acts – it was indeed founded on apostles first, with everyone else coming alongside, not in a subservient, secondary role, but as one block on top of another. Each as important as the next, but with the apostolic and prophetic as the under girding for the rest. It's my humble opinion that this is Church Building 101.

Again, "first apostles, second prophets…" to me is not speaking of some strict hierarchy, where one position is greater than another. It's not an "I'm more important than you because *I'm* the apostle" kind of thinking. In fact, let the first among you be the least. (See Luke 9:48.) Here's my test for a true apostle or prophet: do they act as the floor for the other individuals to build up from? Does the apostle or prophet serve the "average" person in the church to equip them for body ministry in their daily lives; do they release others into their destinies? Because of great power and great grace, apostles and prophets have to be the *most* humble of the Body (in that broad sense of thinking), otherwise they aren't serving the greater good and should be removed. I don't mean "removed" as in cast aside, I mean "set straight" or "taken down a notch," if you will. I trust you understand my intent.

(By the way, as an important aside, my emphasis on an "apostle" is in his/her *function*, more than their title. I believe I operate in an apostolic flow, but I don't use the title "apostle." I believe it's OK if one does, but I don't care who calls themselves what; I just want to see the supernatural anointing to back up their claims. If you're a bishop, great. If you're a prophetess, that's wonderful. If you're an apostolically motivated Prophet/evangelist, with a big "P" and a little "e," then that's fine with me. I once ministered with a guy who called himself "apostle, prophet, evangelist, pastor and teacher".... I think that might be a *little* excessive. It was like he had the fullness of Christ in his own ministry operation.... Anyway, the point here is to place the emphasis on the person's function, not their title. You may have someone in your church who operates apostolically but doesn't call themselves an apostle. That's OK. The proof is in the pudding, as they used to say.)

One last tidbit before moving on. (This one's free and wasn't included in the book price....) Concerning the prophetic teaming up with the apostolic, I've noticed in recent years that some churches have a tendency to leap over the prophetic to get straight to the apostolic, since it's what's "hot" right now in the Charismatic Body.

This is a mistake. Just as a church cannot be functioning to its fullest potential without evangelistic or pastoral influence, we cannot negate the office of the prophet and prophetic movement in a church setting in order to have "the apostolic." This can be a problem with some apostles, thinking they're above prophets, so the prophet's place is minimized. My point here — and don't forget this is an apostolic book — is that each position must be *maximized*, including our dear friend the prophet. Just as "apostle" can refer to apostolic people, "prophet" can refer to prophetic people. Prophecy, in all its forms, is vital to apostolic anointing in a church.

See, the prophetic flow hears the vision from God — the prophetic person *gets* what God wants to do in the Spirit. Teaming up with the apostolic, which releases a breaker anointing to pave the way for what God wants to do, the evangelist (and evangelistic people) take that vision and runs it out into the streets, with his or her own signs and wonders proving the vision to the people. The pastor/teacher (and pastoral/teaching people) feed the people whom the evangelist brings in, equipping them with his or her own supernatural anointing to start the cycle all over again. At the risk of sounding childish: lather, rinse, repeat. Lather, rinse, repeat. See, we cannot neglect the prophetic for the apostolic.

A BIT ON CHURCH GOVERNMENT

This chapter is not intended to cover the entire gamut of church rule. There are literally hundreds, possibly thousands, of works that deal with this subject, and the scope of this book is not to "preach" on church government. I just want to address a few issues here relating to the release of the apostolic anointing.

"We, however, will not boast beyond measure, but within the limits of the sphere which God appointed us — a sphere which especially includes you." (2 Corinthians 10:13)

Often, I have heard of apostles with no release of authority, no approval from God or even the majority of the people in the church, try to insinuate themselves into the structure. To put it mildly, it causes problems. Here's the bottom line, friends: God operates through relegated authority. Authority, here, is defined as "a measure of the rule of God lent to mankind." In His wisdom, boundaries have been measured to each minister; territorial lines have been set in motion, where each person has a specific sphere of influence in which to operate. If an evangelist or a pastor or a prophet or an apostle tries to step out of that sphere, difficulties can ensue and people can get hurt.

Further, with the new novel thing in the Charismatic Church being the Apostolic Reformation, there are literally thousands of people who are coming into the knowledge that they are called to be apostles. They might have been operating in an apostolic flow for years and never known what it was called. I think that's amazing! Good thing the Apostolic Reformation came along to sort it all out — that's its purpose! There are pastors, evangelists and prophets who feel they are being "moved up" (but that's probably a really poor term, I suppose) into the office of an apostle. And for many, they're absolutely right.

But for some, they have been moving many years in prophetic, evangelistic or pastoral giftings who now feel they've been called into an apostolic office. Sure, the signs and wonders will prove the gifting, but some people should remain in the giftings to which they were called to begin with. (again, 2 Corinthians 10:13) I've heard of some people who were wonderful pastors or prophets or teachers who suddenly have been demarcated apostles, and I've thought to myself, *What was so wrong with being a pastor or a prophet?* Hey, I'm just happy to be in the ministry at all — I don't care what you call me.

Why this becomes a problem is that some people feel they're being called into something they're not (again, there are hundreds of exceptions — it's not a blanket statement.) But, in these cases, they should remain as what God called them: prophets, pastors, evangelists, deacons, whatever. They should not get caught up in the "new thing" that God has brought into the Church (and the apostolic is not really a "new thing," dear readers.) If they do, it can bring confusion to the people, because their anointing is *not* in the apostolic vein, and the people get hurt. This turns some people off to the apostolic altogether, and the supernatural, breaker anointing is stunted in their lives. I'd hate to be responsible for something like that. Wouldn't you?

I'm not saying people are moving to be called apostles out of wrong or malicious reasons — they may genuinely feel they're called, but I hope they're not jumping onto the apostolic bandwagon in the name of recognition, in hopes of being identified with the "new thing" God is doing. It will cause problems for them, and for those they have an influence with. You know, I think we'd all be better off if we stayed in the spheres of influence God has graced us with; and if someone's called to be an apostle, then an overwhelming amount of anointing, signs, wonders and miracles will be evidence to that fact. And we all won't have any doubts in our minds: that man or woman is an *apostle!*

Just because one has established a bunch of churches, or has spiritual sons and daughters that look up to them as father or mother, that doesn't necessarily make one an apostle. Pastors establish churches and have spiritual sons and daughters.

It's more than just having a deliverance ministry from demons that proves one's apostolic authority. As important of a ministry as that is, one's authority must move deeper than casting out demons — it takes a miraculous edge in various expressions to bring an apostolic unction to the deliverance ministry, the signs and wonders that accompany the deliverance anointing.

I am always wary of extreme aggressiveness in an apostolic person. True apostles, as I've seen them, tend to have an excessive amount of humility in their expressions. I'm not talking about wanting to see a lack of dominion — just the opposite, in fact. But I want to see meekness and a true servant-leader's heart, rather than an opinionated man or woman who knows how something should be done, but has no supernatural anointing for dominion in that particular field. Again, the proof is in the pudding. (I just love that old adage!)

I am always seeking to find humility in ministers' lives. Let me see what you have done in other churches; let me examine your fruit in the day-to-day activities. Let me find you loving these precious people more than your ministry. Let me experience the miraculous operation consistently in your ministry. Let me see the signs of an apostle accomplished. And then you can be the foundation of the Lord's Church.

I am speaking caution here, not fear. Wariness, not abandonment. Note this: the release of the gifts of an apostle increase the measure of Christ in an environment — they expand the boundaries of an experience in Him. Can an apostle facilitate this? Or does he or she make you feel bad, because they know what to do and you don't? The idea here is to decrease paranoia towards the apostolic, but increase discernment in church operation. In my experience, one of the greatest lacking gifts in the Body today is discernment.

Pastors are right to want to protect their flock — it *is* their job. But protection does not imply an apostolic embargo (yes, another made-up phrase) or a prophetic moratorium (I can do this all day) at the expense of a genuine encounter with Christ's supernatural power. Look, we don't live in a perfect world. Fact: there are people out there, wolves in sheep's clothing, who would damage the Church, maybe not out of maliciousness but of *a veiling of their own.*

Don't get caught up in every new whim and fad, but do exercise true, unbiased discernment for genuinely regulated apostolic authority, backed up by supernatural operation.

Should apostles be over churches? There is no simple, blanket answer. Yes, I believe apostles should be the *foundations* of churches, along with prophets. Their influence should be present in the congregation. Their counsel should be sought on church matters. But does this negate the pastor's role? Absolutely not. In fact, I think it only increases the need for good pastors. It takes all three to release a fuller expression of Christ in a church, not one or two operating out of sync with the other. Here's the prophet who hears or sees what God is doing. Here is the apostle who provides a breaker anointing to clear the spiritual way by developing the strategy to fulfill the words of the prophet. Then, here is the pastor instructing the people on how to respond to this new move of God. After all this is accomplished, then the people are equipped and empowered and sent out as warriors of their own, returning to base camp for a recharge as needed, or to give report on the victories achieved out there in the world.

Does this mean that if a church does not have a prophet or an apostle that it is in the wrong? Not necessarily. It just lacks a completeness of what God wants to show His people. With that lack of completeness a lack of anointing can happen. The people aren't properly equipped and activated. They can become frustrated and bored. Their growth can become stagnated, and they are kept in a perpetual state of infancy regarding their callings and gifts.

As stated before, if the release of the gifts of the apostle increases the measure of Christ, expanding the boundaries of an experience in Him, then the opposite of this is true as well. A hampering of the apostolic anointing hampers an experience in Him. The rule of God, and thus His glory, is unveiled in the foundation of the Church on apostolic, prophetic anointing. Apostolic miracles are used to unveil the rule and glory of Jesus and recover the fullness of His testimony to the world.

All of the signs, wonders, miracles and mighty deeds of an apostle fall under three major categories. The first is miracles of *life*. "For the law of the Spirit of life in Christ Jesus has made me free from the law of sin and death." (Romans 8:2) This speaks of a restoration to life. Apostles and prophets unveil the deceptions that hinder or limit life and life in all its fullness. They breathe fresh life into otherwise dead situations by lifting off the betrayals of the enemy and other people.

Secondly are miracles of *creation*. "In the beginning God created the heavens and the earth. The earth was without form, and void; and darkness was on the face of the deep...." (Genesis 1:1-2) This speaks of rebuilding. Situations that are without form and void can be brought into order, reconstructed in creativity and with purpose. A place that is chaotic, empty, full of waste, of no usefulness and in a state of disarray can become "lifed" again when the glory of God is unveiled through the apostolic and prophetic anointing. That which hindered creativity is removed.

Thirdly are miracles of *conquest*. Take a moment to read Joshua, chapters 3-6, the initial conquest of Canaan. Then read Acts 19:1-20, followed by 2 Kings 2, if you haven't already. All these passages speak of retaking what was lost. The release of the apostolic miraculous undoes that which hindered dominion authority. Remember Acts 19:11, the "special" miracles of Paul. The *dunamis* released under the hands of the apostle removed territorial demonic authority and glorified Christ. Also, read Acts 8:1-18 for great accounts of apostolic miracles of conquest.

For someone who operates in these kinds of miraculous ministry, they possess the breaker anointing necessary to unveil the glory of God — they are the apostolic person. Through the miracles wrought by God, they establish a church of great power and great grace.

RECOVERING GREAT POWER
AND GREAT GRACE

I hope you've been taking breaks while reading this and the previous chapter — there is a lot to absorb, thoughts and truths that need ample time to meditate upon. These two chapters and the next will prove to be the springboard for the rest of the book. I daresay these chapters are the most important to make sure you fully understand what is being said here. Take a few moments, mull it around, refill your coffee (or pop open another can of soda, if you prefer) and then come back. We're plowing along here. You're doing well!

Now, how many people out there reading this right now have ever complained to the Lord? Oh, quit it! I see you sitting there in your armchair, eyes darting around, whistling. You know you've complained to God before. I certainly have!

In my early days at pastoring, I'd find myself complaining to God. "How am I supposed to build a big church for You, Lord?" You know, in small communities out in the Midwest, a pastor didn't have a whole lot of opportunity to preach to new folks. The biggest day of the year was Resurrection Sunday. That'd be the day everyone came out to a service — the one day a year people would darken the door of a church. So I'd always pray before the service, "Oh, God, please don't let something *weird* happen today. Just let it be a normal service, please!"

And invariably, some witch (and I mean a bonafide, spell-casting witch) would show up out of the blue and wig out in the praise and worship! She'd start gagging and screaming. The elders would just look at me and shake their heads, sighing. Yeah, *that'll* make a good impression on the visitors....

They'd bring her up to the front, and I'd spend fifteen minutes casting demons out of her (oh, your theology can accommodate *that!*), she'd be rolling around, foaming at the mouth, (maybe not *that*....), the visitors' eyes as big as saucers. Then the witch'd get saved — the devil would go out and God would go in. I'd bumble through the rest of the service and the moment the benediction was given, it would be, like, major exodus time. I mean, folks would fly out the back doors, the windows (I'm serious); it was just terrible.

And I'd complain to God. "Oh, Lord, how can I grow You a big church if You let stuff like that happen? I can't get people to stick around when we've got some voodoo woman foaming at the mouth!"

To which God would simply reply, "Well, you've got *one* new member...."

My eyes would drift over to the ex-witch, boo-hooing on the carpet. "Not the witch.... That's hard work! I wanted that *doctor* to join the church...."

But you see, God wasn't interested in my desire to have the largest church in Backwater, USA. He was interested in a church of great power and great grace — a church that would turn that witch into a testament of His miraculous dominion.

See, God is establishing a *Church* of great power and great grace. Acts 4:33, "And with great power the apostles gave witness to the resurrection of the Lord Jesus. And great grace was upon them all." Let's use the Antioch church as an example for other churches.

I'll provide you some notes here that I got from listening to Emmanuel Cannistraci, wherein he outlined some of the hallmarks of the Antioch church. There's a list of scripture references at the end that you can peruse later at your leisure. The church at Antioch was known for its *discipline, gracefulness, benevolence, charisma, integration, giftings, teachings, prophecies, worshipfulness, prayerfulness, structure, intimacy* and ultimately its *apostolic anointing.* (See Acts 11:23, 26, 29-30; Acts 13:1-3.) (Emmanuel Cannistraci)

See, the apostolic spirit recovers great power and great grace — it creates a grace-filled church that operates with impressive authority and dominion. Note here, it's not just the *apostles* that provided these qualities, but the people under their *apostolic influence*. This is why apostles are called to equip the saints, so that they can reproduce similar works.

These qualities tell us *why* the church at Antioch was successful. They mark a church that is *attractive, involved, reproducing* and *multiplying*. After the infilling of the Holy Spirit on the Day of Pentecost (Acts 2), the church grew to 3,000 members in one day. That's a pretty impressive growth curve, wouldn't you say?

We've looked at *megadunamis* (great power) already. Now let's look at "great grace." This is the Greek word *megacharis*. You recognize *mega*, I'm sure, and *charis* is where we get the word "charisma" or "charismatic." It translates as "God's grace freely given [manifested] in the ordinary course of people's lives." Why people will come, stay and grow in your church will correlate directly to the level of grace and power that operate in your services. It's not just about your community outreach programs (and, yes, those are *vitally* important — don't stop doing them!) It's not just about your rockin' praise and worship (keep it up! I like loud drums and bass.) It's not just about your carefully constructed, three month membership program (don't stop that either!) Ultimately, working in combination with all of the above, it is your desire to permit the prophetic and apostolic anointing to have a place of eminence in your services. It becomes your passion to maintain a legitimate expression of God in your meetings.

God must peel the exterior level of your church off and reveal the muscle underneath — that is His power moving apostolically and prophetically through the Body... your flock. You have to want to get back to the rawness of the Holy Spirit moving like a rushing, mighty wind through your congregation. This only comes from the leadership of the church having a sense of security in God. They know that He will not lead them astray, so they permit Him to move as He sees fit.

When that kind of operation is permitted in the service, the people gain a certain level of acceptance and recognition among their peers. In other words, the glory they receive in church rubs off on the people around them, at work, at home, at the grocery store. In essence, powerful Christians become extremely attractive to the outside world. It's a divine magnetism where people are drawn to them, saying, "I want what *you* have!"

People will come, stay and grow in your church because multiplication is a by-product of reproducing, meaning that the manifestation of God's grace and power entices the people to stick around. The local church will become exceedingly enticing to the community because others will see the glory reflected in your congregation.

And, yes, you might have to put up with a little foaming at the mouth at first; but once they're set free, some of those people become the greatest movers and shakers for the Lord. And I don't know about you, I want *those* kinds of people.

A CHALLENGE TO AN EXPERIMENT

I have heard from many pastors that they are afraid if someone speaks in tongues or gives a word of prophecy in a service because some uninitiated individual sitting in the back might become uncomfortable and not return. I understand this concern. This may indeed happen. Yes, we need to exercise wisdom. But the fact remains, that when that person is dying of cancer, or when that person's friend can't beat their alcoholism, he or she will say, "Look. I don't want it, but if you want healing, or if you want counsel — go to *that* church because they have something you're in need of." And then you've hooked them.

Remember Isaiah 62:11-12: the redeemed of the Lord shall be called "Sought Out." Check it out.

I daresay the people that will be turned off and leave will not outnumber the people who come seeking a true, tangible touch of God. The world is crying out for an expression of supreme authority and reality in love. For goodness' sake, give it to them!

I'd love to see churches try an experiment. Permit the supernatural to manifest in the services, and see how many people flock to it. I think it's funny that millions of people switch on the TV to see some magician perform his newest act, or some psychic call up dead Aunt Sarah out of the New Age goop to speak to little Nancy... But the churches are afraid the public will be scared of some person calling them forward to say, "Two years ago your cancer went into remission, and the Lord spared your life; He has called you out to be a mouthpiece for His love and mercy. He wants you to work in the soup kitchen, 'cause there are dozens more with your same infirmity. He has given you a healing anointing to reach out to those people." And, yes, still have your bake sales, country fairs and trips to the day spas. Why must it be one or the other? Can it not be both? Dear friends, the supernatural is not *that* scary!

Why is *Harry Potter* so famous? Why are so many of the television programs and movies about some supernatural manifestation? I'm not exaggerating here, folks; turn on your TVs! For the most part, the people aren't frightened off by the supernatural. If they see it in true operation, backed up by the wooing of the Holy Spirit (because it has to be the Holy Spirit drawing them anyway) and the love, meekness and grace of the Church, would they not turn the boob tube off and set ol' Harry aside to come meet God face-to-face? I would venture to say for every person turned off by the supernatural, there are two out there who want it, if not more. At least, that's been my experience.

All right, so great grace speaks of *quality* and *quantity* and an *organic* flow of power manifested. What I mean by "organic" is that life is found, nurtured and expressed in the body that is assembled in a particular locality. The church that has come under apostolic and prophetic influence produces a *zoe*-kind of life. And again, it makes that church *extremely* attractive. Take a look at Antioch! This was a church that had the favor of God, having obtained grace in His sight. So much so that it spawned other churches throughout the land. Again, this is not just speaking of the apostles or the prophets, but of the entirety of the congregation — each person found his or her identity in representing the gifts God bestowed to each one of them. It truly was the Dancing Hand of God!

"How is it then, brethren? Whenever you come together, each of you has a psalm, has a teaching, has a tongue, has a revelation, has an interpretation. Let all things be done for edification." (1 Corinthians 14:26)

This is the Householder's Anointing; all of these things "build up" the Church by expressing God to the masses, who in turn come into the Church to learn and see more. Then, *they* are sent out to do the same. These manifestations are not for the exclusive experience of just those already in the household. It's also for the people who are outside it. See, the Householder's Anointing has a *sending* quality to it, setting people apart and sending them before the congregation and the world. "...'As the Father has sent Me, I also send you.'" (John 20:21) **Again, these gifts are always to be in the context of expressing God to the masses**. This quality is not just a benefit; it is a mandate!

Look, God wants souls, plain and simple. God wants His Church to be unafraid of His Church. You know what I mean? He's not afraid of working in His Church. Why should we be?

"For the Lord will rise up... that He may do His work, His awesome work, and bring to pass His act, His unusual act." (Isaiah 8:21)

Hey, then let's let Him do it!

THE AMBASSADORIAL ANOINTING

If the "first" in 1 Corinthians 12:27 speaks of a prototype (speaking of atomic ingredients building together to bring about a solid object) and the first in order must come first fully to release the next, then we are speaking of apostolic anointing as an infusion of a dynamic that trickles down to others. A linking pin to the next phase of expression, Act I leading to Act II. Therefore, apostles as "sent ones" bear an ambassadorial authority with dominion that comes from the Father, the glory and rule of God in manifestation. The word *ambassador* grew into a biblical principle from a Greco-Roman secular term for someone being sent on the behalf of another. It literally means "to be sent." In modern vernacular, it is a special envoy being "sent out" to expand the kingdom or the empire.

As Jesus was sent first, we in turn were sent in His behalf, in His name, with His full backing and authority behind us. (See John 20:21.) To bring it to an earthly illustration, the apostolic spirit – indeed, the spirit of the Book of Acts – possesses three attributes that can be shown in an ambassador sent, say, in the name of the Emperor of Rome. My friend and colleague, Dr. Larry Hill, presented it to me this way, and it really drove the point home in my mind. I will share with you his thoughts for your benefit.

Firstly, the ambassador came with *authority*; in the name of his sovereign, all of Rome's might was behind him. Secondly, he came with *strategy*; a planting of values that entrenched the people in the mindset of the Roman way of life. Thirdly, he came with *resources*; the accoutrements and people necessary to be sent out to make war, to conquer and subdue if need be.

It's the same for an ambassadorial, apostolic anointing. I want to thank Dr. Hill for crystallizing this concept in so clear a fashion.

We of an apostolic spirit are the righteous unleavened lump (see 1 Corinthians 5:7) that is sent to instruct, teach and equip the people in the mindsets of His Kingdom, with the strategies of a Master Tactician, to subdue all that raises itself against the Kingdom. The difference between our military vehicle and that of an earthly empire is we have an ambassadorial grace and authority that brings *freedom* to the people. Freedom to express oneself to God, freedom to express oneself to others and, most importantly, freedom for God to express Himself to us. This is the rule and glory of God revealed through apostolic anointing.

Freedom is a very important concept that we'll be looking at in a later chapter. It falls in line with the Parrhesia Principle I briefly mentioned in the previous chapter. It's a focal aspect of the apostolic anointing to release this, so we'll dedicate some time to it later on.

THE MILITARY ANOINTING

"...As you know how we exhorted, and comforted, and charged every one of you, as a father does his own children, that you would walk worthy of God who calls you in His own kingdom and glory." (1 Thessalonians 2:11-12)

The attributes of a strong, grace-filled church full of an apostolic spirit are exemplified by strong, militant apostolic leadership. We seem to be afraid of the word "militant" as if it carries some Fascist, manipulating connotation. But true military might is found in people fighting for the cause of freedom under the guidance of great generals magnificently schooled in the tactics of warfare. This apostolic anointing creates fathers, and it creates generals. People with a dominion spirit and supernatural strategy for winning over hearts and winning battles. They are people who don't simply *declare* the Kingdom of God, they *demonstrate* it. Men and women of military prowess who are well-equipped to move this regiment here and this regiment there to maximize the achievement of a successful campaign (i.e., winning the lost.)

Just as soldiers will follow good generals who have proven themselves knowledgeable and ready in battle, children submit to fathers when the fathers position themselves in a stance of ready acceptance, sound judgment and true authority. A poorly equipped general gets his men killed, and a poorly equipped father turns his children away.

What is being loosed in this time of apostolic reformation is not only the Fathering Anointing, but also the Military Anointing. They are infusions of life and dynamics that will ultimately put a stop to the Church's issues and struggles. If the Body of Christ were made to understand the necessity of these anointings, embrace them as God's ordained order for His people, the vast, vast majority of our troubles would be bound; and His Spirit would be loosed upon us in unhampered measure. Let me say this: leaders of a grace/power-filled church are going to be generals in the faith and fathers in the faith. We must align and submit ourselves to such as these.

We have got to understand that Christianity is not a democracy. It is not a republic of severally minded men and women, each with their own agendas, their own interpretations, their own hang-ups.

Christianity is a theocracy — it is the rule of God, and no other!

The only way we can know the rule of God is through His Word, without undue influence from us, adding or subtracting that which we don't like, changing the black and white scripture to fit our own needs at a given time. That is called "Situational Ethics" — that morality is based upon each individual's decisions in their own circumstances; what is right for one may not be right for another in a different scenario. It leads to anarchy, and ultimately destruction. The Bible leaves very little in the "gray area" regarding God's will where glory and anointing are concerned. Who are we to change His mind?

Pastors, your church is to be a militant church. Yes, a loving church. Big smooches all around, love-dovey, sloppy-*agape*. Your church should be the huggingest, lovingest church in the city. (How's *that* for good English?)

But not at the expense of taking the battle to the streets. God does not want a church full of pansies. Oh, you know where I'm coming from here. I can just see you shaking your heads, thinking, *Did he just use the word* pansies *in a Christian book?!?*

Now, now, don't go all religious on me. My grandsons watch that cartoon *Madagascar*. Have you seen it? You know, with the lion, the zebra, the giraffe and the hippo? That's my favorite cartoon because there's this little squirrel-thing who sees these huge animals freaking out over a tiny spider, and he deadpan quips, "They're just a bunch of pansies," with this great, foreign accent. It's so funny!

Anyway, back to the point: you know I love you, and I'm not trying to pick a fight here, but I *am* trying to show that your church can be full of love and full of might at the same time. You are called to operate in a military anointing!

A strong, militant apostolic anointing creates strategies for church evangelism utilizing the cutting edge of God's power. That's how a church should grow big. It creates a movement toward a revolution — not just renewal and revival, which are also important, but ultimately only change the environment of your church, not your community. We need a breaker anointing to provide some insight on how we are to evangelize the community, because, dear friends, the way we're presenting Christianity to the world at present is not cutting it.

Let's get down to brass tacks here. The best way to grow a church is to have apostolic insight in the community, using the miraculous in key, specific points of interest — say, a civic leader getting healed of AIDS for example — that so stirs the rest of the community up, they've just *got* to come out and see what the hoopla's all about for themselves. We need miracles that culturally touch people where they're at.

What we experience in the four walls of the church has got to be translated into the world out there. For too long has the Church reveled in certain manifestations of the Holy Spirit at the expense of the unsaved. I'm not saying it's wrong to enjoy ourselves in the Lord, but not at the expense of the dying, hurting masses. I want to see Holy Ghost laughter translated into blind eyes being opened, so that the blind persons return to their families and say, "Guess what happened to me — you can come and get this, too!"

Viva la revolucion!

THE EMBEZZLED ANOINTING

I believe I have shown, based on the literal Word of God without unwarranted interpretation on my part, that the rule of God is implemented through delegated authority. One either has it, or one doesn't! You can't make up a military or ambassadorial anointing. God must give it to you. The spirit of excellence isn't just made up; it's loaned out from the Dancing Hand of God. It comes from knowing Him in increasing levels of intimacy.

People who try to manipulate apostolic anointing will always phase in and out of great power or great grace because ultimately they are pirating something that God didn't authorize them to have in the first place. What will create a revolution in the Body of Christ is a truly delegated governmental, fathering, militant authority expressed by called men and women. Only that will birth a strong, apostolic strategy for church evangelism exploding with power. The grace- and power-filled church recognizes that even though anyone can have an apostolic motivation, it does not mean they are an apostle. We can all support the apostolic movement, but we are not all called to be generals or ambassadors. We have to develop a knowing discernment between the two.

But before you start feeling bad that you're only a lieutenant instead of a four-star general, or a twenty-something-year-old parent instead of a great-great-grandparent, learn to focus on what can be and what will be by aligning yourself with true apostolic authority — don't focus on what currently is (or is not) happening around you in your church. If you are truly a subject of theocratic rule, seek out those who have the breaker anointing backed up by miraculous expression. That single act of obedience is what will create the movement toward revolution in your home church and hopefully your community.

"Paul, an apostle (not from men or through man, but through Jesus Christ and God the Father who raised Him from the dead), and all the brethren who are with me.... But I make known to you, brethren, that the gospel which was preached by me is not according to man. For I neither received it from man, nor was I taught it, but came through the revelation of Jesus Christ." (Galatians 1:1-2, 11-12)

True apostolic authority establishes great encounters with the presence of God. Those who have purloined apostolic authority will always end up with a weaker expression of the presence of God, a mixture; and in some cases, if the mixture's bad enough, it can even open the door to a counterfeit expression of God, which is never a good thing. The Father uses apostolic authority to create an encounter with Him, and then He will stand back to see how the people respond. Some of the saints will strive to hide these encounters at the expense of the unsaved, but in the end the rule of God will always break through, and no one can convince me otherwise that these encounters will become very attractive to the unsaved.

An apostolic spirit is a spirit that provokes people to act — it releases them where they are at so they can respond. The miraculous impacts the unsaved not only physically, spiritually and mentally but culturally as well. It changes the very fabric of their corrupted society when they come under the rule of God. Millions of people out there in the world are sick of the slop they deal with on a daily basis — any change would do them good.

Be one of those people who help facilitate a change, not stifle it! And for heaven's sake, come *under* God's authority, don't filch it!

A Season for War

In keeping with our militaristic theme, think of miracles as aiming devices so the weapons (the gifts of the Spirit) achieve maximum "damage" to the enemy. Without miracles, we are not in correct position to "Ready, Aim, Fire!" We are not on the cutting edge (another weapon motif) of wretched human need for the release of the gifts. It's like the Holy Spirit is saying, "If you aim Me at the most difficult situation out there in the world, I will become a powerhouse of miraculous expression to blow that situation outta the water! However, if you aim me at a spiritually fat, overfed Christian, I'll dwindle down into a trickle." See, we need the miraculous, but we need it aimed at the right target, otherwise we *lose* the miraculous.

Most of us in Charismatic circles have had many prophetic words. Some of us might have prophetic words coming out of our ears! (Again, it's not a blanket statement; some of us *desperately* need to hear more from God.) I don't begrudge God's people hearing from Him one bit — far from it. We need more! Bring it on!

But don't you think it's a little sad that the average Charismatic churchgoer may have so many words from God, and the poor soul out there on the street corner doesn't have *one*? Why not spread the anointing around a bit? What would happen if we aimed that miraculous power at him or her? I guarantee you, nine times out of ten, if you walked up to someone on the street and gave them a true, genuine word from the Lord — they'd listen to it. "Sure, I wanna hear from God!" And then you've hooked 'em.

Otherwise, the miraculous can be wasted and it begins to wane away.

Do you ever get upset hearing about some evangelist going over to India and coming back with all these heart-stopping stories of miracles getting whole villages saved? Ever wondered why that doesn't happen in your city? There are reasons. For most people, out in India, if they come to a Christian service in search of a miracle, they either get *healed...* or they die. We come out to miracle services to get *blessed*. See the difference? The miraculous has been misaimed at the wrong problems, and it starts to fade away.

A loss of miracles yields a loss of divine order. The miracles prove the governmental doctrine of the apostles. The message they bring is verified by the manifestation of their authority (miracles.) See 2 Corinthians 12:12 and Acts 2:22.

Let me give an example of the loss of miracles in the Body of Christ. Whatever happened to deliverance in the renewal expressions? I'm talking about great deliverances, notable in mainstream society. Deliverance with strategic influence. I mean, unsaved people coming in off the street and getting delivered of demonic oppression (or possession, or suppression, or whatever.) That would be something, wouldn't it?

Of course, I know this has happened to a certain extent, but what would be the impact in your community if the town treasurer came out to your river church, the demons came out of him and he went back to work on Monday talking about what happened?

Apostles, don't waste the anointing on only the saved! Reserve some of that power for the unsaved. I would love to see a radical explosion of mass deliverance for the people in the community, along with the laughing, and the crying, and the silence.

But not to worry! A revolution is coming in the form of intercession — the spirit of faith will fall on the intercessors, and an awesome concert of prayer will arise from their midst. A roar of prayer, a shout to the King, to come and restore His miracles to the saved and the unsaved alike. Divine order will be restored in divine miracles, and we'll see the kinds of deliverance I'm talking about. Thousands of individuals from many nations all over the world will come out from under the curse and into blessing!

"'He has not observed iniquity in Jacob, nor has He seen wickedness [trouble] in Israel. The Lord his God is with him, and the shout of a King is among them. God brings them out of Egypt [that's deliverance on a societal scale!]; He has strength like a wild ox.'" (Numbers 23:21-22)

You know, I hear fellow members of the Body of Christ talking about the imminent return of Jesus. And I want you to know, I *do* believe He is coming again quickly. But I will say that I believe Christ will *not* come back until the ethnic groups in the nations have had a viable, explosive confrontation with His Kingdom in expression. I'm not talking about the simple salvation plan being preached. For the most part, people have heard about that, especially in first-world countries; but since Paul's time, there has been a dramatic decrease in the demonstration of the power behind salvation (i.e., signs, wonders and miracles.) That demonstration is the gospel of the Kingdom, with salvation being a by-product of the miraculous; and by-product is not a demeaning word in this instance, but of the utmost preeminence and importance — without the by-product, the demonstration is fruitless.

"'And this gospel of the kingdom will be preached in all the world as a witness to all the nations, and then the end will come.'" (Matthew 24:14) What was Jesus talking about, "this" gospel? What was Jesus' gospel? Dear readers, it was signs, wonders and miracles! All of His teaching, all of His preaching, was put into action by using the miraculous. "I am the Son of God; I am salvation. Now to prove it to you, bring Me the sick."

And then His apostles went around doing the same thing. "Jesus is true salvation. To prove it, bring us your sick." It's *this* gospel of the Kingdom that must be preached in all the nations as a witness — which implies the people must be *witnessing* something, right? — and then, and only then, shall the end come.

So, folks, we've got some time. Some people in Iraq haven't seen *this* gospel yet. Some people in North Korea haven't seen *this* gospel yet. Some people in Venezuela haven't seen *this* gospel yet. I'd even venture to say Americans as a group haven't seen *this* gospel yet in the level that God wants us to see it. I'm talking about entire ethnic groups, even nations — I know people have been having some success in these places for years, but indigenous people as a whole have not yet been confronted with *this* gospel. Look, it's been 2,000 years since the resurrection of Christ, and we're still here. That tells me we've got work to do. If it was simply a matter of saying, "Jesus is salvation; come get saved, or not if you don't want to," then we would've gone home a long time ago. Christ is waiting for His Church to **SHOW** the world He is salvation; that means the people out there have to *see* something, not just *hear* something.

It is the people in your church that will affect that kind of demonstration to the ethnic groups of the world. Don't wait for me to do it, or Billy Graham, or Benny Hinn. The point is your people must be equipped and then sent out to demonstrate *this* gospel. In fact, they are to be made into soldiers for war.

Now, before I am wrongly labeled, I am not one of those who subscribe to an "ultra-dominion theology" if you understand that terminology. As I understand it, ultra-dominion theologists basically believe that everything God intended for His people to do in the name of ruling and reigning here on literal earth will happen before He returns — I know there's more to it than that, but it's the basic premise. They're not entirely wrong, but I think it's a faulty basis for establishing an entire doctrine. I do believe in dominion, but I also believe in ultimate dominion coming from the rule of Christ on natural earth.

In my most humble of opinions, and I believe I'm right (insert big smile here), the ultimate expression of King Jesus' rule over all the earth comes when He sets His feet on the Mount of Olives and establishes a literal rule on this literal earth for 1,000 years. (See Revelation 20.) If you didn't understand what I just said, I believe in an actual millennial reign. I know some people disagree with me, but I advocate a literal second coming of Jesus for the purpose of establishing His rule on the face of the earth. Notice my excessive use of the word "literal" here. I'm a literalist when it comes to interpreting God's Word. I take a look at the black and white letters for face value before I try to delve too deeply into their hidden meanings. So, yes, I believe Balaam's donkey actually spoke – it wasn't just a voice in his head. (Numbers 22) I believe it was a real serpent in the Garden of Eden, not some archetypical personification of Satan's ultimate evilness taking the shape of a creature commonly disliked by womankind. (Genesis 3) Wow! That's a mouthful!

Do you still love me? Good. Basically, ultra-dominion theology purports, as I've seen it, that the full rule of Jesus Christ here on earth comes entirely through His *people*, apart or before His second coming. And I believe that for the most part. I do believe it's possible entire cities, entire people groups, will come to Christ before His return. That's awesome! In my missionary ventures, I've seen practically entire villages saved. But ultimately, it is the literal rule of Christ on earth that establishes the fullest expression of His authority.

But that doesn't negate our role in giving them *this* gospel with signs, wonders and miracles following. Until His literal return, the gospel of the Kingdom must bring reform in the hearts of people before it can change entire societies. So our dominion, the expression of the Kingdom, can be found in the *hearts* of God's people. We currently have a spiritual Kingdom; we eventually will have a literal Kingdom. His rule is currently expressed through our lives, rather than His actual throne sitting in New Jerusalem. But I believe in that literal throne, too.

Declaration and demonstration of the apostolic gospel serves as confrontation to ignite that rule in the hearts of people. They are forced to make a decision. In the Middle East, the best way I've found to reach Muslims is through demonstration of God's authority – that means the miraculous. I don't actually *rule* over the Muslims. Does this make sense?

My point in sharing all this is to show balance. Yes, apostles must have a dominion philosophy. They are not escapists or pacifists just waiting for the rapture to come bail them out — if they believe in a rapture. Pre-Tribulation, Post-Trib, Mid-Trib. Doesn't matter. (My own beliefs are irrelevant to the scope of this book. Insert another big smile here.)

So while I don't believe the whole world will come under God's rule before His return, I do believe in Isaiah 60:1-3, "'Arise, shine; for your light has come! And the glory of the Lord is risen upon you. For behold, the darkness shall cover the earth, and deep darkness the people; but the Lord will arise over you, and His glory will be seen upon you. The Gentiles shall come to your light, and kings to the brightness of your rising.'"

I do believe dominion gospel — salvation through signs, wonders and miracles — will be shown to every people group on a societal scale. I am convinced we can change the world, one soul at a time. However, ultra-dominion theology can cause frustration for the Body of Christ, because we aren't seeing His rule like we think we should. Something like one in six people on the face of this world live in the country of India — a piece of land somewhere near the size of Texas — and I don't think it's exaggeration to say 90% of those people have never had the gospel presented to them with signs and wonders following. Why, 90% of Christians living in the United States have never seen the gospel presented with signs and wonders!

But don't get disheartened here! I do subscribe to an anointing that causes confrontation. And I do subscribe to an anointing that releases His spiritual Kingdom in the hearts of many thousands and millions that were once lost. And we're approaching a time of vast increase where the apostolic spirit is going to ignite the hearts of churches, and the *people* – that's you and me and the guy working at Subway – will show other people the rule of God out there in the workplace. This is one of the most exciting times in all of Christian history to be alive!

I do subscribe to a strong, militant anointing in discipleship that preserves the harvest and restores stewardship among the saints. That's a key attribute of a grace-filled church – a church that gets people saved and then *keeps* them saved, in that sense of the word. It gets people employed and fruitful, and since everyone is called for some type of ministry, it equips them to that end. See, the apostolic spirit promotes people to *act*. When people are acting, the greatest expression of the church turns away from Sunday morning or singular miracle services. The culture of the miraculous becomes a daily way of life.

Now, I'm not talking about an ultra-discipleship movement that demands your pastor tell you what color socks to put on in the morning, or what kind of car you are permitted to drive. Don't take these few paragraphs out of context here. Consider the theme of the entire book. I'm talking about a true, apostolic discipleship anointing that provokes people to act. It drives people to become spiritually employed, to make ready for war.

"It happened in the spring of the year, at the time when kings go out to battle, that David sent Joab and his servants with him, and all Israel; and they destroyed the people of Ammon and besieged Rabbah...." (2 Samuel 11:1)

There was a certain season when the Israelites went out to war. True apostolic discipleship prepares the people for that season. The people are *called*, *trained* and *activated* for making war. Think of it as a three-fold anointing – one that is priestly (called), prophetic (trained) and kingly (activated.) Now tie that philosophy into the general populace of the saints. Can you see where a workplace ministry anointing might come from? That people are properly discipled and then, in the proper season, sent out to make war. It's more of a balanced dominion, discipleship theology that I'm talking about here. Not sending ill-equipped soldiers will-nilly out into the battlefield in the middle of winter only to meet their doom at the sword edge of the enemy or from starvation.

You want to know how to make your cell groups flourish? Then implement *this* kind of apostolic anointing, one tied into the rule of God, under proper authority, with the miraculous backing it up, and then watch what happens. Don't forget, the ministry is out there! Not just within the four walls of your sanctuary.

We need to have decentralization, a moving away from the Sunday morning experience and out into the workplace, Monday through Friday. We've made Sunday morning services the entire time of body ministry in North America, and other parts of the world as well. That must change! Sunday is supposed to be the Lord's time. And, yes, have soul winning and all of that. But the Lord's day should be a time when the people gather to celebrate what God did in the previous week out there in world, not use it as the one time a week where the Christians can get their problems taken care of, or the only time an altar call is given for the unsaved. I mean, really, the apostolic spirit creates an attitude so intent on bringing in the lost that soul winning becomes a by-product of *breathing*!

The apostolic spirit is a *spirit of initiative*. It is a pioneering spirit that carries with it an impetus to tame the wilds around it — it causes the people to progress, so that others may be brought in.

Does that mean if your church is possessed of an apostolic initiative that your church will be perfect? Absolutely not. You wanna know why?

'Cause it's made up of people. Hey, my ministry is by no means perfect... because it's mine! But that doesn't negate our desire to press into a more perfect gospel presentation to portray to the world! We have got to unlock people's potentials!

In the vein of *megadunamis* and *megacharis*, of a church founded with great power *and* great grace, we need to see that apostolic anointing creates a miracle ministry that creates other miracle ministries. Those with an "excellent spirit" cause other people to become innovative, people that are ultimately productive in fulfilling the Great Commission.

Remember the excellent spirit that was upon Daniel? He was possessed of knowledge, understanding, interpretation of dreams, dissolving of doubts, showing of hard sentences, dissolving of things that were tied up and bound (these are found in the Old King James.) Go back to Daniel 5-11:12 and then read Daniel 5:14, 16. These attributes were so fiercely displayed in Daniel — along with his salvation from the lions' den — that Darius the king issued the following:

"I make a decree that in every dominion of my kingdom men must tremble and fear before the God of Daniel. For He is the living God, and steadfast forever; His kingdom is the one which shall not be destroyed, and His dominion shall endure to the end. He delivers and rescues, and He works signs and wonders in heaven and on earth, Who has delivered Daniel from the power of the lions." (Daniel 6:26-27)

It is the excellent spirit that unlocks the people's potential! It is the apostolic anointing that causes even kings to know the rule of God. People of an excellent spirit are not afraid to face challenges. Now, keep in mind, excellent people might not always be understood by the people of the world until the people of the world become recipients of those apostolic blessings; but in the end, the rule of God is unveiled in a proper display of His great grace and great power through the Church.

Let's sum this all up into one simple thought: your church is supposed to be a training center, not just a spiritual feeding stall. With ambassadorial, military, apostolic anointing present, your church will equip its members for the season of war. People will find purpose and desire and proper instruction. Your church will be attractive to the people out there in the cities and towns, despite what you may have heard or tend to think. Your church is to be a militant church, sending its soldiers out to make war!

Look, you can have all the anointing in the world, but if you don't have people to send out, it does no one any good. That's why tithes and offerings to the storehouse are so important — it follows the same guidelines. You may have some of the most talented people in your church, but if you don't have the money to get them down the block, they're not able to impact the environment at the level God wants them to. And of course, I hear pastors all the time crying out, "Oh, Lord, send us the millionaires!" Hey, I'll admit it — I've prayed it, too! But you know what, the people in your church now are possessed of enough unique qualities and talents — believe for *them* to become millionaires. Train and equip *them* for utilizing their gifts. And you'll have your millionaires. People properly taught to sow their money in good churches with good visions for demonstrating the gospel before the world. It's the people in your church that will catch the vision and fulfill the Great Commission.

It's like that story (and I think it's probably true) of Bishop Wright, in the late 1800s, who took his two sons to a meeting where a prophetic minister was proclaiming that in the near future mankind would fly as birds flew, with two wings, and society would be revolutionized. The right reverend Wright proclaimed it as heresy and took his two sons home. He just couldn't see the prophet's vision. People *flying* — it was ludicrous. He couldn't see it happening. But his two boys could.

Their names were Orville and Wilbur....

OK, that's enough food for thought on the rule of God. One last notion before we end the chapter: the apostolic anointing creates a strong and militant praise and worship that in turn creates a prophetic atmosphere. By the grace of God, we need to capture that robust, vibrant new sound of heaven because it will captivate the people — it will cause people to sit, walk and talk as if they were in heavenly places, experientially not just positionally. They will be caught up in the glory of God, and from that position prophetic destinies unfold.

We need that new sound that restores effervescent relationship with the Father. We need the praise, not just the worship — although I don't minimize times of worship in relationship to the Father. It takes both, but it seems that churches have placed a higher premium on worship, and sometimes we forget to celebrate life! You know, we *are* supposed to enter into His gates with thanksgiving and His courts with praise. (Psalm 100:4) When you offer a sacrifice of praise and thanksgiving, it releases a celebrant spirit — the apostolic spirit — that prepares you to enter into worship by removing all that emotional baggage you brought into the service. Again, keep balance, but don't forget to rock on! I guess you can blame my Hippie upbringing for that....

Restored intimacy with God's rule restores godly encounters wherein people are thoroughly changed, and no one is ever the same again. Try it out in your church!

Chapter Seven Outline
"Unveiling the Rule of God"

OUT OF ORDER

- Something is out of order in the structure of the Church at large — we are not seeing the greater miraculous moves of God on a continual basis
- "...God has appointed these in the church: first apostles, second prophets, third teachers, after that miracles, then gifts of healings, helps, administrations, varieties of tongues." (1 Corinthians 12:28)
- The Law of First Things: "one thing must come first fully to release the next" (see excerpts on biblical hermeneutics for further study)
- So, "*first* apostles, *then* prophets, etc." "First" is the Greek *proto*, as in *prototype* or *proton*, implying a building block for an atomic release of molecules designed of first protons, then neutrons, then electrons
- The initial building of God's Church is rooted in the foundation of apostles and prophets for the dynamics of Church-life, with Christ being the chief Cornerstone. (Ephesians 2:20)

A BIT ON CHURCH GOVERNMENT

- "We, however, will not boast beyond measure, but within the limits of the sphere which God appointed us — a sphere which especially includes you." (2 Corinthians 10:13)

- God operates through relegated authority. Authority, here, is defined as "a measure of the rule of God lent to mankind"
- The release of the gifts of an apostle increase the measure of Christ in an environment — they expand the boundaries of an experience in Him
- A hampering of the apostolic anointing hampers an experience in Him. The rule of God, and thus His glory, is unveiled in the foundation of the Church on apostolic, prophetic anointing
- Apostolic miracles are used to unveil the rule and glory of Jesus and recover the fullness of His testimony to the world
- The signs, wonders, miracles and mighty deeds of an apostle fall under three major categories:
- Miracles of life: apostles and prophets unveil the deceptions that hinder or limit life in all its fullness. They breathe fresh life into otherwise dead situations by lifting off the betrayals of the enemy and other people
- "For the law of the Spirit of life in Christ Jesus has made me free from the law of sin and death." (Romans 8:2)
- Miracles of creation: situations are rebuilt; situations that are without form and void can be brought into order, reconstructed in creativity and with purpose. A place that is chaotic, empty, full of waste, of no usefulness and in a state of disarray can become "lifed" again when the glory of God is unveiled through the apostolic and prophetic anointing. That which hindered creativity is removed

- "In the beginning God created the heavens and the earth. The earth was without form, and void; and darkness was on the face of the deep...." (Genesis 1:1-2)
- Miracles of conquest: the release of the apostolic miraculous undoes that which hindered dominion authority, retaking lost ground
- See Joshua Chapters 3-6, Acts 8:1-18, Acts 19:1-20, 2 Kings 2
- Apostolic people possess the breaker anointing necessary to unveil the glory of God — through the miracles wrought by God, they establish a church of great power and great grace

RECOVERING GREAT POWER AND GREAT GRACE

- "And with great power the apostles gave witness to the resurrection of the Lord Jesus. And great grace was upon them all." (Acts 4:33)
- The church at Antioch was known for its *discipline, gracefulness, benevolence, charisma, integration, giftings, teachings, prophecies, worshipfulness, prayerfulness, structure, intimacy* and ultimately its *apostolic anointing.* (See Acts 11:23, 26, 29-30; Acts 13:1-3.) (Emmanuel Cannistraci)
- These characteristics mark a church that is *attractive, involved, reproducing* and *multiplying*
- *Megacharis* is "great grace," meaning, "God's grace freely given [manifested] in the ordinary course of people's lives"
- Why people will come, stay and grow in your church will correlate directly to the level of grace and power that operates in your services

- People will come, stay and grow in your church because multiplication is a by-product of reproducing, meaning that the manifestation of God's grace and power entices the people to stick around
- The local church will become exceedingly attractive to the community because others will see the glory reflected in your congregation

A CHALLENGE TO AN EXPERIMENT

- Great grace speaks of *quality* and *quantity* and an *organic* flow of power manifested. It is an organic, integral part of meeting the people's needs. The church that has come under apostolic and prophetic influence produces a *zoe*-kind of life found, nurtured and expressed in the local Body, making the Church extremely attractive to the outside world
- This is not just speaking of the apostles or the prophets, but of the entirety of the congregation — each person finding his or her identity in representing the gifts God bestowed to each of them
- "How is it then, brethren? Whenever you come together, each of you has a psalm, has a teaching, has a tongue, has a revelation, has an interpretation. Let all things be done for edification." (1 Corinthians 14:26)
- This grace has a *sending* quality to it, setting people apart and sending them before the congregation and the world
- "...'As the Father has sent Me, I also send you.'" (John 20:21)

- These gifts are always to be in the context of expressing God to the masses. This quality is not just a benefit; it is a mandate!
- "For the Lord will rise up... that He may do His work, His awesome work, and bring to pass His act, His unusual act." (Isaiah 8:21)
- Let's let Him do it!

THE AMBASSADORIAL ANOINTING

- Apostles as "sent ones" bear an ambassadorial authority with dominion that comes from the Father, the glory and rule of God in manifestation
- *Ambassador* grew into a biblical principle from a Greco-Roman secular term for someone being sent on the behalf of another. It literally means "to be sent." In modern vernacular, it is a special envoy being "sent out" to expand the kingdom or the empire
- The ambassador comes with *authority*; in the name of his sovereign with all of the king's might behind him
- The ambassador comes with *strategy*; a planting of values that entrenched the people in the mindset of his/her way of life
- The ambassador comes with *resources*; the accoutrements and people necessary to be sent out to make war, to conquer and subdue if need be
- The difference between our military vehicle and that of an earthly empire is we have an ambassadorial grace and authority that brings *freedom* to the people

- Freedom to express oneself to God, freedom to express oneself to others and, most importantly, freedom for God to express Himself to us

THE MILITARY ANOINTING

- "...As you know how we exhorted, and comforted, and charged every one of you, as a father does his own children, that you would walk worthy of God who calls you in His own kingdom and glory." (1 Thessalonians 2:11-12)
- True military might is found in people fighting for the cause of freedom under the guidance of great generals magnificently schooled in the tactics of warfare
- This apostolic anointing creates fathers, and it creates generals. Men and women of military prowess who are well-equipped to move this regiment here and this regiment there to maximize the achievement of a successful campaign — winning the lost
- Just as soldiers will follow good generals who have proven themselves knowledgeable and ready in battle, children submit to fathers when the fathers position themselves in a stance of ready acceptance, sound judgment and true authority. A poorly equipped general gets his men killed, and a poorly equipped father turns his children away
- Christianity is not a democracy. It is not a republic of severally-minded men and women, each with their own agendas, their own interpretations, their own hang-ups

- Christianity is a theocracy — it is the rule of God, and no other!

The Embezzled Anointing

- You can't make up a military or ambassadorial anointing. God must give it to you. The spirit of excellence isn't just made up; it's loaned out from the Dancing Hand of God. It comes from knowing Him in increasing levels of intimacy
- People who try to manipulate apostolic anointing will always phase in and out of great power or great grace because ultimately they are pirating something that God didn't authorize them to have in the first place
- The grace- and power-filled church recognizes that even though anyone can have an apostolic motivation, it does not mean they are an apostle. We can all support the apostolic movement, but we are not all called to be generals or ambassadors. We have to develop a knowing discernment between the two
- If you are truly a subject of theocratic rule, seek out those who have the breaker anointing backed up by miraculous expression. That single act of obedience is what will create the movement toward revolution in your home church
- "Paul, an apostle (not from men or through man, but through Jesus Christ and God the Father who raised Him from the dead), and all the brethren who are with me.... But I make known to you, brethren, that the gospel which was preached

by me is not according to man. For I neither received it from man, nor was I taught it, but came through the revelation of Jesus Christ." (Galatians 1:1-2, 11-12)

- True apostolic authority establishes great encounters with the presence of God. Those who have purloined apostolic authority will always end up with a counterfeit of the presence of God

- The Father uses apostolic authority to create an encounter with Him, and then He will stand back to see how the people response

A SEASON FOR WAR

- A loss of miracles yields a loss of divine order. The miracles prove the governmental doctrine of the apostles. The message they bring is verified by the manifestation of their authority (miracles)

- Divine order will be restored in divine miracles

- A revolution is coming in the form of intercession — the spirit of faith will fall on the intercessors, and an awesome concert of prayer will arise from their midst. A roar of prayer, a shout to the King, to come and restore His miracles to the saved and the unsaved alike

- "'He has not observed iniquity in Jacob, nor has He seen wickedness [trouble] in Israel. The Lord his God is with him, and the shout of a King is among them. God brings them out of Egypt; He has strength like a wild ox.'" (Numbers 23:21-22)

- The gospel of the Kingdom brings reform in the hearts of people before it can change entire societies. So our dominion, the expression of the Kingdom, can be found in the *hearts* of God's people
- Declaration and demonstration of the apostolic gospel serves as confrontation to ignite that rule in the hearts of people. They are forced to make a decision
- Apostles must be dominion in philosophy; they are not escapists or pacifists
- "'Arise, shine; for your light has come! And the glory of the Lord is risen upon you. For behold, the darkness shall cover the earth, and deep darkness the people; but the Lord will arise over you, and His glory will be seen upon you. The Gentiles shall come to your light, and kings to the brightness of your rising.'" (Isaiah 60:1-3)
- "It happened in the spring of the year, at the time when kings go out to battle, that David sent Joab and his servants with him, and all Israel; and they destroyed the people of Ammon and besieged Rabbah...." (2 Samuel 11:1)
- True apostolic discipleship prepares the people for a season of war. The people are *called, trained* and *activated* for making war.
- It is a three-fold anointing — one that is priestly (called), prophetic (trained) and kingly (activated)
- We need to have decentralization, a moving away from the Sunday morning experience and out into the workplace, Monday through Friday

- The apostolic spirit is a *spirit of initiative*. It is a pioneering spirit that carries with it an impatience to tame the wilds around it — it causes the people to progress
- A church founded with great power *and* great grace hosts an apostolic anointing in a miracle ministry that creates other miracle ministries
- Those with an "excellent spirit" cause other people to become innovative, people that are ultimately productive in fulfilling the Great Commission
- The apostolic anointing unlocks the potential in other people

Chapter Eight

Unveiling the Availability of God

MOVING RIGHT ALONG

My adoptive parents weren't too pleased with my decision to quit football and not attend the Naval Academy, and instead head out to Dallas, Texas, to attend some Bible school. I can definitely understand that. I had no idea what I was doing, I'll be honest. I just showed up on campus and sat outside the registration office with a suitcase and a Bible. I hardly had any money saved up, no job, no transportation. Nothing but the advice of an elderly woman I barely knew. Still, I knew this was where God wanted me. So I'd just somehow make the tuition payments. Easy enough.

Christ for the Nations Institute (CFNI) was witnessing some amazing moves of the Spirit among the student body. It was the early '70s, a time coinciding with the Jesus Movement of Southern California, which crescendoed into the Charismatic renewal. Literally thousands of Hippies were getting saved and Spirit-filled. I'm very glad to consider myself as being birthed out of that movement. Back then, these people didn't really have to worry about whether or not they believed healing and deliverance were for today. Potheads on the street were just sovereignly coming into sobriety, repenting, getting saved and speaking in tongues. It was a very exciting time! I believe it was a divine appointment of God's to counteract all the junk that went on in the '60s, something to bring a little balance back to the United

States. CFNI was caught up in that wave of the Spirit, and revival was running rampant on the campus.

Back to the story, I was dirt poor. Somehow I paid tuition, but I didn't really have much money to buy food. So I fasted a lot. All I could do was attend the powerful classes and read forty chapters in the Bible a day – none of which I really could understand. Because of malnourishment in my early upbringing, I suffered from some learning disabilities. I wasn't stupid, *per se*, but I had to struggle a lot harder than most to maintain decent grades in high school. Reading the Bible began to renew my mind. I could actually feel synapses starting to fire in my brain, and I began to overcome the disabilities as the term progressed. I was beginning to understand what I was reading.

The Lord began to work on me in great depth, pointing out issues and insecurities I had because of my early childhood, things I had long thought buried and forgotten. It was as if His finger would point to some area in my life and calmly say, "Let's deal with that." It wasn't a comfortable time for me at all. I constantly felt the need for a lot of prayer and fasting. It seemed to me that prayer and fasting was to be a school in and of itself. I had the ability to do this with nothing else begging for my time, so I'd set my clock at four in the morning and just pray in tongues until seven. School started at eight.

For several weeks I felt nothing at all, no anointing, no presence of God. Just this wall in my mind and in my soul that mimicked the wall in front of my face. I'd faithfully go into my prayer closet – which was the bathroom – and stand there facing that wall, praying in tongues and feeling miserable. I had to stand, because if I sat on the toilet I'd fall asleep. I tried not to wake up my roommate, who was a very gracious young man, tolerating all my idiosyncrasies. God bless you, Randy!

This went on for three or four months, me getting up in the middle of night, just crucifying the flesh, pressing on but getting no breakthrough. I was reading a book entitled *The Release of the Spirit* by Watchman Nee. It dealt with attitudes and motives of the heart, oppressions of the soulish life that would bind up the move of the Spirit. It showed me I was desperately in need of a breach that would let the spirit man come through.

I began to get desperate. This breakthrough just wasn't coming. No matter what I did. I began to feel like I wasn't fitting in at the school because I would go into classes where people would be laughing and rejoicing in a tremendous outbreak of God's Spirit, but I was always the exact opposite. They'd be whooping and hollering; I'd feel grieved, full of humility, weeping and sobbing, a portrait of brokenness and condemnation. Then when everyone else was weeping in somberness, I would want to laugh and dance, feeling like I was getting a breakthrough. Always opposite with me, and it became very confusing.

It was getting worse and worse. I felt myself spiraling down into a sense of despondency. Finally I decided I had to go into a serious time of fasting. I know that sounds super-spiritual, but really it was because we didn't have a cafeteria back in those days, and I didn't have any money to eat, so I didn't have any other choice *but* to fast!

Still, God used it. He understood my heart. At first I went seven days, then I'd wait a week or so and go another eight days. Then it was fourteen. Four or five of these fasts in a row. I dropped so much weight, it was freaky. And nothing was changing, because I felt every time that I wanted to enter into a greater relationship with God, something would raise itself up in my soulish life, a barrier. Just something I couldn't put my finger on. And I couldn't break it off. What was it? What was this hindrance?

I studied God's Word; I knew what it said. "Draw near to God and He will draw near to you.... Humble yourselves in the sight of the Lord, and He will lift you up." (James 4:8,10) Yet there was *something* that made me feel I didn't have the right or the power to draw unto Him, no matter how humble I tried to be. With all the issues in my life, the rejection, the mental hindrances, the lack of esteem, I couldn't convince myself I warranted that kind of intimacy with God. Who was I to think He'd want to get to know me? I was an emotional basketcase! A wreck!

Now I was really desolate. It was the night of the fourteenth day of this particular fast. Once again, it was four in the morning, and I'm in the bathroom crying out to God. What was wrong with me? I was going to quit the school. I thought, *God, if You don't show me what this barrier is, what's isolating me from You... if You don't unveil Your heart to me... I don't know. I just can't go on any further. I have to share in Your secrets and in Your desires. I can't do this. I can't handle it anymore. You have to reveal Yourself to me like You did when we first met. Show me what's wrong!*

When I said that, I felt something tear out of me. It ripped right out of my emotions, like God took His hand and tore something out of me. And I saw something that had tormented me my entire life.

THE NIGHTMARE OF REJECTION

I had this dream my whole life, a recurring nightmare that would haunt me every few months, time and again, for years on end, harassing my sleep and my waking hours. It was always pressing on the envelope of my subconscious, just waiting for the moment when it could pounce on me again. The dream was always exactly the same. Isn't that strange? The identically same dream, over and over again?

In the dream, I am at a party, and I'm just a child — like six or so. There are many, many other children at this party with me, all nicely dressed in crisp trousers and dresses in pinks and yellows. The colors are quite vivid. Bright streamers are strewn across the ballroom where this party is being held. There are balloons everywhere, and music. We are running around, playing, dancing, twirling, but we can't seem to touch each other. When I run up to touch one of the little boys, he pulls ahead of me, just out of reach. The music continues, and we play tag some more. Everyone seems happy, but also lonely, because we can't touch. Just when we get close enough to touch, one veers to the left or to the right.

The colorful balloons and the cheery music attempt to provide an outward happiness for the children. However, each of us feels totally isolated, unable to reach out and really get to know one another. So we grope about. I am so close to grabbing one of the boys or girls; my fingers brush their clothes, but they speed up, blurring out of my grasp.

That's when the black cloud appears. This huge, monstrous face appears above us, billowing out of this dark cloud. What an ugly face it has! Snarling fangs and sharp claws. Many teeth and dark red eyes. It makes terrifying noises, slurps and growls. We all scream in fear and scatter.

All the other children run and hide from its fierceness. They scramble away.

Except for me.

I'm frozen to the ground, moving in slow motion. I'm in molasses or superglue. I am not going to make it. I know this. I smell the stench of its breath, the heat from its mouth.

The monster engulfs me, swallowing me down its maw, and I suffocate in pitch-black death.

I awaken, screaming. My bed is soaked with sweat, and I can't breathe. I wheeze, trying to catch my breath, gasping and crying. I feel physical pain throughout my body, like something had tried to eat me.

The nightmare had gotten me again.

A HOLE TORN IN HEAVEN

Something was torn out of me that night in my bathroom at CFNI. This *thing.* Something plaguing my emotions. I could literally feel it tearing out of me.

I heard God speak from behind me. He said, "Look up, My son."

I did. And there it was. That same demon from my nightmare, the eyes, the teeth, the black cloud.

God spoke again. "This is the spirit of rejection. It entered into you from your mother's womb."

I shivered.

"Point your finger at it and tell it to leave, for it *has* to flee in My name."

I raised my finger at that vile monster, that demon. I yelled out, "Spirit of rejection, you have tormented me my whole life! Not anymore. I *command* you to leave me in the name of Jesus!"

I wish I was eloquent enough to describe the look of shock and abject terror that settled on its grotesque face. It was a fear I have never known, something I can't even begin to write. It was paralyzed with absolute panic. I can only describe it like this: the demon puffed up, its red eyes bulging in horror. And it shattered like a mirror into thousands of pieces.

Heaven instantly filled my bathroom, and glory came down and filled my soul. I looked up at where the ceiling should've been. But after the demon exploded, there was a hole in heaven, like a funnel made of purplish clouds. (Again, see Exodus 33:9.)

And God the Father granted me a glimpse into His throne room. I don't know exactly how long; I'd say several minutes. I cannot even begin to tell you what I heard. It was the most unique music — I've never heard anything like it on earth. I don't think we can make music like that. Just beautiful and maybe a little strange, not in a scary way, but it sticks with you in the back of your mind. You *feel* it.

The best word I can come up with for heaven is *synergism*. Everything flowed in perfect harmony to the music. The colors I saw are not here on this earth — they're alive, if that makes any sense at all. They are *part* of the harmony of the music. Your eyes are in high definition, everything seems 3-D but with absolute clarity. Everything is ultra-vivid. The colors we have on earth pale in comparison.

I did *not* see the Father on the throne. But I did have a quick glimpse of the winged creatures with eyes all around them, the seraphim that worship Him continually. They're strange looking, but in a really neat way. I don't know how to describe them. They exhibit the Father's creativity, let me say that.

Even though I couldn't see the Father with my eyes, I immediately knew I had perfect and complete access to His throne room, anytime I needed. Just as a son would enter into a father's room. I had total right of entry.

I heard His voice again. "You have all authority and power to call on Me. I have given you the right, as there is no wall of isolation between us."

The best way I can depict His voice is to say it sounds like multiple cracks of lightning at the same time, layered upon each other. Or maybe several waterfalls, a few just milliseconds behind the others. It's not really an echo, but more like a hum, a vibration. I guess I would say it carries life in and of itself. That may not be very clear, but it's the sense I got. Bear with my inability to illustrate it properly. How does one describe the God of all creation?

His voice continued. "What is it you would desire of Me?"

I was absolutely floored. *He* asked me a question. I had His complete and total attention, nothing else was happening at that moment, but His conversation with me. Here was God, the ruler of all that is made, He who holds the stars up in the sky, makes the earth rotate at just the correct speed, counts the sparrows as they fall to the ground, numbers the hairs on every person's head; and He still has time for a chat with me. I had been given a private audience with Him. I didn't know what to say. How thick is that? God asks you a personal question, and you don't know what to say!

"Share your desires with Me." The Lord prodded. "What do you want in your life? What do you want to accomplish? What makes you creative? I don't want you to see My thoughts only. Surrender your heart's desires to Me, and I will give them back to you. I have made you with tremendous potential."

My whole life I had never believed that. I had been on mute, stunted from excellence, unable to express myself creatively. I would strive to achieve acceptance through football, but it wasn't enough. Because of my upbringing, being locked in that closet as a toddler with nothing but a bottle of water and a filthy diaper, the enemy had convinced me I was still in that closet, emotionally and spiritually. I could not break free. I had suffered from bouts of panic and terror because of that nightmare demon. I was hampered from believing I could ever amount to anything. Do any of you ever feel like that? Something hits your life and you go into a panic, feeling that nothing you do matters anymore. It is simply not true.

The Father told me that night that every human being is born with creativity and massive potential, secret desires and tremendous innovation. He said it was His desire to develop that in everyone's life, as they yielded to Him and grew to know Him.

"What do you want Me to do for you to help you facilitate this?" He asked me.

So I began to voice desires for my ministry and personal fruitfulness, things I wanted to accomplish in His name and to further His glory. After each thing I would say to Him, He would respond. "Mmm-hmm." I would tell Him something else. "Yes." And another thing. "OK."

I don't know what else to say about this. It was the best conversation I've ever had. It was just incredible. How weak is that? Well, I will say that after my bathroom reappeared, I was changed from then on. My life has never been the same. I went to school that morning and laughed when everyone else laughed, and I cried when everyone else cried.

Roar if You're Pro-Life

"But speaking the truth in love, may grow up into him in all things, which is the head, even Christ: from whom the whole body fitly joined together and compacted by that which every joint supplieth, according to the effectual working in the measure of every part, maketh increase of the body unto the edifying of itself in love. This I say therefore, and testify in the Lord, that ye henceforth walk not as other Gentiles walk, in the vanity of their mind, having the understanding darkened, being alienated from the life of God through the ignorance that is in them, because of the blindness of their heart: who being past feeling have given themselves over unto lasciviousness, to work all uncleanness with greediness. But ye have not so learned Christ; if so be that ye have heard him, and have been taught by him, as the truth is in Jesus: that ye put off concerning the former conversation the old man, which is corrupt according to the deceitful lusts; and be renewed in the spirit of your mind; and that ye put on the new man, which after God is created in righteousness and true holiness." (Ephesians 4:15-24, KJV)

That's a massive excerpt, I know, and it's in the Old King James, which most of you are probably not familiar with — even though it *is* the truly inspired translation! (That was a joke.) But the original King James is quite eloquent and points out several phrases I want us to take a look at. The first being, "Fitly joined together." That's a wonderful expression, I think. "If I move, you feel my movement; if you move, I feel *your* movement." That's what it's saying. Or, in other words, when I move toward something, you're to experience that same movement and vice versa. When you are blessed, I am blessed. When I hurt, you hurt, too.

"Every joint" speaks of relationships which make the entire Body increase, lifting itself up in love. Because of who we are fitly joined together with, I am increasing, and you are increasing. Oh, Lord, let us increase!

In your Bible, circle that word "alienated" — it's OK, God doesn't mind if you mark in His Book, and underline "put off" and "put on." We'll come back to this later. I'm going to ask you to bear with me a few pages here, because I believe the Lord is giving us another unveiling of His Person, an apostolic anointing for lifting off a barrier of seclusion that might prohibit our perceptions of His availability to us. Just as that nightmare of rejection kept me from knowing my position with Him for many years, it's quite possible people we know, maybe even ourselves, suffer from a similar hindrance.

I'll be brutally honest here, there is something that is hindering the fullness of God's life from flowing in many people's lives; and because we are fitly joined together, one person's inability to overcome their barrier may affect someone else in overcoming theirs. We're not seeing the breakthroughs we should be seeing. But I'm convinced that's changing! These people need an unveiling to occur, so that they might choose His life.

Some of you dear readers may not really know this yet, but you have a choice to have *that* kind of life. "...'I have set before you life and death, blessing and cursing; therefore choose life'...." (Deuteronomy 30:19) God has set before you the choice: life or death, blessing or cursing. Therefore (and I paraphrase here)... don't be ignorant. Choose life. It's the obvious selection, right?

"'For as the Father raises the dead and gives life to them, even so the Son gives life to whom He will.'" (John 5:21) This "life" the Father and Son give is *eternal life* — a quality of life that comes from heaven itself. This life abides within us if we are born again. We know this, and this life inside should cause us to roar like lions! Hey, that's scriptural: "Look, a people rises like a lioness, and lifts itself up like a lion...." (Numbers 23:24) But for many Christians, their *roar* sounds like a "meow," doesn't it? Well, thank God, the apostolic miracles have come to tap into that kind of life, and the roar of the people will be heard throughout the land!

"For we who live are always delivered to death for Jesus' sake, that the life of Jesus also may be manifested in our mortal flesh." (2 Corinthians 4:11) The life of Jesus *fully* manifested in yours will cause you to roar. So go ahead and do it. You know you want to roar! I won't tell anybody....

The problem is "the god of this age has blinded" the minds of those who do not believe. (2 Corinthians 4:4) We could say it has made them choose death. So many people, even some who call themselves Christians, have been strapped with these "mind-blinders" of the enemy; yet, don't fret overly, because there is a Law of the Spirit of Life in Christ Jesus! (Romans 8:2)

I teach there are basically three laws operating in the world today. The Law of the Flesh – which must be crucified. That's the only way to deal with flesh: to put it to death. My brother-in-law, David Alsobrook, has a very witty teaching concerning flesh, sins and demons. It's the Three C's to victory – cleanse, crucify and cast out. He teaches that sin needs to be cleansed, flesh needs to be crucified, and demons need to be cast out. We in the Church tend to get it all turned around sometimes, huh? It seems everywhere I go I find people who are trying to cleanse flesh, or cast out sin, or crucify demons – and the slimy devils won't stay put on the cross! We need to use the right C for the right problem!

Anyway, back to the three laws. There is the Law of Flesh, and there is the Law of Death, which came through sin and disobedience. (See Romans 5:12-21.) Death is an inevitable happening. No one here gets out alive. I hate to be blunt, but let's face it – someday we are all going to die. (Hebrews 9:27) It's part of the curse brought about when sin entered into the Garden of Eden. Now, I am under the firm persuasion that death can be delayed so that we might fulfill our destinies in the Lord, so our days might be full on the earth, but death *is* a law. "As there is a law that can claim your body at death, there is a law of death that can claim your soul as well." (John G. Lake)

Thankfully, we can nullify that law, for we have a third law – the Law of the Spirit of Life in Christ Jesus! We can choose His life and make it our own. The body may eventually die, but our souls live on forever in Him. Coming to Christ is the only element to stopping the process of death in our souls.

You know, when people lose their souls, it's not so much because they're horrible sinners; it's because they're naturally careless – they reject Christ. Or rather, they're not "putting on" Christ. See, when one is born again, one is *initially* putting on Christ; and then throughout one's life, one is *continuously*... putting on Christ. I'm trying to show a progression here.

The Greeks used not only present tense, but a present-continuous tense. "Therefore, if anyone is in Christ, he is a new creation; old things have passed away; behold, all things have become new." (2 Corinthians 5:17) Here's an example. Old things are "passing" away; behold all things are "becoming" new. To the Greeks, it was both. So while one was a new creation, one was continuously becoming more and more released into the fullness of the life of that new creation. One was not just set free from the sin principle initially, but then from the *consequences* that came from the sin principle. Sin originally generated decay, which is sickness and death, which is disillusion (read "a veiling.") Yet there is an antidote found in choosing the life of Christ. So then "put on" Christ, so much so that the operation of the Law of Life negates the operation of the Law of Death. It's time to roar again: "Oh Lord, *life me!*"

Without His life, where do we find ourselves? "Alienated from the life of God." That's an interesting word choice there, alienation. What does that mean exactly? I can rephrase it this way, alienation creates an isolation. I have seen that there are tens of thousands of well-meaning Christians bound under an isolation from the availability of God. In my case, the isolation was rooted in the demonic, but since I don't want to rustle anyone's theological feathers here, I would also say it can be rooted in a mindset, or an emotional trauma and wounding. They are all veilings of deception. Whatever the case may be, let's just break it off in the name of Jesus, all right? Let us tear down the wall of isolation.

THE WALL OF ISOLATION

There is acceptance as the beloved of God, and, remember, where there is *acceptance*, there is *access*. (again, Ephesians 2:18) The Father does not change in His position of availability. I have not forgotten James 4:8, but one must realize that when one draws nigh to God, He has not really moved. He was always right there, but it is one's own weights, sins, mindsets and veilings that make it *seem* as if God has moved away.

Yet His position toward you is unchanging. He is never distant from you. He is never unconcerned regarding your well-being. Here is the key to this chapter: **God accepts you with the same level of fervency that He accepted His own Son.** He will intervene on your behalf just as readily and as quickly as He intervened on Jesus' behalf. The challenge is making *yourself* see that. It is a lie of the enemy that isolates and alienates us from the life of God. So something must be choking out the life of God, and I don't know about you, but I wanna know what that *something* is! It is a mental strangulation that needs to be put off. I want to know what that barrier is that raises its ugly head against us, even though we preach and we teach and we prophesy. Yes, we see measurable successes, all of us as Christians, and I do not minimize those in the slightest. I'm so thankful that *anything* of eternal worth happens in someone's life. Any level of healing is worthwhile. I couldn't heal a gnat if I wanted to! It takes a certain level of Christ's life within for anything to be accomplished. Please, please don't misunderstand my point here.

But there's so much more! There are levels of life in God we have not begun to touch, and partly this is due to that wall of isolation. So I want to identify the wall, tear it down, and put on more of Christ in an ever-increasing progression. Don't you?

First Thessalonians 5:19 says, "Do not quench the Spirit." The Greek word translated "quench" (Strong's #4570) carries the notion of suppressing the Spirit – stifling His work from proceeding. So from "quench," I extrapolate the following phrase: "Don't allow anything to *repress* the inner workings and dealings of God that abide within you." What is experienced inwardly is to rise up and push its way to the *outside*, but so often we lack a sense of confidence to express outwardly the Holy Spirit. Something is lying to us, and it has isolated us from that *zoe* kind of life, because God is not withholding His acceptance in the slightest.

"Every good gift and every perfect gift is from above, and comes down from the Father of lights, with whom there is no variation or shadow of turning." (James 1:17) That tells me God wants to bless His people lavishly. His eyes are upon the righteous; His ears are tuned to the people's cries. "The eyes of all look expectantly to You, and you give them their food in due season. You open Your hand and satisfy the desire of every living thing." (Psalm 145:15-16) God is infinitely more available to touch our lives than what we realize! We've got to be renewed in our understanding of God's availability. That comes from the breaker anointing of the apostolic which crumbles the wall of isolation.

Let us not be as Cain was in Genesis 4:11-16. After murdering his brother, the Lord isolated Cain from His presence. What became of Cain? Firstly, he became a wanderer and a vagabond. Secondly, he could find no rest. Verse 16 says Cain "dwelt in the land of Nod," literally the Land of "Restlessness or Wandering." Thirdly, he cried out because his punishment was too great to bear. Lastly, fear came upon him because of his alienation from God. We have to recognize the wall of isolation affects thousands and thousands of people, in the Body of Christ let alone out there in the world, in the same ways. We wander aimlessly, restlessly, fearfully, crying out for release, unable to trust in a relationship with God. And that fear affects our relationships with others. Intimidation smothers us from acting out creatively in the desires God wrote into our very genetic code. We *must* break down the wall of isolation! We *must* destroy intimidation!

Because so many feel a vibrant relationship with the Law of Life is a futile effort, they enter into a "survival mode" of living. Scraping and scratching by. Many people don't *live*, they just exist. They simply go through the motions with no understanding of life in its abundance. I don't minimize these issues in people's lives, but the Word of God is the Word of God. "...'I have come that [you] may have life, and that [you] may have it more abundantly.'" (John 10:10) Either Jesus was lying or He was telling the truth. I think we all agree He is a trustworthy Person, so the problem must lie within our scope of dealings.

Yes, there are the "bread issues" of life — the needs that must be met. The basics for survival, physically, emotionally and spiritually, the battles with the concerns we face — but, dear friends, we have to rise above the bread issues, for "...'It is written, "Man shall not live by bread alone, but by every word that proceeds from the mouth of God."'" (Matthew 4:4) Again, since Jesus is truthful in His speech, we must believe this, also, is true. The apostolic people rise up on the inside and cast off the bread issues of life, laying hold to the Law of Life found in close proximity to the Father. He will always meet their needs because He wants His people to prosper, and no wall of isolation will prevent them from seeing life in all its abundance! We must also have this mentality.

God has no desire for us to labor under mental harassment or emotional traumas, these things that alienate us from Him. He desires for our complete health, not just for our sakes, but so we can give out that health to others. It is a poor testimony to Jesus' authority when His people live entire lifetimes of mere existence. We must rise up!

We have all been there, had these issues that make us feel we can't draw nigh unto Him. This vanity of the mind — for that's really what it is — carries with it a downward spiral into nothingness, an existence void of creativity and passion. It creates mediocrity, introversion, self-indulgence, addictive behavior, the seekers of the quick fix, all entertainment driven for the mind to escape reality. It's amazing the kinds of crises this world faces, but what are the people interested in? Which Hollywood celebrity will date so-and-so this month! But see, if we don't tap into the resources and potentials within ourselves, we begin to live vicariously through other people's experiences.

Metaphorically, we fall off the wall of isolation and destroy ourselves on the rocks of nominalization below, but I am convinced this is changing. God's apostolic people have brought enough dynamite to clear any wall out of the way. Nothing will prevent them from giving every opportunity to enter into the availability of God.

Quite possibly this wall of isolation is the number one problem in people's lives — it has been the antagonist for this entire book: rejection, fear, emotional remoteness, distance from the Father. It all stems from a misconception, a perceived gulf between deity and mankind, the "mind-blinders" mentioned earlier. It takes the breaker anointing to unveil the people's minds; yes, combined with the other facets of ministry, but it is the breaker anointing that starts shaking the wall to its foundation.

DOWN WITH THE BAD, UP WITH THE GOOD

Let's sum all of this up into a two-fold problem, so we can get over the negative and move on to the positive. You know, there *is* a positive! This is a good news book, not a bad news book. But we must first identify the bad to overcome it with the good, right?

So there are two problems to address here. One, many people live a life full of futility. People isolated from God are isolated from themselves. They cannot perceive the fullness of potential they possess. So they become failure orientated. They're pessimists. They're indecisive. They're easily discouraged, throwing in the towel at the first sign of opposition.

Two, many people are the walking wounded — many have used that term before. They're full of pain, anguish, anger, bitterness, hostile toward themselves and others. Distrustful, withdrawn, fearful of others, torn between opposite emotions, fragmented, broken, without self-control. They lash out and crawl back inside themselves. And to top it all off, they suffer with shame and guilt, and no wonder the life of God is not flowing!

We need God's Word to be laid as an axe to the root. (Matthew 3:10) Let's stop dealing with symptoms here, folks! Instead of just praying with people for the torment to subside, we need to tear up the plants of wounding by the roots. This goes back to the concept of things being bound, but then the Spirit being loosed. Matthew's Gospel, chapter twelve, says bind the strongman and spoil his goods. (Verse 29)

If you study the kings of the Old Testament, as a general rule, over a forty or fifty year reign, "each king would face between two and four major battles." (Bill Hamon) If they overcame, the rest of their reign would be prosperous, not excluding a few minor skirmishes. Now in a sense, I believe Satan is bound to that principle in the life of a believer or in a ministry. Take a look back at your life, in retrospect I bet you will see two to four major strongmen that needed to be overcome. And once you bound the strongman, did it not unchain the next course of your life in that particular level of your walk with God? Give it some thought, and be encouraged! For most of you, you've already been through one or two or three strongmen. Some of you may be thinking of two or three dozen! But I'm convinced after you've finished this book, you will be propelled into a new level of victory — these strongmen are being bound as you mix what you read with faith. Your future is bright in the Lord!

We are approaching the greatest days in Church history! Here is the catalyst. The answer, as it were. We now know what to put off; here is what must be put on. Ephesians 4:23, "...Be renewed in the spirit of your mind...." Life has everything to do with choice. It has everything to do with attitude. You must be renewed to that kind of thinking! You can choose to remain a basketcase (I mean that in love!), or you can choose to rise up!

I had to get to that point in my walk with the Lord — it was the key to 90% of my victory over the spirit of rejection; the deliverance part was easy. I had to choose to rise up and say, "I'm not permitting this anymore! I won't allow *anything* — no sin done against me by another person, no lie of the enemy — to prohibit me from entering into the fullness of what God has destined for me to experience!"

Let me define being renewed in the spirit of your mind. It is the activity of a work of grace, the stirrings, the movings, the churnings of the Holy Spirit in your mind. It is the essence of unveiling. Did you know there are measures of your mind that need to be enlarged? You may experience complete victory in one area of your mind. "Here, I see total faith for God's power to work." But in this area? Mmmm, not so much.... Remember, the battlefield for your complete victory is in your mind. So while one battle may be won; another needs to be waged.

All of us have certain veilings, yokes, that must be broken off. Remember, all true apostolic miracles break those veilings off of people. Then the anointing fills in that area of the mind, enlarging it, so that the person sees God's availability, His glory, His otherness, whatever we want to term it. It is the miracle in and of itself that sparks the unveiling, that wages the battle in your mind, or in your body, as the case may have to be. This is why we need miracles today, people!

Aren't you tired of the accusations of the enemy that say you can't be close to God in this particular area? Maybe it stems from your upbringing – like mine did – rejections, woundings, slanderings. Maybe your parents spoke negatively over you. All words are images, and negative words transform a person into a negative image. "A wholesome [healing] tongue is a tree of life, but perverseness in it breaks the spirit." (Proverbs 15:4) Has your spirit man been breached?

Then permit the apostolic anointing to make you know you are a son or daughter of the Most High God! Be unveiled in your understanding; let you mind be renewed! Knowing God as your Father is the single greatest release you'll ever have to make you a success in this life. Knowing your sonship, your daughtership, in Him will pour into you the needed confidence to overcome any strongman you face in this life! Maybe you didn't receive that vital confidence from your earthly upbringing. Then you have to get in the Kingdom of God! Your past, your parents' failures, cannot be permitted to dictate your future!

Let me tell you the Christian answer to a bad past. You know what it is? A Holy Ghost present! No bad childhood can restrain you from greatness, unless you let it. Rise up! "But as many as received Him, to them He gave the right [authority, power] to become children of God, to those who believe in His name...." (John 1:12) You just have to be made to *know* this. And in the context of being *in* Christ, "For the Father loves the Son, and shows Him all things that He himself does, and He will show Him greater works than these, that you may marvel.'" (John 5:20) *You* are the greater works, and we should marvel! The Father loved you before you got saved, when you got saved, and after you got saved. *He accepts you with the same level of fervency that He accepted Jesus Christ. God loves you with the same zealousness that He loves His firstborn Son.* You *have* to know this!

The devil lies and creates this isolation. Don't believe his falsehoods. Tear down his wall of isolation!

Now, let's tie this into apostolic ministry. The wall is one of the greatest hindrances in seeing creative miracles in the Body of Christ. Because we stand there, looking at some person who, in the natural, is absolutely unable to be healed. Whatever they suffer under — perhaps it's something terminal, say — cannot be broken in this world. And we know who God is, that to Him, it is all the same. Healing the terminal patient is identical to healing the bruised pinkie toe. But what happens?

That terminal patient stands in front of us, and we become overwhelmed. So when we attempt to exercise our faith — *whoompf!* — something is raised up. Again, it's all in our minds. Nothing has changed on God's end. He is still just as available as He was ninety seconds ago. But we think to ourselves, *Do I really have the right to ask this of Him? Is there some sin I've forgotten to confess? Should I really presume my relationship with Him warrants authority over the cancer? Am I just being foolish to assume I can so engage the grace and zoe life that this person can't help but recover? Is this arrogance?*

See, it's not so much the disease issue here, folks. In God's mind the person is *already* healed. Their healing was already provided for at Calvary. But, rather, it's that barrier — that wall of isolation again. I *hate* that wall!

Turn the tables now. The terminal patient has smacked into the same wall. *Am I worthy to ask this of God? Do I have the right to expect Him to heal me? What about that time I backslid for six months? I mean, I think I'm a good Christian now, but what if I'm not?*

But God loves us with the same zeal that He loves His Son! What that tells me is this, in Jesus' earthly ministry, the Father was completely available to Him. When Christ faced the dead girl, when

Christ faced the leper, when Christ faced the cripple. The Father was equally available, the same measure as when Christ healed the pinkie toe. (I'm sure that probably happened, too, at some point. What is it with pinkie toes and them getting hurt all the time?)

"[For] of His **fullness** we have all received, and grace for grace." (John 1:16, emphasis added)

What I think this scripture means is that once you have a sufficient amount of grace at the moment of time in ministry (say, to heal the sick), you experience God's *fullness* to see the completion of the miracle. Then you move on to another situation, another moment of need, another condition in a person's life, and then there's further grace to experience the fullness of God. It's almost like grace for grace for grace for grace. Jumping from this grace to that grace. We should be receiving grace to experience His *fullness* (that is, the answer to whatever need is in one's life.) We could say this: in each circumstance where you require God's grace to meet a specific need, it is made available to you the *fullness* of whatever you're lacking at that particular time. When that need is met, you will move on to the next circumstance and find you have sufficient grace (fullness) for *that* need as well. It's a short verse with a really powerful meaning!

If we have His *acceptance*, and we have His *availability*, we have *access* to His life. And if we have access, we can take *advantage* of His grace. Oh, don't let it bother you! Yes, God wants you to take advantage of Him! Why else would He have given you His Son? So just do it. Swallow your religious über-humility and go take advantage of the power He's conferred on your behalf. You're only taking what's rightfully yours!

You know what God Himself says? "Thus says the Lord, the Holy One of Israel, and his Maker: 'Ask Me of things to come, concerning My sons; and concerning the work of My hands, you command Me.'" (Isaiah 45:11)

Scrreeeeeching halt.... What? "You command Me"? Huh?! What does that mean? I'm glad you asked. That phrase, "you command Me," means this: "Prove Me right! Test Me! Accost My heart!"

It's OK if you feel like roaring again....

All right, then, Lord, I will! I will prove You.

You've just got to get a revelation of this, my dear friends. Some of us are just waiting for God to do something. We spend too much time waiting around. I tell you what, it's a wrong concept of the sovereignty of God. "You... move... Me!" Yes, humbleness. Yes, discernment. Balance, balance, balance. Yes, meekness. But not weakness, and not at the expense of taking what Jesus rightfully purchased for you at the cost of His own blood. Don't waste His blood!

Yes, I know God is sovereign, but I'm convinced that in some respects God limits His expression of sovereignty based upon our responses, our engagements of His power. And wouldn't a sovereign Person be able to do that? It only makes sense. He's so sovereign, He doesn't have to be. *Selah.* It's like He's saying, "I don't change. I'm here. I haven't moved. You move toward Me! Come mobilize My arm." That's availability!

Now before I'm labeled an arrogant, presumptuous faith healer, let me give you the reason why I know I'm right in this matter, and you won't convince me otherwise. I mean, I love you all deeply, and there is *sooooo* much I don't know. But I *do* know this as a fact. And here's why:

The Raising of My Daughter

My daughter is adopted from India. On one of my mission trips to that poor country, I went into an orphanage and saw this tiny, little Indian girl who weighed all of three pounds. She was just a few days old, and she fit in the palm of my hand. Her mother was homeless, illiterate and unmarried (a great reproach in certain Indian cultures.)

But rather than toss the baby in the garbage as many do, she decided to give the girl to the orphanage.

When I held her, my heart leapt in my chest. I just knew she was for me and my wife. So I claimed her. I said under my breath, "Lord, I want this child."

I returned to the States, and we started the process of adopting the baby. It was a very expensive, time-consuming process that took eleven months before she was in our home. During this time a telegram came to us, having taken several days to find us because we traveled so much on the road, and Indian communication abilities are a joke in the more remote areas I go to.

The wire said this: "The baby has come down with dysentery. She has been placed on intravenous fluids. She has been in a coma in the hospital." Keep in mind, this telegram was almost two weeks old when it caught up with us in a hotel in California. More than likely, she was already dead. Dysentery is the number one killer of children in India, a place that faces a 50% infant mortality rate. In the natural, she could not have survived.

As dejected as we were upon receiving the note that morning, I finally left with my son to go to the evening service. My wife, Joy, stayed behind to intercede. I felt miserable the whole time, but the service actually turned out pretty good in spite of my feelings. We had the church praying for her. We had no idea if the baby was alive or dead. It had been thirteen hours of intense prayer that day, wrestling between life and death for our daughter, by the time my son and I returned to the hotel room late that night.

When I opened the door, I couldn't even see Joy because of the light that was in the room. We picked our way into the room and found her with this great, big smile on her face. The glory of God was tangible throughout the place.

"Our daughter will live," she said, still grinning. "God spoke to me. He said, 'Surely she would have died, but just because you have asked Me, she will live and not die. I have raised her for your sake.'"

I don't know if His voice came from behind her or not. I've never asked....

It was three more weeks before we received an answer to our reply telegram. In the natural, that would have been the most horrible period of time imaginable, not knowing if your daughter was alive or dead. Just picture it. But we were the happiest people on earth. We had assurance from the Father above she would be all right. We slept like babies.

Sure enough, another wire found us in some other State where we were holding meetings. It said, "The doctors call it a miracle! At precisely such-and-such time... the baby came out of her coma and began to cry. She was released from the hospital and returned to the orphanage in good health." My wife did the calculations for the time change, and it was to the very hour when she had heard the voice of God that our daughter awoke from the coma.

Don't tell me we can't move the Dancing Hand of God!

Keeping the Perspective of Life

See, in faith you just got to keep breaking through the wall of isolation. Nothing can stand in your way, if you won't let it. And if it doesn't happen in your timeframe, don't cave into the wall and say, "Well, it must not be God's will." It's time for us all just to grow up. I speak to myself as much as to you.

When a person no longer sees the face of God (remember that's His availability and favor), he or she will lose His perspective of life, and the person will turn inward, becoming isolated from that life.

But in this apostolic and prophetic time, God is keeping His face just where it is — turned toward us with high favor. We must not break eye contact with Him!

I have been through all the spiritual gymnastics. My times of fasting (I don't minimize fasting when God leads you to do it, understand.) My times of intense prayer (also worthwhile.) But I used to use those as reasons for why I would see greater miracles. If I fasted more, if I prayed more, they would come. And I suppose, after a fashion, there is a principle in that. We need to set ourselves apart, dedicated totally to knowing God more.

But I've learned the hard way that sometimes I'd spend all day and all night in forceful prayer, eat nothing for the whole day, get up behind the pulpit, feeling like God's gift to humanity... and nothing would happen. And then the next night, I'd chow down the thickest steak around, burping through the whole sermon, and God would blow through the congregation like a windstorm. It's funny how He moves like that.

It's when I've looked up to the Father, and I've just known I am His son. He is as available to me as He was to Jesus. The same power and authority in Him could be mine if I wanted it. That's when the miracles have come.

You have to understand you are His *sons*. Ladies, don't count me sexist here. You're sons, too. Get over it. And hey, fellas, don't worry, you're part of the Bride of Christ. Deal with it. Wow. What deep revelation....

Anyway, we *are* sons. That implies intimacy with the Father. It demands closeness to the Father and to Jesus. But the day that you experience intimacy with God without fruitfulness is coming to an end! Remember Hannah's story. She wasn't satisfied with intimacy — she had that with God, so much so she felt capable of making a request of Him. But she wanted more than intimacy, she wanted a son. She wanted fruitfulness. You should, too.

Some of you may have truths and revelations in the bag. Maybe you've got it all worked out. That's great. But what about the child molestation victim living in a crackhouse downtown? What about the embittered Vietnam vet begging from his wheelchair over off 5th Street? Or the drunk who comes home from the office to beat his kids? Are you so over the wall of isolation that you have no problem going up to those walking wounded under the unction of the Holy Ghost and doling out a little of the open-heavens above your head?

Hey, I'm not trying to make you feel bad here. There are situations I've found myself in where I didn't know how I would react. Sometimes I was the victor, sometimes I was a colossal failure. The point is, we need to keep scratching away at that wall of isolation. Keep pressing through. We have to keep that perspective of God's kind of life.

It's all got to do with blindness. Blindness on those poor people's parts, blindness perhaps on yours. To make God real to people, we have to know just how real He is for ourselves. The apostolic knowledge from above, that you know exactly how to respond to the molestation victim, the drunk, the invalid. You know, if the average person you met on the street had an incredible unveiling of the truth in God's Person — be that from a Holy Spirit-inspired word of knowledge you gave them, a startling sign and wonder, a notable miracle — they would receive Jesus. To reject Him would make no sense. Now, of course, there are just going to be some people with a spirit of stupid (I think it might be a real spirit) that if Christ stood before them, they'd still choose their own way, but that's the smaller minority of a hurting world desperate for God to be made real to them through you and me.

You know how I know the majority of people would come to God?

Well, you did.

What makes you think you're more qualified than they are?

I'll say it again, it's got everything to do with blindness, that barrier, that wall, that veiling of His right Personage. *The greatest fear you will ever have to face as a person in ministry — lay or otherwise — is that you won't have what you're in need of at the time you minister to someone.* There's that blasted wall again!

We need to be renewed; we need a work of the Holy Spirit to take the knowledge we have in our heads – that we are, indeed, sons of God – and make it real down where it really matters, our spirits. That no matter what weakness, mental issue, or imperfections we might have in our lives, our position is not changed with Him. His availability stays the same throughout eternity. We must keep our perspective on life!

Chapter Eight Outline
"Unveiling the Availability of God"

ROAR IF YOU'RE PRO-LIFE

- "But speaking the truth in love, may grow up into him in all things, which is the head, even Christ: from whom the whole body fitly joined together and compacted by that which every joint supplieth, according to the effectual working in the measure of every part, maketh increase of the body unto the edifying of itself in love. This I say therefore, and testify in the Lord, that ye henceforth walk not as other Gentiles walk, in the vanity of their mind, having the understanding darkened, being alienated from the life of God through the ignorance that is in them, because of the blindness of their heart: who being past feeling have given themselves over unto lasciviousness, to work all uncleanness with greediness. But ye have not so learned Christ; if so be that ye have heard him, and have been taught by him, as the truth is in Jesus: that ye put off concerning the former conversation the old man, which is corrupt according to the deceitful lusts; and be renewed in the spirit of your mind; and that ye put on the new man, which after God is created in righteousness and true holiness." (Ephesians 4:15-24, KJV)
- "Fitly joined together" means, "If I move, you feel my movement; if you move, I feel *your* movement"

- "Every joint" speaks of relationships which make the entire Body increase, lifting itself up in love. Because of who we are fitly joined together with, I am increasing, and you are increasing
- Apostolic anointing lifts off a barrier of seclusion that might prohibit our perceptions of His availability to us
- Something is hindering the fullness of God's life from flowing in many people's lives, and because we are fitly joined together, one person's inability to overcome their barrier affects everyone else in overcoming theirs
- These people need an unveiling to occur, so that they might choose His life
- "...'I have set before you life and death, blessing and cursing; therefore choose life'...." (Deuteronomy 30:19)
- "'For as the Father raises the dead and gives life to them, even so the Son gives life to whom He will." (John 5:21)
- This "life" the Father and Son give is *eternal life* — a quality of life that comes from heaven itself
- "Look, a people rises like a lioness, and lifts itself up like a lion...." (Numbers 23:24)
- Apostolic miracles have come to tap into that kind of life, and the roar of the people will be heard throughout the land
- "For we who live are always delivered to death for Jesus' sake, that the life of Jesus also may be manifested in our mortal flesh." (2 Corinthians 4:11) The life of Jesus *fully* manifested in yours will cause you to roar

- The problem is "the god of this age has blinded" the minds of those who do not believe. (2 Corinthians 4:4)
- So many people have been strapped with these "mind-blinders" of the enemy; yet, don't fret overly, because there is a Law of the Spirit of Life in Christ Jesus! (Romans 8:2)
- The Law of the Flesh — which must be crucified. That's the only way to deal with flesh: to put it to death
- The Law of Death, which came through sin and disobedience (see Romans 5:12-21) and can be nullified by the Law of the Spirit of Life in Christ Jesus
- Without His life, we find ourselves "alienated from the life of God"
- Alienation creates an isolation. There are tens of thousands of well-meaning Christians bound under an isolation from the availability of God

The Wall of Isolation
- There is acceptance as the beloved of God, and where there is *acceptance*, there is *access*. The Father does not change in His position of availability
- God accepts you with the same level of fervency that He accepted His own Son
- It is a lie of the enemy that isolates and alienates us from the life of God. It is a wall of isolation
- "Do not quench the Spirit." (1 Thessalonians 5:19)

- The Greek word translated "quench" (Strong's #4570) carries the notion of suppressing the Spirit — stifling His work from proceeding.

- So from "quench," I extrapolate the following phrase: "Don't allow anything to *repress* the inner workings and dealings of God that abide within you."

- What is experienced inwardly is to rise up and push its way to the *outside*, but so often we lack a sense of confidence to express outwardly the Holy Spirit. Something is lying to us, and it has isolated us from that *zoe* kind of life, because God is not withholding His acceptance in the slightest.

- "Every good gift and every perfect gift is from above, and comes down from the Father of lights, with whom there is no variation or shadow of turning." (James 1:17)

- "The eyes of all look expectantly to You, and you give them their food in due season. You open Your hand and satisfy the desire of every living thing." (Psalm 145:15-16)

- God is always available, desiring to bless the righteous. It is a lie that says otherwise, but the breaker anointing of the apostolic crumbles that wall of isolation

- Because so many feel a vibrant relationship with the Law of Life is a futile effort, they enter into a "survival mode" of living. Scraping and scratching by. Many people don't *live*, they just exist

- God has no desire for us to labor under mental harassment or emotional traumas, these things that alienate us from

Him. He desires for our complete health, not just for our sakes, but so we can give out that health to others. It is a poor testimony to Jesus' authority when His people live entire lifetimes of mere existence

- The wall of isolation is the number one problem in people's lives: rejection, fear, emotional remoteness, distance from the Father. It is a misconception, a perceived gulf between deity and mankind
- The breaker anointing unveils the people's minds, shaking the wall to its foundation

DOWN WITH THE BAD, UP WITH THE GOOD

- Many people live a life full of futility. People isolated from God are isolated from themselves and cannot perceive the fullness of potential they possess. They become failure orientated, pessimists, indecisive
- Many people are walking wounded, full of pain, anguish, anger, bitterness, hostile toward themselves and others, distrustful, withdrawn, fearful of others, torn between opposite emotions, fragmented, broken, without self control, lashing out and crawling back inside themselves, suffering with shame and guilt
- God's Word needs to be laid as an axe to the root — stop dealing with just the symptoms. Instead of just praying with people for the torment to subside, tear up the plants of wounding by the roots

- Kings of the Old Testament would face between two and four major battles in their reigns. (Bill Hamon) If they overcame, the rest of their reign would be prosperous, not excluding a few minor skirmishes

- "...Be renewed in the spirit of your mind...." (Ephesians 4:23)

- Life has everything to do with choice, everything to do with attitude. One must be renewed to that kind of thinking

- "Renewed in the spirit of your mind" means, "the activity of a work of grace, the stirrings, the movings, the churnings of the Holy Spirit in your mind — the essence of unveiling"

- Apostolic miracles break those veilings off of people, then the anointing fills in that area of the mind, enlarging it, so that the person sees God's availability, His glory, His otherness as they were meant to

- "But as many as received Him, to them He gave the right [authority, power] to become children of God, to those who believe in His name...." (John 1:12)

- "'For the Father loves the Son, and shows Him all things that He himself does, and He will show Him greater works than these, that you may marvel.'" (John 5:20)

- God loves you with the same zealousness that He loves His firstborn Son

- The wall of isolation is one of the greatest hindrances in seeing creative miracles in the Body of Christ

- The minister thinks, *Do I really have the right to ask this of Him?*

- The recipient thinks, *Do I have the right to expect Him to heal me?*
- This is a veiling, for God has given you the right
- "[For] of His fullness we have all received, and grace for grace." (John 1:16)
- If we have His *acceptance*, and we have His *availability*, we have *access* to His life, and if we have access, we can take *advantage* of His grace
- "Thus says the Lord, the Holy One of Israel, and his Maker: 'Ask Me of things to come, concerning My sons; and concerning the work of My hands, you command Me.'" (Isaiah 45:11)
- "You command Me" means, "Prove Me right, test Me, accost My heart"
- Yes, humbleness, but not at the expense of taking what Jesus rightfully purchased for you at the cost of His own blood. Don't waste His blood!
- In some respects God limits His expression of sovereignty based upon our responses, our engagements

KEEPING THE PERSPECTIVE OF LIFE

- When a person no longer sees the face of God (His availability and favor), they lose His perspective of life, and they turn inward, becoming isolated from that life.
- But in this apostolic and prophetic time, God is keeping His face just where it is — turned toward us with high favor. We must not break eye contact with Him!

- Isolation has to do with blindness on people's parts — yours and others. To make God real to people, we have to know just how real He is for ourselves

- If the average person had an incredible unveiling of the truth in God's Person — be that from a word of knowledge, a sign and wonder, a notable miracle — they would receive Jesus. To reject Him would make no sense

- The greatest fear you will ever have to face as a person in ministry — lay or otherwise — is that you won't have what you're in need of at the time you minister to someone — the wall of isolation

- We need to be renewed; we need a work of the Holy Spirit to take the knowledge we have in our heads — that we are, indeed, sons of God — and make it real down where it really matters, our spirits. That no matter what weakness, mental issue, or imperfections we might have in our lives, our position is not changed with Him. His availability stays the same throughout eternity

James Maloney has been in full-time ministry for nearly forty years, traveling extensively across the United States and abroad in more than 40 countries, averaging 250-300 services yearly. In America, he speaks in healing and prophetic seminars, teaching the mechanics of ministry anointing release, and in leadership conferences, ministering to hundreds of pastors. He preaches in many local and regional church conferences, hosting schools of the supernatural, helping to equip the people of God in a release of the miraculous so they can extend the rule of His Kingdom in their own communities. He has made numerous media appearances on Christian television programs and radio shows.

As a revivalist, his work is marked with an apostolic/prophetic anointing for the release of God's power. In his revival conferences, one of his main messages is the release of the glory, drawing people into encounters with a mighty God. Ministering in a prophetic flow, he has spoken the personal word of the Lord to thousands individually, producing a greater sense of identity, motivation and clarity of direction. Operating in the revelation gifts of the Spirit, physical conditions are revealed, creating faith to receive healing.

He actively hosts international crusades and has preached to crowds of tens of thousands, evangelizing in extremely remote areas of the world, with heavy influence in closed countries of the Middle East and

Asia. He has worked with indigenous ministers in establishing many churches worldwide, licensing and ordaining hundreds of pastors.

James holds a D.D., a Th.D. and a Ph.D. He has taught for over twenty years in several Bible schools, including Christ for the Nations Institute in Dallas, Texas, and Kingdom Faith Training College in Horsham, England.

Dr. Maloney is the president of The ACTS Group International (AGI), an apostolic network that provides peer-level accountability and mentoring to this generation of ministers, and the next, who are eager to see a fuller release of the miraculous power of the Lord Jesus Christ by hosting teams in overseas crusades and conferences.

James and his wife, Joy, live in the Dallas-Fort Worth area.

For more information, please contact:

The ACTS Group International
P.O. Box 1166
Argyle, Texas 76226-1166
www.answeringthecry.com